Economic Crisis and the
Politics of Reform in Egypt

Economic Crisis and the Politics of Reform in Egypt

Ray Bush

A Member of the Perseus Books Group

Copyright © 1999 by Westview Press, A Member of the Perseus Books Group

Published in 1999 in the United States of America by Westview Press, 5500 Central Avenue, Boulder, Colorado 80301-2877, and in the United Kingdom by Westview Press, 12 Hid's Copse Road, Cumnor Hill, Oxford OX2 9JJ

Find us on the World Wide Web at www.westviewpress.com

Bush, Ray.
    Economic crisis and the politics of reform in Egypt / Ray Bush.
        p. cm.
    Includes bibliographical references and index.
    ISBN 0-8133-3676-7 (hc)
    1. Structural adjustment (Economic policy)—Egypt. 2. Egypt—
Economic conditions—1952–   . 3. Business cycles—Egypt. I. Title.
HC830.B875 1999
338.962—dc21
                                                                                                      99-41454
                                                                                                          CIP

The paper used in this publication meets the requirements of the American National Standard for Permanence of Paper for Printed Library Materials Z39.48–1984.

10   9   8   7   6   5   4   3   2   1

*This book is dedicated to my
father and the memory of my mother*

"Know-how" is not one of the things that its [Egypt's] agriculture lacks, nor was ignorance of agricultural techniques a cause of peasant poverty. On the contrary, the fellahin are excellent farmers, skilled and hard-working. In these respects Egypt was not an under-developed country; it was not the land which was neglected, but its cultivators.

Doreen Warriner, *Land Reform and Development in the Middle East* (1962)

Contents

Tables and Illustrations

Maps

Weights and Measures

1 *feddan*[t]=[t]1.038 acres or 0.42 hectares
1 *feddan*[t]=[t]24 *qirat*
1 *qirat*[t]=[t]175 square metres
One U.S. dollar was worth between 3.3 and 3.4 Egyptian
    pounds (LE) after 1991.

Acronyms

APCP	Agricultural Production and Credit Project
ASU	Arab Socialist Union
CAPMAS	Centre for Public Mobilisation and Statistics
ERSAP	Economic Reform and Structural Adjustment Programme
ESRC	Economic and Social Research Centre
EU	European Union
GDP	gross domestic product
GoE	government of Egypt
HIES	Household Income and Expenditure Survey
IFI	international financial institution
IMF	International Monetary Fund
LDCs	less-developed countries
LE	Egyptian pound
MALR	Ministry of Agriculture and Land Reclamation
MEED	Middle East Economic Digest
NDP	National Democratic Party
O&M	operation and maintenance costs
PBDAC	Principle Bank for Development and Agricultural Credit
PL480	Public Law 480 (of the U.S. Congress)
SAP	structural adjustment policies
SDR	Special Drawing Rights
UNDP	United Nations Development Programme
USAID	U.S. Agency for International Development

Acknowledgments

I learned a lot from others while writing this book in both the UK and Egypt. Pandeli Glavanis and Kathy Glavanis were both generous sharing with me, almost ten years ago, their knowledge of Egypt and suggested a number of fruitful avenues of enquiry relating to its rural political economy. Two spells of research leave from the Department of Politics, University of Leeds, have enabled me to take full advantage of being a guest researcher with the Norwegian Nobel Institute and of field visits to Cairo.

The bulk of the fieldwork for this book was funded by the Economic and Social Research Council of the (UK) grant number L320253119, as part of a project "Coping with Poverty and the Environment: Social Transformation in Egypt." I am very grateful to that funding, and I benefited from working on that project with Simon Bromley. He was an excellent colleague to collaborate with and he has offered many insights. I also thank Jonnie Rau and Philip White for help in data analysis and Sidgi Kaballo for help with translation. That project would not have been possible without the late Professor Mohemad Abu Mandour. His death was a significant loss for Egyptian social science. He was a staunch critic of structural adjustment and hounded its defenders in the Egyptian press and in his scholarly work, which included the establishment of Cairo University's Centre for Agricultural Economics.

Field data were collected in Cairo by Hassanine Kishk, Mohemad Hakim, Ibtissam el Gafaarawi, and Lamia Raai. Hassanine Kishk is an outstanding and committed researcher, and it has been a privilege working with him. Ibtissam el Gafaarawi has also been indispensable in helping with this work, and I am delighted she not only helped in Cairo but joined the Leeds department of politics to successfully write her doctorate on the Egyptian economic reforms.

I have benefited enormously by being involved in discussions with a range of researchers and commentators in Egypt. Although some of them might not agree with what follows, I do want to record my gratitude for the time they have spent helping me fathom the complexity and simplicity of Egypt's political economy. They include Hoda Rashad, Moheb Zaki, Mohemad Atif Kishk, Mohemad Abdel Aal, Hassan Abu Bakr, Ismail Sabri Abdullah, Mustapha Kamel El Sayyid, Hani Shukrallah,

Gouda Abdel Khalek, Soheir Mehanna, Yasser Sherif, Nicholas Hopkins, Liz Taylor, Karam Saber, and his colleagues at the Land Centre, Cairo. A special thanks to Amal Sabri, who has helped me think through many different issues and from whom I continue to learn a great deal. Ashraf Hussain provided essential help in the finishing stages of the manuscript, and I am very grateful for his attentiveness and accuracy. I have also gained a lot from working alongside several Egyptian research teams that were funded by the Ford Foundation Cairo Middle East Office. That work and the support of the foundation's directors, first Humphrey Davies and later Steven Lawry, have been very fruitful. I have learned a lot from working with Mohemad Atif Kishk and Mohemad Abdel Aal.

I must also thank the people I spoke to at the USAID (U.S. Agency for International Development) and the U.S. Embassy in Cairo for their candour and openness—a contrast with other international financial agencies.

Work in Leeds over many years has benefited from support and discussions with Lionel Cliffe. He is an invaluable critic and source of encouragement. He also read early drafts of some of what follows and helped me think through the consequences of what I was trying to argue. I also benefit from working with Morris Szeftel. He provides enormous help in understanding the topsy-turvy world of late capitalism. Thanks, too, for comments on parts of the earlier manuscript from David Keen and Alex De Waal. Tess Hornsby-Smith has been very efficient in helping with tables and laying out the bibliography, and Alison Haskins reworked the village maps with great care and clarity.

I owe a special thanks to Timothy Mitchell and Simon Bromley. Tim read and gave detailed comments on the first draft. His advice on changes in the manuscript's organisation and structure has vastly improved this book. Simon took time to read a later complete version of the manuscript, and his grasp of detail and the argument improved what follows. I am very fortunate that they both read and spent time giving me their perceptive observations. Of course I'm alone with the responsibility for what follows.

Thanks to the editorial staff at Westview, especially Jennifer Chen and Michelle Trader and to the careful copyediting of Margaret Ritchie. All have been extremely efficient in taking this project to publication.

I want to thank my father, who has usually supported the things that I have chosen to do—although perhaps not always with the same eagerness. I dedicate this book to him and the memory of my late mother. Their increased impatience with injustice and inequality has been a wonderful example for me.

Finally, thanks to Mette, Emile, and Leo. I'm not going to thank them for their forbearance. That is so often the final comment from authors, and I'm pleased to say I don't think I have to join the list—although the final month of manuscript preparation did sometimes make it touch-and-go. Although Emile has at times commented that I should "go back to Egypt," it's also the case that they have shared with me the excitement and vibrancy of Cairo. With their love they remind me that life is much more about people than about myopic research.

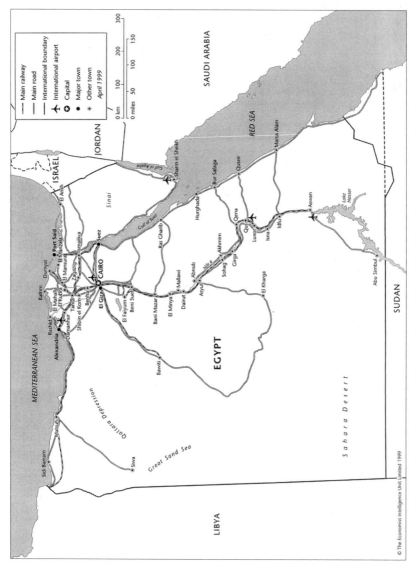

Map 1 Egypt

1

Introduction and Argument

This book examines the character and consequences of Egypt's economic reform and structural adjustment programme (ERSAP) of 1991, along with the second stage of reforms in 1996. Despite the very specific conditions pertaining to Egypt's political economy, its experience with the World Bank has relevance elsewhere in the Middle East and Africa. I will argue that, although economic and political reforms have been necessary, the strategy promoted by the international financial institutions (IFIs) and the government of Egypt (GoE) is inappropriate to the needs of Egypt. ERSAP does not address a significant number of issues, and there is continuing resistance within the GoE to reform. Among other things, the economic reforms focus too much on changes in the structure of prices and incentives and not enough on issues of productivity, growth, and the sustainability of markets, including the types of commodities for production, and the importance of political reform.

My focus is agriculture, where liberalisation began in the mid-1980s under Yusuf Wali, the Minister of Agriculture and Land Reclamation (MALR) and deputy prime minister. Agricultural reform has been preoccupied with market deregulation, cash crop promotion, and changes in land tenure. Reformers seldom mention the needs and interests of Egypt's much-maligned fellahin and especially the vast majority of small landholders, with access to 5 *feddans* or less. These farmers represent about 96 percent of the country's landholders and agricultural producers, and the policies pursued by the IFIs are undermining their productive capabilities.

I offer a direct critique of most orthodox commentary on Egypt's political economy. Most of the historical and contemporary characterisations of Egypt's economic malaise are based on fundamental misunderstandings of the social organisation and economic dynamics of rural Egypt. Most accounts of Egypt's economic reform, moreover, use a crude conception of the market as an instrument of economic progress. I now argue for the importance of understanding the household rather than the farm as the primary unit of social and economic organisation. I also stress the variety of strategies that households create, the important role of women in economic production and social reproduction, and the nature of local responses to environmental problems. In short, I stress the importance and significance of class and gender inequality as factors that shape the character of Egypt's countryside and the organisation of agricultural production. Until these themes are properly accounted for in the strategies of the IFIs and the GoE, as well as in the discussions of academic apologists for structural adjustment, it is likely the reforms will accelerate rural inequality and be economically and politically unsustainable.

This book now puts centre stage the position of Egypt's small farmers and especially those that populate the northern Delta area of northern Egypt. Discussions about agricultural modernisation have for too long failed to include Egypt's farmers, and the negative view of the fellahin has been a continuous thread throughout Egypt's recent past. I examine the ways in which Egypt's farmers have coped with poverty, economic change, and aspects of environmental transformation during structural adjustment. I also indicate how the policy paradigms of the reforms fail to recognise the needs and interests of the majority of Egypt's farmers.

This book also has another concern. Most of the existing consensus on Egypt's economic crisis locates the cause of the country's difficulties in an overburdening state. That state, especially since the Nasser revolution of 1952, is seen to be at best intrusive and inefficient, at worst rent seeking and corrupt. The set of remedies offered by commentators and international agencies is to create a more limited and effective state. In agriculture, this includes rolling back the state from its historically important position and liberalising markets to stimulate export-led growth of cash crops. Yet this set of policies grossly misunderstands a far more complex set of relationships between the state and dominant social classes in Egypt. Capitalist classes are too weak in Egypt to pursue their interests without a labyrinthine collaboration with the state. The "market," in which so much faith is invested by the reforming lobby, is simply not equipped to disentangle the competing interests around the state—or to provide an efficient substitute for government intervention in the economy.

I essentially counterpoise two sets of assumptions. The first are those of the IFIs and increasingly, especially in the agricultural sector, those of the GoE and academic commentators. The IFI argument is that distortions in the Egyptian economy are promoted by the dominance of an unproductive, rent-seeking state. The solution is for the state to retreat from economic activity. The IFIs argue that liberalisation and privatisation will allow Egypt to discover its true comparative advantage in international markets. They also argue that rising overall levels of welfare will offset increased inequality associated with the reforms. The retreat of the state, moreover, will allow a productive private market sector to emerge. A further IFI assertion is that reforms will promote a more open and transparent policy framework.

In contrast with the assertions that underpin Egypt's economic reforms is the view that the strategy has underestimated political obstacles to reform within the state. The strategy has also ignored the need (even in Egypt's authoritarian context) to sustain support among Egypt's working class and fellahin. The strategy is based on a static rather than dynamic notion of comparative advantage, and therefore, liberalisation is unlikely to generate sufficient growth to sustain increases in welfare. It is also a gross simplification for the IFIs to characterise the Egyptian state as merely rent seeking. My argument is that a retreat of the state is insufficient to generate a healthy private agricultural sector. There has, moreover, been no attempt to promote governance and transparency in decisionmaking between the IFIs and the GoE. If anything, the trend in Egypt since 1991 has been towards greater authoritarianism and deliberalisation. That has been reflected in the way in which it has dealt with a perceived threat from Islamists and in the way the "election" of 1995 was conducted, riddled with incidences of intimidation and accusations of corruption.

Beyond the issue of transparency at the level of the state, there has also been the absence of any meaningful attempt to construct rural institutions of decisionmaking and rural empowerment. The absence of this dimension to academic discourse relating to civil society is an indictment of the way in which Egypt's farmers continue to be perceived. At its worst, this view is reflected in comments made by a senior official in one of the IFIs that the problem of Egyptian agriculture was that "the Egyptian village has not changed for 100 years" (Interview 1995). In fact, as we will see, there is very little about the Egyptian countryside that is reminiscent of Egypt in the nineteenth century. Moreover, it is the failure of policymakers to grasp the *dynamics* of *change* in the countryside that will hinder sustained agricultural growth.

There is a further problem with Egypt's reform strategy. The IFIs and other policymakers apply an undifferentiated view of reforms to Egypt's rural political economy. It is one based essentially on price and institutional change, and it fails to grasp the realities and dynamics of agricultural production and social reproduction in the countryside. The GoE and the IFIs have failed to establish an empirical understanding of the way in which rural production is organised. They have also failed properly to grasp the nature of social differentiation in the countryside, and this failure will lead to greater inequality and social divisiveness. That inequality is not only between larger landholders and owners, and those who are not, but also between men and women and between small holders and landless. The World Bank has for some years conceded that the role of women in agricultural production needs to be put much more centre stage in policy calculations, but there is little evidence of this in Egypt. The triple burden carried by women, of child rearing, household management, and production has long been recognised to marginalise women in their relations with men. Nevertheless, what still needs to be situated more clearly, in the discussions relating to policy is the impact on women of the precise way in which they are integrated into every sphere of economic and social existence. Debates about the gender division of labour, and the changes that are taking place in Egypt, need to capture the dynamics of incorporation and marginalisation: how women themselves transform their opportunities and with what impact, if any, on decisionmaking structures. These structures include those in the household as well as beyond in the village and the national decision-making environment, and they take on particular importance during a period of economic reform.

Policymakers are concerned only with monetary aggregates of the productive economy and not with human resources, issues of the reproductive economy, and indicators of health, nutrition, and skill development (Elson 1994a). Male bias of policymakers may also disregard women's work because it is not part of the economic matrix constituting national accounting figures. Women's work is not accounted for because much of it takes place on family farms or is income earned within the household. It is also the case that women are assumed to be able to withstand the rigours of adjustment of agricultural "modernisation" because women's time is seen to be infinitely flexible. There is also the overall assumption that economic policies of the IFIs are gender neutral yet this view fails to recognise the differential way in which women enter into economic (market) relationships. The IFIs and the GoE assume all economic relationships are solely structured around tradable activities. They therefore fail to recognise the range of activities done by women and the way in which they are incorporated into markets (see also Dasgupta 1993:305–342).

The IFIs and the GoE fail to understand the different types of rural production system, the levels of inequality within them, and the struggles that they create. To illustrate that, I draw on new data from four villages in the governorates of Qalyubiya, Dumyat, and, to a lesser extent, Giza and Daqahliya. These data focus especially upon villagers' access to resources and responses to changes in economic life chances. I have not tried to make a direct correlation between household responses and adjustment, although evidence does indicate an intensification of economic hardship since 1991. ERSAP has failed to recognise the character of rural structures and patterns of coping with crisis. That failure has been either because of ignorance by the IFIs or because it is part of an integral strategy for social engineering in the countryside. The GoE and the IFIs are colluding to undermine the existing vitality and vibrancy of rural Egypt. And they want in their place to substitute a strengthened and emboldened landowning class. Yet by failing to grasp the nuanced way in which production is organised and social reproduction of communities sustained, the policymakers in Cairo will exacerbate rural social differentiation and undermine the ability of communities to withstand stress.

Among other things, the period of adjustment has elevated (or confirmed) the mistaken belief of neoclassical orthodoxy that the farm unit is a single economic actor. The theoretical notion of the farm unit, which appears in agricultural economics textbooks, is assumed to have real empirical meaning in Egypt as the unit, which performs the allocation of resources for goal maximisation. This is a fundamentally flawed perspective. The IFIs fail properly to grasp the importance to Egyptian peasants of issues like the persistence and dominance of labour migrancy; the crucial role which women play in economic production as well as in sustaining the maintenance and reproduction of households, and therefore labour power; and the problems of continuing structural rural poverty and the mechanisms which generate it.

This book indicates that households follow very different and varied strategies for production and reproduction and that strategies and patterns of survival include more than just responses to market mechanism and pricing strategies seen as panacea by the IFIs. These rural strategies, which are currently being threatened and challenged by ERSAP, emerge from different relations of production within the household and village in relation to local markets and the interaction with the state. They also relate to households' differential access to resources and means of production—in short, the village class structure. They relate to shifts in the character of national economic crises that in turn are inextricably linked to global capitalist crises and restructuring. Central to my argument is the importance of the interrelationship of the policies pursued by the IFIs, the GoE response to them, and the way in which Egypt's fellahin have coped with changes imposed on them. The impositions come from outside their communities although often by actors, like landlords and merchants, who may live among them. Most research in Egypt, and elsewhere, has tended to have a rather compartmentalised view of the world—as if you can talk about adjustment without having a sense of the political realities shaping the states' actions and interventions. I have also tried to move away from a top-down view of social and political change in order to bring the actors, classes, and social forces that shape the character of political and economic realities in Egypt into focus. This is difficult. The usual portrayal of the fellahin is to see them as passive subordinate actors who will do anything that they are told and put up with any policy even if it may worsen their drudgery.

This book now contributes to the debates underpinning the political economy of economic reform and structural adjustment in Egypt. Although the issues of political reform, environmental crisis, and Islam have received a lot of the debate relating to the nature of Egyptian politics and society in the late 1990s, I raise issues that run alongside these more openly debated concerns but that seldom become the focus for debate, namely, the continuing influence of the IFIs in shaping Egyptian economic policy and especially the changing position of Egyptian farmers and the relationship between economic production and social reproduction in the countryside during economic reform. I seek to show the interconnectedness of the impact of the policy debate and action on rural people's livelihood strategies and the efficacy of the agricultural reform strategy.

Chapter 2 discusses the origins of Egypt's current crisis. It does so by tracing a historical narrative from Nasser to Mubarak. It exposes the recurrent themes of Egypt's savings and investment gaps, the difficulties successive regimes have had in accessing sufficient quantities of revenue for sustainable industrial and agricultural development, and the recurrent crises that these difficulties lead to. Chapter 3 assesses the remedies for the crisis of Egypt's political economy. It does so by detailing the post-1987 economic reforms and situating these within the context of the IFI and GoE explanations of the need for those reforms. The chapter documents the academic consensus that has emerged in the treatment of Egypt's economic and agricultural crisis.

Chapter 4 also assesses the impact of the reforms revealed by an examination of aggregate data like productivity levels, exports, poverty levels, and income. These are the indices most often used by the protagonists of reform to assess the success of liberalisation. This provides the material to indicate the weaknesses in the impact of the reforms that follow from the defective characterisation by the IFIs and the GoE of the country's problems. Chapter 4 begins the critique of the ERSAP. I assess the difficulties surrounding the conceptualisation of agriculture that are used by reformers, the fallacy of comparative advantage, and the tyranny of the market. In addition, I lay out the importance of having a clearer understanding of what actually happens in the countryside, the form that the agrarian question has taken in Egypt, and the importance of situating women and labour migrancy, among other things, centre stage in plans for economic reform.

Chapter 5 extends my general critique to an assessment of new data from Delta governorates. The data demonstrate a range of strategies adopted by farmers to cope with economic transformation and an indication of the complex ways in which households manage resources. The pressures of liberalisation have become acute and have been uneven in their impact, yet the strategy of economic reform has been universal in its application.

Chapter 6 suggests that Egypt is at a turning point. There remains little evidence that the state has significantly erased rent seeking to promote greater efficiency to ensure the declared possible benefits of market reforms. Changes in land tenure legislation, Law 96 of 1992, allowed landlords to raise rents and evict tenants, abolished Nasser's 1952 agrarian reform law, and have generated sustained, albeit uneven, opposition from poorer tenants and farmers throughout the country. The pursuit of grand development projects, moreover, like Tushka, to irrigate the western desert, promise to devour available resources before proper assessments have been made of their impact. Most disturbing of all, however, is the issue of Egypt's increased authoritarian polity. Market liberalisation has been accompanied not by improved governance arrangements and democracy, but by political deliberalisation. Complaints regarding the regime's clumsy handling of elections, vote rigging, and abuse of electors' rights are the most obvious aspects of deliberalisation. But there is another side, and one that will be much more difficult for political actors to reform even if they have the desire to do so: the abuse of human rights. Amnesty International and other independent auditors of global human rights have noted that the GoE has failed to prevent the fundamental abuse of human rights, of wrongful imprisonments, unfair trials, and ill treatment of detainees and prisoners of conscience. Torture by police and security forces has become routine and therefore far more difficult to exorcise. Amnesty's calls in 1997 and 1998 for the end to trials of civilians before military courts and for political prisoners to be given fair trials seem to have gone unheeded by the GoE. So, too, has the call for an independent body to investigate accusations of torture. In addition, these abuses are not restricted to the forces of law and (dis)order. In 1997, armed opposition groups claiming radical Islamist credentials took the lives of at least 100 civilians. The *Gama 'a al-Islamiya* has attempted to use sectarian murder to mobilise support for its opposition to the GoE. It has attacked Coptic Christians in Upper Egypt and also claimed responsibility for the slaughter of fifty-eight foreign tourists in Luxor in November 1997 (Amnesty International 1998; Humana 1992).

Although increased hardship and accelerated levels of poverty might increase the sympathy Egyptians have for radical Islam, it is unlikely to pose a serious challenge to the GoE. The authoritarian structures of government seem impenetrable by the weak forces of insurrection. The structures of government, however, may not have such a strong influence with the IFIs, at a time when the regime's strategic influence is dwindling. Notwithstanding President Mubarak's pretension to replace the late King Hussein of Jordan as the region's elder statesman, the IFIs are impatient for the GoE to deliver a decent return on their investment: a successful vibrant model of liberalisation. Although the IFIs cannot risk another failure, they are also aware of the need to break down state resistance to reforms and to demonstrate the declared efficacy of private capital rather than the continued dominance of the public sector.

2

The Origins of Egypt's
Economic Crisis

This chapter traces the background of the post-1991 economic reforms. It does so by examining the ways in which successive Egyptian regimes have tried to generate economic growth and development. I also look at the historical influence of international involvement in Egypt's liberalisation and the importance of the United States to that. One commentator has suggested that Western involvement may have retarded the pace of liberalisation. Springborg has argued this because Washington policymakers have been torn between, on the one hand, promoting economic liberalisation and U.S. business interests and, on the other, not undermining the authority and political stability of the Egyptian state, which might be jeopardised if Egyptians reject the consequences of reform (Springborg 1993:153). At different times, Egypt has used its strategic rent to maximise economic returns from the United States, but these returns have never been as great as Egypt's policymakers would have liked.

This chapter also shows that there are many parallels in the emergence of Egypt's economic crisis and the recurrent ways in which the government has responded to it. There are many similarities, for instance, between the strategy of Sadat's *infitah* and the push by the IFIs in the 1990s to liberalise the Egyptian political economy. Although liberalisation began after the 1967 war with Israel, it was accelerated following Sadat's October Paper in 1974 (el-Sadat 1974). Although the *infitah* began with optimism, it led to a fourfold increase in imports (especially of food), without a corresponding level of domestic production and exports. The principal effect of *infitah*, aside from an oil-financed boom in infrastructure and construction, was to provide the opportunity for speculative investment and the consolidation of Cairo as a place for Gulf Arabs to spend their summer vacations.

In ways very similar to the promises of Sadat, the IFIs in the 1990s pledged economic growth based on liberalisation of investment and trade. Yet as Abdel Khalek understood in the 1970s, and as he has reiterated in his critique of liberalisation since, limited growth might occur with *infitah*, but it was unlikely to promote sustained and balanced *development* (Abdel Khalek 1979). Of course, the political and economic stakes seemed much higher in the early 1990s than they did in the 1970s. The reason is the threats posed to Egypt's stability by Islamist opposition that may have been fuelled by increased economic hardship after 1991. Islamist terror has led to a misplaced fear of an Algerian scenario in what is perceived as perhaps a more strategically important country. Moreover, the levels of surveillance maintained and orchestrated by the IFIs was more detailed and intrusive in the 1990s than in earlier experiments with liberalisation. The scope of the contemporary programme is much wider than before, introduced as it was on the back of an acute economic crisis and President Mubarak's support for Operation Desert Storm.

Nasser's Break with the Ancien Régime

The Free Officers and the Revolutionary Command Council inherited in July 1952 a stagnant and corrupt economy. "Statistically Egypt stood still in the 40 years before 1950" (Yapp 1996:62). Economic growth in the period had been about 1.5 percent per annum. The average Egyptian was about as well off in 1950 as in 1910—in fact, probably rather worse off because of worsening terms of trade and poorer income distribution.

The July coup d'état signalled a major new beginning—the Egyptian revolution. The key features were a major agrarian reform begun in 1952, the disbanding of political parties, and the abolition of the monarchy, leading to the establishment of the Egyptian Republic in 1953. A year later, Britain was forced out of the Suez Canal Zone (to return momentarily with French and Israeli forces in 1956), and after 1952 institutions emerged that were intended to promote and consolidate economic production.

Nasser's agenda focussed on four major issues: the economic and social development of Egypt; the spread of the Egyptian revolution to the rest of the Arab world; the promotion of the Non-Alignment Movement; and conflict with Israel. My concern is with the first of these issues and the impact that Nasser had in ultimately creating the conditions for Sadat's *infitah al-iktisadi*.

Nasser tried quickly to make Egypt a major industrial power (Waterbury 1983; Mabro 1974). To do this, he had to encourage investment in areas of manufacturing and capital goods production to generate economic growth with a strategy of import substitution industrialisation.

Nasser's presidency fell into three broad periods. During the first of these, between 1952 and 1956, he sought to modernise Egypt's economy, and to mobilise investable sources of income and savings when taxation was nonexistent and public service provision lamentable. This period witnessed an incrementalist approach to generating growth by seeking to establish a dialogue with the private sector (Aliboni et al. 1984; El-Kammash 1968). Private interests were represented on the Board for National Development, light industry was seen to be largely the preserve of private capital, and the Federation of Egyptian Business was respected by the military government. But although this period was marked by the protection of private sector interests, Nasser grew impatient with the reluctance of business to commit resources to industrialisation at the *pace* he thought important and, in the heavy goods sector, that he saw as necessary to reduce dependence upon Western technology. Impatience was not one-sided. Private business grew anxious about Nasser's 1955 arms deal with Czechoslovakia and the increased policing of private capitalist interests. For example, new ventures needed to apply for permission from the state, and the nationalisation of the Suez Canal and the banks in 1956 shocked private capitalists, as did the short-lived 1958 political union with Syria that created the United Arab Republic. The 1952 land reforms were also perceived as acts of dispossession.

The Struggles for Land

Nasser's land reforms of 1952 and 1961 involved the seizure of estates belonging to the royal family and the prohibition of landowning by foreigners. The value of rents was reduced to seven times the land tax, and a limit was imposed on the amount of land that an individual could own: 300 *feddans* in the 1952 act, and then 100 *feddans* after the 1961 reform. A further reform in 1969 limited a person's landownership to 50 *feddans*.

There were three dimensions to Nasser's 1952 and subsequent land reforms: the redistribution of rural resources; the attempt to shift the balance of political power in the countryside away from landowners; and the desire to drain surplus from agriculture to subsidise urban growth and industrialisation (Radwan and Lee 1986). The reforms went beyond the political concern of simply minimising opposition to the Free Officers by Egypt's pasha class. The reforms tried to improve the efficiency and effectiveness of the agricultural sector. The reforms aimed at expanding irrigation, establishing legal rights for tenants and minimum wages for agricultural labourers, and providing improved production and marketing infrastructure.

On the eve of the revolution, about 60 percent of Egypt's cultivated land was worked under very tough tenancy agreements. Landlords and foreign companies generated monopoly profits, and they evicted tenants without providing compensation. Between 1931 and 1950, rental values increased fourfold, opportunities for rural credit were limited—controlled by two foreign banks—and rural poverty increased. There were only very limited earning opportunities for Egypt's 45 percent of agricultural households that neither owned nor rented land. As El-Ghonemy has summarised, "The pre-1952 land based power structure obstructed rural development and stratified the rural society into an upper class minority of rich landlords and cotton merchants and a mass of very low income and poor *fellaheen*" (El-Ghonemy 1990:226–227).

In the period 1810–1835, Mohemad Ali granted land-use rights to clients and officeholders who were valuable in maintaining rural order (Cuno 1992). Landholdings were converted to private ownership between 1835 and 1897 with the principle aim of facilitating the generation of income from land taxes. By 1858 land tenure laws had been reformed. Individual ownership was allowed, and community usufruct rights and nonhereditary rights controlled by officials were reduced. This different legislative framework was a major precondition for the growth of capitalist agriculture. It certainly facilitated the emergence of estate agriculture with foreign investment, as well as growth of royal family interest in landownership (Saunders and Mehanna 1986).

Although the evidence is scanty, the period between 1835 and 1897 suggests a dramatic increase in total cultivable area by 60 percent, a doubling of the cropped area, and an increase in land-use intensity of 37 percent (El-Ghonemy 1992:176–177). This period was one of public investment, especially in irrigation, and the growth of European interests in estate agriculture and cotton production. Growth slowed in the period 1897–1952, as levels of investment fell, absentee landlordism prevailed, and peasant impoverishment increased.

After the 1952 revolution, Nasser tried to use the fellahin for two purposes. First, to promote a rhetoric of equity and social justice, the fellahin became a bulwark against a politically antagonistic pasha social class, and second, they continued to be a vehicle for generating economic surplus to assist rapid industrialisation.

Nasser's land reforms meant that those owning 5 *feddans* or less gained from redistribution. In 1952, they represented 94 percent of all owners and controlled 35 percent of cultivated area. After the first reforms, they owned 52 percent of cultivated acreage. Those who probably gained most, however, were the middle peasants—those owning 11–50 *feddans*. The reforms led to this class representing 3 percent of all landowners and owning 24 percent of the cultivated area. Middle peasants strengthened their position by purchasing land sold as a result of the 1952 reforms, and they were also able to shape the character of, and control the benefits derived from, the post-1952 system of agricultural cooperatives (Abdel Fadil 1975).

The system of cooperatives dominated the lives of the fellahin. It provided farming inputs and the allocation of tractors, the supply of credit, and the purchase of crops through marketing agencies. In addition to undermining the power of the pashas, the land reforms for the first time provided a legal and institutional framework within which the peasantry gained access to farming implements and fixed minimum wages, land rents, and improved tenancy agreements. These gains were not effectively challenged until Law 96 of 1992.

The land reforms had the declared intention to "build Egyptian Society on a new basis by providing free life and dignity to each peasant and by abolishing the wide gap between classes and by removing an important cause of social and political instability" (Land Reform Act No. 178, 9 September 1952, cited in El-Ghonemy 1990:228). Yet by 1980 only 13.9 percent of the total cultivated land was redistributed to 9.6 percent of total agricultural households. This act was characterised as a partial land reform, which included compensation to those dispossessed, the maintenance of the institution of private property, and different limits on the size of landholdings at different times, and wide variations continued in the size of landholdings between classes and especially among those households with less than 5 *feddans*.

Nasser's Move to the Left

The second period of Nasser's presidency is noted as a period of "directed capitalism" and spanned 1957–1961. Although it may still be seen as a period of partnership with private capitalist interests, Nasser became more and more impatient with the lack of entrepreneurial support for the state's role in promoting industrialisation and declared a "socialist-democratic-co-operative society" where the role of the state was to prevent excessive exploitation. By the end of 1961 the state had nationalised the majority of large and medium-sized firms and had promoted urban rent control and free health and education provision.

The third period of Nasser's presidency 1961–1970 is characterised as a period of "national capitalism." Investment policy focussed on seeking a rapid and broad-based industrialisation. Between 1952 and 1966 about 700 million Egyptian pounds (LE) in shares and assets were transferred to the public sector (Waterbury 1983:75). Nasser stressed that socialism was the only road to justice, where socialism meant equality of opportunity and the greater sharing of national assets according to need. Yet he also noted that the specific quality of Arab socialism was not to dispossess but to allow private ownership without exploitation (Mansfield 1969; Stephens

1971; Ginat 1997). The contradictory assertions about the specificity of Arab socialism were consolidated in the National Charter of 1961. The National Charter reaffirmed the Arab character of Egypt, attacked reactionaries and "feudal" elements in the rest of the Arab world, and declared the banner of freedom, socialism, and unity. The charter served two important functions: it set out the rationale for policies of nationalisation and the importance of the state being actively involved in development when local entrepreneurs failed to deliver investable surpluses, and it confirmed the increasingly authoritarian character of the regime. Described as a "populist," Nasser had step by step erased the opportunity for political expression and representation. He did that while simultaneously declaring that the single government party, the Arab Socialist Union (the successor to the Liberation Rally and then the National Union), increased the formal participation of workers and peasants while downgrading the historical power of feudal landowners and emerging businessmen.

Nasser's populism was rooted in his rhetorical promotion of Arab nationalism and his real delivery of improved living conditions for Egypt's middle classes and poor. Nasser essentially delivered a "social contract" in which political repression was extracted from the working class and peasantry in return for the government's delivery of basic services. Job guarantees were given for all young Egyptians as well as promises about salaries and housing provision. Expectations were high, and Nasser managed to deliver goods and services to a much wider group of Egyptians because he had success in increasing Egypt's GDP (gross domestic product) that doubled between 1961 and 1970. The rate of economic growth from 1955 to 1965 was about 7.0 percent. Per capita income also grew, although by only about 2 percent as many gains were offset by increasing population growth. Schools were built at a rapid pace (an average of one a day) between 1952 and 1966, and the numbers of children receiving free primary education rose by 1.3 million to 3.4 million, of which more than a million were girls. The period 1955–1965 was also marked by a high rate of investment, averaging 17.0 percent of GDP.

In addition to its authoritarianism, however, there emerged another recurrent dimension to Nasser's presidency: debt. Total civilian debt at the time of Nasser's death in 1970 was $1.7 billion. Much of this had resulted from the building of the Aswân High Dam and industrial projects during the First Five-Year Development Plan, 1960–1965. This debt had also been accumulated because Nasser took the view that using foreign loans to maintain investment levels was preferable to cutting domestic consumption. Nasserism had set high expectations, and the president did not want to lower these. Nasser feared the scorn that might emerge from elements of a not altogether subordinated working class and peasantry, Western critics, reactionary Arab neighbours, and Islamists who had tried to assassinate him on several occasions. Although between 1965 and 1966 imports were reduced to finance the deficit, Egypt was hit with dramatically increased bills for its wheat imports.

The major watershed accentuating the economic crisis was the defeat by Israel in 1967. Although Nasser managed to survive the personal humiliation, the war added to an increasing deficit. Between 1967 and 1973 expenditure on armanents increased 600 percent, from LE150 million to LE1 billion. Defeat resulted in the occupation of Sinai, destruction of oil-processing facilities, loss of revenue from Suez rents, and increased migration to Cairo by displaced Egyptians. It also led to a rethinking by Nasser of the need to relax state control of the economy—for a degree of liberalisation. The 30 March Programme of 1968 conceded, among other things, the need for greater freedom for Egyptians with overseas deposits of foreign currency to import it without restriction.

Nasser had established the strength and spread of the Egyptian state, and he endowed "it with a nationalist-populist legitimacy" (Hinnebusch 1990:188). He also promoted a modernisation of the economy through the use of a large public sector, bureaucracy, and the mobilisation of subordinate classes against the old landed elites and private business elites. The mobilisation of popular support was facilitated by the establishment of a new social contract: The state delivered new economic rights and the working class and peasantry submitted (often reluctantly and unevenly; Pripstein-Posusney 1997) to an authoritarian and unrepresentative new military and bureaucratic elite.

Despite Nasser's many successes, his reification of control of the economy at the expense of promoting democratic and participative structures failed to institutionalise Nasserism and meant that no successor would continue to carry the torch. Although Nasser had in many ways accommodated the bourgeoisie in the new state structures and public sector activities, he had never fully conferred on them the authority that would enable them to accumulate capital independently of the state. This perpetuated a crisis that Nasser had tried to resolve, namely, generating local savings for domestic investment. These savings were desperately needed to sustain the strategy for industrialisation that was necessary to deliver the goods to the working class and poor, enabling populist rhetoric to be sustained. There emerged with Nasserism an inherent contradiction "between the ideological superstructure and the socio-economic base of the regime which ultimately would be bridged, once the charismatic leader passed, by a bourgeois recapture of state power" (Hinnebusch 1990:190). Nasser failed to ensure the longevity of the revolution because he was repeatedly confronted with the difficulty of generating sufficient amounts of investible resources for industrialisation. He also failed to create an organic relationship with Egypt's rapidly increasing population of industrial workers and farmers. Both were needed to entrench industrialisation and provide a balance between capital goods production and consumption goods. Nasser's heritage was the rhetoric of populism, the gradual surrender of statism, and the maintenance of coercion.

Sadat and *Infitah*

The 1967 defeat by Israel and mounting foreign debt created conditions for President Sadat's policies of *infitah*, or "open-door economic policy." This became the cornerstone of Sadat's policies of de-Nasserisation. *Infitah* began with optimism and ended with the food riots of January 1977. Sadat set about reversing Nasser's heritage, including the legal framework of security set in place for Egypt's peasantry. Specifically, Sadat sought to break links with the Soviet Union; to end any notion of socialist policy or rhetoric; and to end the Israeli occupation of Sinai. These measures were enacted, initially at least, by Sadat maintaining Nasserist rhetoric but undermining the state's hold on the economy— Cairenes joked that he told the chauffeur to indicate left while moving right. He exercised initial policy caution until he erased opposition within the state, the military, and the Arab Socialist Union (Henry 1997:66).

Sadat's strategy was to bring together Arab capital, Western technology, and Egyptian resources (Cooper 1992). This combination was an attempt to reduce the development constraints of both a savings gap and a foreign exchange gap. Nasser had tried to bridge these by an interventionist state mobilising private sector resources. Sadat now wanted to remove the Nasserist "statist shackles" seen as restrictive of incentive and economic growth. And Sadat sought to do this by invoking Nasser's heritage, arguing that the former president would have been an advocate of *infitah* because the path to economic liberalisation had already been prepared by Nasser's 1968 March Programme.

Infitah was launched after the October 1973 war with Israel. The war gave Sadat confidence and established him with greater credibility and authority among many Egyptians. Sadat's October Paper of 1974 called for a return to pre-1965 growth rates. The mechanism for doing this was to attract inward investment and to encourage Western banks to operate from Egypt and promote joint investment ventures. These policies were aided initially by the increases in oil prices following the October 1973 conflict. Millions of Egyptians migrated to the Gulf and other Arab countries for work and remitted billions of dollars from the mid-1970s. Arab countries benefiting from enhanced oil revenues also invested in Egypt. One estimate is that remittances and capital from Arab oil-exporting countries in the mid-1970s accounted for $3 billion of the annual flows to Egypt and that Western aid, especially from the United States, averaged $2 billion a year (Ibrahim and Löfgren 1996:162).

Underpinning Sadat's economic policy was a crucial political consideration. Sadat needed first to properly establish and then consolidate his political power base. He needed to establish his own legitimacy and authority. He received support for *infitah* from sections of the working class that perceived possibilities for improved employment at home and overseas. He also got more robust support from Egypt's upper classes, landed interests, and professionals. And there emerged a relatively new group of businessmen and intermediaries with links to international companies.

Sadat's first and crucial group of supporters was found in the state bureaucracy. Nasser had largely denied this group free-and-easy control over their economic assets, but Sadat promised liberalisation that would free them to engage more easily in their interests in Egypt's business community. Sadat did not go unchallenged in his promise that economic liberalisation would generate widespread benefits across Egypt. But the opposition, notably from Ali Sabri (one of the claimants to the mantle of Nasserism), had little effective support and was outmanoeuvred. In short, Sadat recruited more widely to the machinery of government from capitalist elements and in so doing linked the state more effectively with conservative social forces, eroding the power of the left and ideologues who believed that the state could remain an effective mechanism to orchestrate economic growth.

Sadat extended his authority by also developing a social base among landowners. He promoted the desequestration of land acquired in the Nasser years. And after 1975, he pushed for the end of a rents freeze on agricultural land that had been in effect since 1952; the abolition of the disputes committee that handled conflicts between landowners and tenants; the erosion of any political functions of the agrarian reform cooperatives in 1976–1977 (whose board members had been elected by peasants); and an increase in the reconsolidation of "agricultural land in the hands of wealthy landowners through purchase and court action" (Springborg 1991:234–235).

In addition to Sadat's policies of economic opening, he initiated political liberalisation. For the first time since 1952, groupings within the ASU (Arab Socialist Union) were condoned in 1976, and then in 1977 five political parties were created by Sadat. Conveniently covering the spectrum of political division—at least on paper—the five parties put forward candidates for elections in 1976 and 1979 and were allowed to publish their own newspapers. These parties were Sadat's Egypt's Party, which became the ruling National Democratic Party (centrist); the Liberal Party (rightist); the Progressive Unionist Party (leftist); the Labour Socialist

Party (left of centre); and the New Wafd (right of centre). Sadat, however, soon became disillusioned with democratic experiments, even the limited excursion into electoral politics that he had stage-managed. The parties were unhappy with the way elections were manipulated by the ruling party. In the 1979 election none of the major parties won a seat, and despite his control, Sadat grew angry with dissent. By 1981 deliberalisation set in—he was assassinated in October the same year.

Although Sadat's regime offered promise of economic growth and development, it foundered on the rocks of being unable to promote sustainable economic expansion. Egypt's external debt rose dramatically from less than $5 billion in 1970 ($1.7 billion civilian debt and an estimated $3.3 billion military debt) to about $30 billion in 1981. The civilian debt was mostly generated in 1970–1975, the first five years of Sadat's presidency, rising 350 percent, from $1.7 billion to $6.3 billion (Ibrahim and Löfgren 1996:164). The regime also developed a reputation for corruption across government, extending to the president's family. The wealthy who benefited from *infitah* became loathed by those who increasingly suffered from accelerated inequalities in wealth. A major outbreak of dissatisfaction occurred in 1977 when food riots, protesting the reduction of food subsidies accompanying IMF (International Monetary Fund) advice, took the regime by surprise. The military was used to quell the rioters, its use perhaps indicating the final death of Nasser's attempts to promote economic justice. Although *infitah* was sustained for a short time by aid from the West, a boost in oil prices, and labour migrant remittances, it still relied heavily upon growing debt, uneven national levels of equality, and escalating poverty. It was helped in the strategy to cope with these increasing costs of economic liberalisation by U.S. support, financial, military, and economic.

The International Context

A major recurrent theme underpinning the Nasser and Sadat regimes was the continuous importance of relations between Egypt and the United States. The two main dimensions to this relationship were the politics of food that I want to discuss now and the increasing importance of USAID that I examine in Chapter 3.

The Politics of PL480

U.S. food aid to Egypt was a major factor shaping relations between the two countries between 1955 and 1992. Food aid took the form of PL480, or to give it the full title, the Agricultural Trade Development and Assistance Act—known also as "Food for Peace." The history of PL480 is significant. At different times it became a measure of the relative bargaining strength of the United States with Egypt. It has been a significant economic lever in Washington's attempts to extract political compliance of states over which the United States wanted to exert influence. Indeed, U.S. agricultural trade policy and its food aid programme after World War II have greatly shaped the character of the "international" food system (Friedmann 1993; Friedmann and McMichael 1989; George 1979).

PL480 was a vehicle for promoting U.S. foreign policy interests under the guise of aid and trade. It was initially a tool to dispose of surplus U.S. food commodities on concessionary terms to client states, or states over which Washington sought to exercise control. It was not always effective in the leverage it sought to exact, and Egypt during the Nasser years is an important case in point.

PL480 was promoted within the United States as an important means to offset economic hardship of U.S. farmers resulting from food surpluses, falling prices, and overproduction. The initial champion of Food for Peace, was Senator Hubert Humphrey. He represented Minnesota, populated by small-scale farmers, who were most vulnerable to the processes of concentration and centralisation of U.S. capitalist farming.

Ultimately PL480 failed to address the structural crises of U.S. farming. It could be only a pressure valve that was periodically used by Washington to placate the strong domestic farming lobby in agricultural surplus years, and to discipline food-deficit states in lean years. Probably the most positive view of PL480 was conveyed by President Eisenhower as it became law on 10 July 1954. He noted that it would "lay the basis for a permanent expansion of our exports of agricultural products, with lasting benefits to people of other lands"(Wallerstein 1980:35). Contrasting with that perspective was one that has become more of a determinant in shaping the character of PL480; a leaked CIA report argued that world grain shortages

> could give the US a measure of power it had never had before possibly an economic and political dominance greater than that of the immediate post World War 2 years. In bad years when the US could meet the demand for food of most would be importers, Washington would acquire virtual life-and-death power over the fate of millions of the needy. Without indulging in blackmail in any sense, the US would gain extraordinary political and economic influence. For not only the poor LDCs [less-developed countries] but also the major powers would be at least partially dependent on food imports from the US. (Wallenstein 1976:287–288)

PL480 is divided into three sections, or titles. Two of these titles, II and III, have been completed in the case of Egypt. Title II involved a programme of selected food commodities on a grant basis to improve the nutritional status of targeted groups, and Title III provided wheat and flour on concessional terms that were then "forgiven"—as long as the Egyptian government could show that receipts from the sale of those foodstuffs locally were used to improve local services.

Title I of this act is the most important and most contentious. This programme helped finance U.S. agricultural commodity imports to Egypt at concessional rates. It involved not free or subsidised food, but balance-of-payments support to finance the import of U.S. agricultural commodities through subsidised loans. In the early 1990s, Title I assistance accounted for at least 20 percent of Egypt's wheat imports. In 1991–1992, credit offered to cover these imports equalled $165 million. It was reduced to $150 million in financial year 1992–1993 and then ceased. Since its inception in 1975, total funding of the programme has been $3.8 billion.

PL480 targeted a particular group of countries that were usually strategically located and accounted for a large proportion of U.S. assistance. Among these in the Middle East are Turkey, Israel, Egypt, and Jordan. In the case of Egypt it is very clear, when looking at the changes in the timing of aid, that it has been inextricably linked with the political character of the regime in Cairo and the leverage that Washington has been able to exert (Morsy 1986; Hussein 1981; Quandt 1988).

Between 1955 and 1964, U.S. food aid shipments to Egypt totalled $690 million or 11.7 percent of its total food aid (Moustapha, n.d., 14). Food aid to Egypt took many different turns and fluctuations. The volume and speed of aid depended upon the interrelationship of the character of the political regimes in Washington and Cairo and how well they coexisted. It also depended upon the particular foreign policies of the United States and Egypt and the willingness of third states, notably the former Soviet Union, to act as a catalyst in providing for regional Middle East stability.

The refusal of the United States to assist with the building of the Aswân Dam in 1956, and thus its reluctance to help Egypt in its ability to promote a degree of autonomous growth, led to the closer ties between Nasser and the former Soviet Union. The Kennedy administration was weary of those links, and Washington tried to undermine them by approving a $390-million three-year PL480 agreement with Cairo in 1962. It was part of the Kennedy administration's general foreign policy initiative to promote limited economic development in countries like Egypt and Brazil, in the hope of defusing any revolutionary (i.e., nationalist) forces in the third world (Chomsky 1969).

President Kennedy sent Harvard economist Edward S. Mason to Egypt in 1962 to assess the prospects for economic growth and political stability. His visit followed Syria's withdrawal from union with Egypt—a mistaken sign in Washington that Nasser was moderating his foreign policy. Indeed, no sooner had Egypt signed a PL480 agreement with the United States than Nasser committed Egyptian forces to intervene in the overthrow of the royal family in Yemen—an episode that arguably undermined Egypt's military capacity in the subsequent war with Israel. And there was an accompanying military buildup in Egypt and a threat to dynastic rule in Saudi Arabia.

Food shipments were renewed in 1965 after Lyndon B. Johnson replaced the assassinated President Kennedy. The shipments were restarted after being held up by Washington in response to Nasser's militancy in 1963 and 1964, and they followed the observation by the U.S. Secretary of State that Egypt had only three weeks' supply of grain remaining. Washington repeatedly kept Nasser hanging onto the promise of aid and then delayed its delivery. The United States would also not agree to a length of PL480 agreements that might give breathing space to enable successful food policy and development planning in Cairo. Uncertainty about the agreements also made it difficult for Cairo to divert money saved from food payments to industrial development and therefore undermined Nasser's strategy of industrialisation.

Strains in the relations between Nasser and the United States led to the ending of aid in 1967. A series of events had led to that cessation of assistance. Among these was Nasser's earlier support for the revolution in Yemen and two years later, in 1964, anti-American demonstrations in Alexandria against U.S. compliance with French intervention in Congo. Egyptian military also shot down a U.S. oil company plane after it had strayed into a military zone near Alexandria: the owner was a friend of President Johnson. The combination of these incidents led to heightened calls in Congress for U.S. assistance to stop. And it did cease following the break of diplomatic relations after the 1967 Israeli war. At that time the Egyptian food reserve was enough for just fifteen days: wheat production of 1.5 million tons left a deficit of 2.5 million tons.

PL480 started again alongside much stronger links between Egypt and the United States. The closer relationship was at the heart of Sadat's policies following the 1973 war with Israel. Sadat's increased bargaining power resulted from, among other things, the Arab oil embargo, although this was partial and brief. The United States also recognised that Sadat offered the possibility of greater leverage in the region for North American strategic interests and relations with Israel. U.S. grain deliveries began in the winter of 1973–1974 after U.S. Secretary of State Henry Kissinger visited the region. The United States wanted Sadat's acceptance of Washington, rather than Moscow, as broker for peace in the Middle East. And it was soon after the restart of PL480 shipments in 1974 that USAID began its Egypt operation.

In the first periods of U.S. relations with Egypt, the political strength of Nasser, the authority of the regime, and the broad respect it had in the less-developed countries for its role in the politics of nonalignment determined when and how much assistance was delivered by the United States. It also seems that the United States recognised that Nasser did not automatically agree with the Soviet line on international relations, and this created an opportunity for the United States to perhaps tease him away from Moscow (Sayed-Ahmed 1993). U.S. food power was important: Washington used the timing, quantity, and character of PL480 to shape its links with Egypt.

Nasser knew that the domestic political costs of automatic compliance with U.S. foreign policy over Yemen, Egypt's military buildup, and confrontation with Israel outweighed any possibility of maintaining his regime's social base. Yet he was not always able to hold off U.S. food power. He was unable, for instance, in 1963 to prevent Washington from stopping supplies and slowing down delivery after an agreement in October 1962.

Washington's relations with Nasser and Sadat were always part of U.S. government attempts to gain a stronger foothold in the Middle East. When aid started flowing again in 1974 to Sadat's regime, it was at a level far greater than the original request from the U.S. Embassy in Cairo. It led one commentator to note: "From the outset, the aid program was overfinanced and the level of funding was politically determined" (Waterbury 1983:403). U.S.-Egyptian relations came to a head with Sadat's 1978 Camp David peace agreement with Israel.

Camp David highlighted Egyptian compliance with U.S. geostrategic interests, and ensured that the most populous Arab state no longer posed a threat to Israel. The United States promised Sadat that funding for Egypt would be roughly equal to U.S. support for Israel, but that was never the case either in volume or in the type of support. And it is significant that President Carter refused to endorse Sadat's call for a "Marshall Plan'" for economic recovery and growth in Egypt (Eilts 1988:137).

U.S. aid since Camp David has been much more closely (and openly) tied to the promotion of economic reform. In both 1988 and 1989, cash elements of support representing some $115 million a year were held back awaiting compliance with economic policy changes in Cairo (Eilts 1988:135). Yet it is the interrelationship between political and economic conditionality, geostrategic interest, and fear of political Islam—the continued need for Egypt's role of moderation in the region—that has ultimately underpinned U.S. policy. This view is best summarised in USAID's own words:

U.S. economic assistance is crucial to support Egypt's moderating role in the Middle East and to help Egypt confront political and economic problems which could endanger Egyptian stability. The rationale for substantial assistance to Egypt in recognition of Egypt's role in maintaining stability in the Middle East has been reinforced by the current Persian Gulf crisis [1990–1991] and by Egypt's leadership role in trying to resolve it. The US national interest is well served by an Egypt which is strong enough to play this constructive role. (USAID 1992a:3)

Mubarak and the Economic Crisis of the 1980s

The Egyptian economy had grown by about 8 percent per annum between 1974 and 1985 (Handoussa 1991:3). Per capita income doubled from $334 in 1974 to $700 in 1984, and current account receipts rose from just $3 billion in the mid-1970s to $13 billion in the mid-1980s. But the 1970s were in many ways falsely hailed as boom years. Growth resulted from the increase in foreign exchange earnings after the October war of 1973. That growth was attributable to the impact that the Egyptian-Israeli peace agreement had on regional stability, the increase in the price of petroleum, and an increase in worker remittances, earnings from the Suez Canal, tourism, and overseas, particularly U.S. aid. Growth, in other words, still originated from "traditional" rents and foreign aid rather than national industrial productive activity.

Economic growth was short-lived. The oil-based boom ended in the mid-1980s and led to domestic and regional unemployment and the reduction in the numbers of Egyptians employed as labour migrants in neighbouring oil-producing states. The frailty of Egypt's economy to changes in the international economy once again became clear. By late 1985 there was net return migration, and "open unemployment" reached unprecedented levels of almost 15 percent, or 2 million out of a labour force of 13.7 million (International Labor Office 1991:3). Resource-based growth did not lead to sustained development, and economic opening had not promoted industrial development, but it did appear to generate agricultural neglect.

The essential weaknesses of the Egyptian economy continued to plague the new President Mubarak: the inability to generate access to local savings for investment, dependence upon foreign borrowing to pay for imports, and dependence upon "windfall profits" from oil and rents. Moreover, income that had been generated in the short term from *infitah* had not been invested in industrial or agricultural production, only in the service sectors, and Sadat's dependence upon the United States had included the import of expensive weaponry paid for with expensive loans—despite the peace with Israel.

Sadat had failed to establish an effective alternative to the public sector statist formula of Nasser, and he left Mubarak with an economic crisis. Indeed, shortly after becoming president, Mubarak set up a three-day economic conference in 1982 to establish a strategy for extricating Egypt from crisis. The policy suggestions included the need to reduce imports and the military budget and reduce dependence upon foreign loans. However, nothing seemed to change in the 1980s compared with the policies of the 1970s in terms of shifting dependence of the economy away from rental income (Ibrahim and Löfgren 1996:164). By the mid-1980s, foreign exchange from rents and remittances still accounted for three quarters of current account receipts and for more than 40 percent of GDP (compared to about 6 percent in 1974). One of Egypt's problems was that by 1987 total foreign exchange receipts, expressed in current 1989 U.S. dollars, were 2 percent lower than they had been in 1981 (Handoussa 1991:3; World Bank 1989b:130).

One of the reasons why Mubarak found it difficult to shift the underlying nature of the Egyptian economy was his caution about the political consequences of radical change. The 1977 food riots that accompanied Sadat's engagement with the IMF and his attempts to reduce food subsidies left a lasting impression on Mubarak. Even on the eve of the 1991 IMF and World Bank ERSAP, Mubarak insisted on the importance of safeguarding "our social and economic situation and the standard of living" (Seddon 1990:96). Because of Mubarak's apprehensiveness and his failure (unlike Nasser and Sadat) to promote a distinctive leadership style and role for himself in the early 1980s, compared with the 1990s, he failed to grasp the nettle of debt. The dramatic fall in the real value of windfall profits after 1982 left substantial external and local account imbalances. The deficit on Egypt's balance-of-payments current account reached a high of $5.3 billion in 1986 (15 percent of Egypt's GDP) and the budget deficit reached LE8.8 billion (23 percent of GDP). (Handoussa 1991:4). The recession that followed was prompted by a fall in the price of petroleum and a worsening in the terms of trade that cost Egypt 11 percent of its GDP. Between 1981–1982 and 1986–1987 Egypt's share of petroleum exports fell from US$3.3 billion to US$1.4 billion.

Nevertheless between 1983 and 1985, the state managed to sustain rates of growth in GDP of 6–7 percent. It did that, however, by running a balance-of-payments deficit and an increased foreign debt. Between 1981 and 1990 external debt rose to its highest ever modern-day figure, from $30 billion to $48 billion—about 150 percent of Egypt's GDP (Ibrahim and Löfgren 1996:165). The irony is that in this first phase of Mubarak's presidency, 1981–1987, he probably had the greatest amount of favourable popular will, which might have enabled him to push through economic reforms less draconian than those he was later compelled to accept.

The ten years from the mid-1970s to the mid-1980s were characterised by continued policies of subsidies for goods and services, rent controls, and price controls. Government deficits continued to be funded by foreign borrowings. GNP (gross national product) per capita declined by 10 percent between 1986 and 1990 ($670 to $610), and the mounting foreign debt made it increasingly obvious that the traditional mechanisms Egypt had to raise revenue from oil rents or the country's geostrategic position were insufficient to keep the creditors at bay.

Mubarak continued to be plagued by savings and investment gaps and an inefficient and corrupt public sector. Despite rhetoric to the contrary, the public sector grew during the Sadat and early Mubarak periods. Between 1975 and 1984 public revenue as a percentage of GDP grew from 34.4 percent to 43 percent (Hansen 1991). The twenty years after Nasser's death failed to usher in a radicalisation of the state that might have improved public sector provision to catalyse social and economic development. It also failed to deliver a market-based economy that promised improved sector investment. As Springborg noted, Egypt failed to "prioritize sectors and projects according to rational and clearly-articulated principles" (Springborg 1993:158; compare Waterbury 1985:78). That failure resulted from a combination of poor public policy and underlying structural resistance in government and the state apparatus to economic and political liberalisation.

Egypt's Recurrent Economic Crisis

There have been several continuous themes running through Egypt's political economy since 1952, including the relationship between state and development, the relationship between international aid and the national economy, and the inability of the agricultural sector to feed growing numbers of Egyptians. These themes, as we will see in the next two chapters, have been polarised around issues of whether the state is a suitable or necessary feature for Egyptian development.

Successive regimes have had considerable difficulty accessing sufficient quantities of local resources for chosen paths of national development. Access to investment has been the major challenge for Egypt's development and underpinned the debate regarding the extent of state intervention necessary to facilitate economic growth. The Egyptian debate has focussed on the Nasserist legacy, the extent to which the public sector was successful in generating economic growth and sustaining a populist appeal and delivering a social contract with the country's poor and working class.

The assessment of Sadat's presidency also focussed on the relative merits of the state in development and the extent to which the rolling

TABLE 2.1   Arab Republic of Egypt: Economic Structure

	1960	1970	1980	1990	1997
GDP US$ m	3,880	6,598	22,913	33,210	75,482
Distribution of GDP %					
Agriculture	30	29	18	17	16
Industry	24	28	37	29	32
Manufacturing	20	–	12	16	25
Services	46	42	45	53	53

SOURCE: Adapted from various World Bank *World Development Reports*: 1960, 1980, 1990, 1991, 1997, 1998–1999.

back of the state was a necessary component of economic liberalisation. Despite growth of the Egyptian private sector, Mubarak inherited a legacy of public sector development, and *infitah* failed to bridge savings and investment shortfalls. Mubarak's inheritance has also been one of an inefficient and often corrupt public sector that has failed to promote sustainable economic growth. One of Mubarak's dilemmas has been the reluctance of the Egyptian state to relinquish some of its political and economic power to encourage capitalist investment independent of government. Mubarak and his officials have also been unable to provide political leadership, authority, and legitimacy to harness national savings and local resources with foreign loans for development that meet the needs of Egyptians throughout the country. Indeed a feature of Mubarak's presidency, as he conceded economic adjustment and the increased role of international agencies after 1991, is accelerated inequality between Egypt's rich and poor and between Egypt's north and south.

The 1970s and 1980s were decades of agricultural neglect. Table 2.1 indicates the decline in agriculture's contribution to gross domestic product from 30 percent in 1960 to 16 percent in 1997. Egypt has experienced a recurrent food crisis. The popular view is that this crisis is best characterised by too little local production of food grains to feed a growing population. As in other countries in the region, the demand for food has been fuelled by population increase and growth in incomes following the oil boom years of the 1970s: food deficits led to the emergence of increasing levels of imports (Richards and Waterbury 1990:139–140; Adams 1985, 1986b; Richards 1982).

Yet this is at best only a partial account of Egypt's agricultural crisis— it is also somewhat inaccurate. Mitchell for example, has argued convincingly that, "the dependence on grain imports since 1974 has been caused not by population growth, which lagged behind the growth of domestic grain production, but by a shift to the consumption of meat".

(Mitchell 1995:134; 1991a; Thomson 1983:179). Although this change in tastes is explained by Richards as due mainly to changes in income and improved standards of living, Mitchell importantly provides evidence that U.S. grain links with Egypt shaped the change in diets, enhancing U.S. leverage with Egypt. After 1974 Egypt became the world's third largest importer of grain. Imports quadrupled in the 1970s to fill the gap between wheat production, which grew at less than 2 percent per annum, and wheat consumption, which grew at almost 9 percent. Subsidised U.S. loans, supplemented by further international borrowing to purchase grain imports, led, as we have seen, to increased external debt. Between 1966 and 1988 grain imports increased by 5.9 million metric tons, but it is probable that 5.3 million metric tons of this was for the tremendous increase in nonfood consumption of grains, notably as animal feed.

A fuller and more accurate account of Egypt's agricultural crisis in the 1970s recognises a change in domestic consumption patterns away from traditional foodstuffs towards meat. That shift was orchestrated by Egypt's increased reliance upon U.S. subsidised grain imports and government policy to bolster the interests of meat producers and consumers at the expense of local staple production. Consumption of corn, barley, and sorghum fell from 53 percent in 1966 to 6 percent in 1988. This decline was offset by increased consumption of imported wheat. The increased dependency upon imported grains and the change in consumption habits thus also began to affect the structure of Egyptian agriculture and not solely the volume of agricultural imports and balance of payments. Farmer priorities shifted away from the production of cotton and other "traditional" crops to focus more on meat, poultry, and dairy products and the cultivation of berseem as animal fodder (Mitchell 1995:135).

The twenty years to the end of the 1980s was marked by the substitution of locally produced foodstuffs by imports. Expressed in per capita terms, imports of basic food grains and pulses rose by just under eight times between 1970 and 1980. Consequently the overall trade balance for the agricultural sector, previously in surplus ($300 million) in 1970, became a deficit of $800 million by 1977 and $2.5 billion by 1980–1981. The annual net deficit in agricultural trade rose to $3 billion in the mid-1980s (USAID and the Government of Egypt 1995:4).

One estimate in 1992 put the cost to Egypt of importing food at $10 million a day, much of it for wheat and wheat flour (Economist Intelligence Unit 1992:19; Soliman 1992). As long as revenue could be generated to offset the cost of such import dependency, there was no obvious worry that reliance upon food imports would have a necessarily negative impact. Agricultural imports grew significantly between 1970 and the mid-1990s, as I indicate in the next chapter. Egypt's difficulty has essentially been twofold. It could temporarily pay for the cost of increased imports in the 1970s and early 1980s from oil rents, but this was only short term. The ability to generate sustained income for grain imports in the late 1980s and early 1990s dwindled. Second, the impact of subsidised U.S. grain imports and the shift in diets towards the consumption of meat rather than locally produced grains and pulses undermined the viability and structure of the agricultural sector. Despite the rhetoric of the international agencies with regard to the persistent intervention of government, agriculture has been neglected by the GoE, and the cost of its neglect is now being borne by the majority of the country's farmers.

We can now look at the strategy of agricultural reform that Mubarak embarked on in agriculture as early as 1986 to redress the problems I have sketched and, after ERSAP in 1991, for policies adopted for the economy as a whole.

3

Economic Reforms and Egyptian Agriculture

This chapter presents an overview of Egypt's 1991 economic reform and structural adjustment programme (ERSAP) and the economic reforms initiated in agriculture in 1986. It examines these reforms in the context of the prevailing understanding of Egypt's problems as described by the GoE and the IFIs. I highlight what has become a consensus in Egypt, and within the international agencies and the academic community, regarding the policy measures thought necessary to resolve the characterisation of the country's agricultural crisis. I pursue the need to understand the rationale underpinning an extensive range of policy suggestions for agricultural reform before assessing the outcome of the reform measures in terms of the broad aggregate of economic data used by most commentators.

My argument is that the economic strategy has little relevance to the concerns and real problems experienced by the vast majority of Egyptian farmers. The reforms, moreover, are unlikely to significantly raise (and sustain) levels of agricultural productivity. The policies that the World Bank, USAID, and the Ministry of Agriculture are applying in the Egyptian countryside may well bolster the economic and political position of large landholders but will undermine the more than 90 percent who have 4 *feddans* or less. Those "really poor" fellahin are seldom considered in the formulations of the agencies and the GoE. The gap in the way the agricultural strategy was conceived is likely to have a disastrous influence on the abilities of rural producers to cope with the economic hardship that accompanies economic adjustment. One of a series of questions that needs to be raised is the extent to which the refusal to grasp the reality of the Egyptian countryside is simply the ignorance of agencies that have not done their homework, or a deliberate policy to promote agricultural modernisation that excludes helping the majority of rural people?

Egypt's Economic Reform and Structural Adjustment Programme, 1986–1998

Egypt's ERSAP took three years to negotiate before it was signed in November 1991. Mubarak in that time became an experienced negotiator with the IMF and the World Bank. In May 1987, the GoE won agreement from the IMF to help Egypt reduce its foreign debt, built up, as we have seen, over the preceding decade during Sadat's *infitah*. Yet that 1987 agreement collapsed, as did later negotiations in 1988 for a replacement, when the IMF called for "shock treatment" to open Egypt's economy. Although Mubarak did make some concessions with the liberalisation of the exchange rate system, he was adamant that more radical action proposed by the IMF to increase interest rates to 20–25 percent, and to increase energy costs, would undermine the stability of his regime. Mubarak kept an eye on the social costs that compliance with the IFIs was likely to create. The irony is that the protracted negotiations, which culminated in 1991 with the IFIs' trumpeting Cairo's success in grasping the nettle of reform, went much further than any previous government affirmation of intent (Abdel-Khalek 1988; Seddon 1990; Niblock 1993; compare World Bank 1991a:30, 129). It is also important to ask why Mubarak felt compelled in 1991 to move ahead with "rolling back the state."

The May 1991 ERSAP agreement provided for an SDR (Special Drawing Rights) 400-million standby accord with the IMF and a $300-million structural adjustment loan (in U.S. dollars) with the World Bank. Agreement with the Paris Club in the same month covered about $27–28 billion (U.S. dollars) in official government and military debt linking relief with economic reform. The ERSAP led to significant reductions in state subsidies; the liberalisation of interest rates; the restoration of private currency dealing; a new sales tax; relaxation of the licensing system for trade; introduction of a single unified exchange rate; and commitment to reduce the budget deficit from 20 percent of GDP in 1990–1991 to 9.5 percent in 1991–1992 and 3.5 percent in 1994–1995 (Butter 1992; Refaat 1991; Bromley and Bush 1994).

The reforms were intended to open the economy to international capital: "to deal with macro-economic imbalances in the economy—to correct inflation and to allow interest and exchange rates to respond to market forces" (U.S. Embassy 1991:n.p.). Egypt has fulfilled many of its macroeconomic targets. There has been a big reduction in government budget deficit, falling from 17.7 percent of GDP in 1991 to about 0.8 percent in 1997. This fall resulted from increases in government revenue, notably from a new sales tax that doubled income compared with a pre-reform consumption tax to LE7.4 billion in 1993. All tax revenue increased from LE7.8 billion to LE13.3 billion between 1990 and 1993—an increase of 71 percent (Ibrahim and Löfgren 1996:171). The GoE has also reduced spending on subsidies to goods and services by 16 percent, from LE4.5 billion to LE3.8 billion in the twelve months following ERSAP.

The IMF and World Bank reforms were completed in 1993, and a new three-year IMF Extended Fund Facility focusing on structural reforms began. The second round of reforms hit the rocks quite quickly, however. There were large disagreements between the IMF and the GoE over the IMF demand for 20–30 percent currency devaluation. There was an extended period of protracted conflict, during which it is likely the U.S. State Department (with its eye on geostrategic stability) applied pressure to the IMF to dilute its preoccupation with devaluation and concentrate more on structural reform. After eighteen months of disagreement, when the IFIs grew ever more impatient with what was perceived as GoE backsliding on the seriousness of reforms, a new two-year standby agreement was signed in October 1996. Significantly, this agreement followed the formation of a new government in January 1996 headed by Prime Minister Kamal Al-Ganzouri. The IFIs and the U.S. Embassy in Cairo identified him as someone with whom business could clearly be done (interview with U.S. Embassy official April 1996). The 1996 agreement also built on the U.S.-Egyptian Partnership for Economic Growth and Development, which had been launched by Vice President Al Gore and President Mubarak in September 1994. That "partnership'" deal, intended to remove blockages to economic reform and to streamline decisionmaking and promote private sector growth, received a further boost in January 1996, at the time of the appointment of Egypt's new cabinet, when Al Gore visited Cairo to reinforce U.S. commitment to accelerated liberalisation.

The 1996 agreement was intended to consolidate the gains of the earlier reforms. It particularly sought to keep the budget deficit as close as possible to less than 1 percent of GDP and inflation to around 5 percent. It was also intended to meet the GoE concern that although ERSAP may have been effective in stabilising the economy, there was little evidence of increasing economic growth. The 1996 agreement was intended to increase the slow pace of privatisation and also to increase growth of 5–6 percent of GDP a year between 1996 and 1998 from the sale of public companies. This privatisation was to include the banking sector. Deregulation has also been signalled as part of the GoE unified business law passed in May 1997, the declared commitment to reduce civil service employment by 2 percent a year in 1996–1997, and the elimination of energy subsidies in petroleum products, gas, and electricity (International Monetary Fund 1997).

Privatisation has been one of the biggest obstacles in relations between the IFIs and the GoE. In 1991, there were 314 public companies with an official book value of LE90 billion and debts of LE77 billion. Law 203 of 1991 provided for public sector restructuring and the creation of 16 independent holding companies. But the Public Enterprise Office, established to oversee privatisation, was ineffective. In January 1996, a ministerial committee was established to oversee privatisation. Despite the GoE's declaration that privatisation was at the top of its agenda, there has been very little progress. Only 6 companies were put up for sale in the first half of 1997 despite a government list of fifty-two privatisations for the year. Serious difficulties remained about government vested interests in the public sector, overstaffing, accurate valuation of assets, and available investors to purchase state assets.

In March 1991 international donors, including the World Bank, the European Union, and the UN Development Programme, established the Social Fund for Development. Its brief was the alleviation of the impact of ERSAP on the poor and marginalised sections of Egyptian society. It began with $613 million supplemented by a second phase of $746 million in January 1997. It has mainly been involved in the initiation and coordination of labour-intensive projects creating employment for the poor women heads of households and establishing service provision in Egypt's poorest, mainly southern, governorates. Supporters of the Social Fund have argued that it has created 50,000–70,000 jobs a year—a quarter of all nonagricultural jobs each year. By the end of 1996 the Social Fund estimated that almost 20 million people had benefited from its activities and that it had created about 350,000 jobs—although just how many of these jobs were permanent, rather than short-term, is unclear (World Bank 1996a; Economist Intelligence Unit 1998:16).

Before examining the precise ways in which the advocates of reform in Egypt have promoted liberalisation in agriculture, it is important to pause for a moment to ask why the ERSAP was agreed upon in 1991. There was a coincidence at that time of international, local economic, and geostrategic processes that gave the IFIs more leverage than ever before. These processes related in particular to the success of Mubarak's leadership in explaining Egyptian support for the U.S.-led Gulf War against Iraq. Considerable repressive Egyptian state apparatus that deflected criticism of the GoE, though little reported, aided that success. It also created a media image of a government capable of "courageous" reforms. Mubarak's position in the war also led to the economic underwriting of his regime. He was rewarded with a considerable debt write-off.

Domestically, Mubarak's call for rolling back the state was an attempt to secure his social and economic base of support from among those

TABLE 3.1   U.S. Aid to Egypt[a] ($ m)

	1992	1993	1994	1995	1996
Commodity export credit guarantees	40	115	160	165	200
Agricultural commodity loans (PL 480)[b]	150	0	0	0	0
Economic grant aid	892	747	592	815	815
Military grant aid	1,300	1,300	1,300	1,300	1,300
Total (obligation basis)	2,382	2,162	2,052	2,439	2,300

[a]US fiscal Years.
[b]USAID programme.
SOURCE: © The Economist Intelligence Unit Ltd. Reproduced by permission of the Economist Intelligence Unit Ltd.

classes that were blocked during the Nasser years and that were not entirely provided for by Sadat. These are the interests located in finance capital, construction, and services, those likely to benefit from economic liberalisation as long as the ERSAP did not crowd them out with foreign competition. The domestic constituency also included the military, which in 1997 took soundings about the possibility of purchasing Chinese military equipment if for any reason the United States got tough with Egypt and cut off military assistance. Egypt has 450,000 people in its armed services, of which 320,000 are conscripts. It was the second largest arms importer in the region in 1996–1997 (July–June) at $2.3 billion, funded mostly from an annual U.S. military assistance budget of $1.3 billion (Economist Intelligence Unit 1998:12). Mubarak may well have resisted the appointment of a deputy president (usually taken from the military), but he has been keen to meet the military's corporate interests and to use them ruthlessly when necessary. He did this in 1986 against a mutiny of 20,000 conscripts and against Islamists in the early 1990s.

Agricultural Reform

Agricultural liberalisation began in 1986, five years ahead of the economic reform programme of 1991. The international agencies have long had an ally in Yusuf Wali, the deputy prime minister and Minister of Agriculture and Land Reclamation. He has fought for market liberalisation and privatisation in agriculture (Sadowski 1991; Khedr, Ehrich, and Fletcher 1996), and the MALR has been a pioneer in applying a strategy of economic reform and adjustment. The GoE has worked very closely with USAID since 1986 in the promotion of the agricultural reform programme. Table 3.1 summarises U.S. aid to Egypt between 1992 and 1996.

The collaboration between the GoE and USAID has had the following elements: the removal of government controls on farm output prices, cropping areas, and procurement quotas with regard to all crops; increasing farm gate prices of cotton and sugar cane to come into line with international prices; the removal of farm input subsidies; and the removal of government constraints on the private sector in importing, exporting, and distributing farm inputs to compete with the Principle Bank for Development and Agricultural Credit (PBDAC). In the words of a recent MALR document:

> The economic reform program aims at: releasing the agricultural sector from all restrictions and distortions; encouraging the private sector; improving terms of trade of agriculture and relieving the burden on it; encouraging the farmers to use modern technology in agriculture; increasing cultivable areas, productivity and farm income; improving the standard of living for the farmers . . . and providing food . . . at reasonable prices; increasing export and raising the share of the agricultural sector in the social and economic development of the country. (Nassar 1993:3–4)

Economic reform in agriculture is intended to redress a recent record of poor growth. Between 1981 and 1992 the average rate of real growth in the agricultural sector was about 2 percent per annum. This was 2 percent less than was thought to be necessary to sustain economic growth and far short of the GoE target of 5 percent. Agricultural growth of 1.9 percent in 1980–1985, down from 2.8 percent 1965–1980, was less than the estimated population growth of 2.7 percent per annum, and government policies that had favoured food imports, discussed briefly in Chapter 2, led to an estimated annual net deficit of $3 billion in agricultural trade by the mid-1980s (Khedr et al. 1996:53).

The MALR has identified excessive government intervention as the cause of a decline in agricultural productivity. These policies included price and marketing controls, the state ownership of major agricultural industries, and an overvalued exchange rate. By the early 1980s the extent of the agricultural crisis had led the GoE to work with USAID to formulate the U.S.-funded Agricultural Production and Credit Project (APCP).

The APCP was initiated in 1986 to deregulate the agricultural sector and increase the capacity of the PBDAC. It has had two main phases and cost $289 million ending in September 1996. The first phase, 1987–1989, examined issues relating to the liberalisation of price and marketing controls and the government system of delivery quotas for ten major crops. This programme freed markets for ten crops, farm gate prices for fertiliser rose by 75 percent, and the PBDAC began to reduce its activities in input provision. The second phase, 1990–1994, concentrated on policy reforms and set quantifiable targets for agricultural output. In particular, attention focused on the relaxation of the cotton sector, including government control of seed and fertiliser provision. Other important accomplishments noted by USAID have been the transition of PBDAC from a specialised agricultural bank to a "viable rural bank." That has involved staff training—about 25,000 in Egypt and 230 overseas. USAID has also helped with the installation of intermediate technology and development of rural financial services—although what exactly these are is unclear (USAID 1998a, 1998b). Beginning in 1977, USAID also invested more than $300 million, notably through a programme called National Agricultural Research. That programme was concerned with what USAID saw as the promotion and dissemination of productivity-enhancing technologies focusing on agricultural research, technology transfer, seed technology, and initiatives that emphasised the role of extension workers and technological packages in agricultural production. This programme finished in August 1996.

The most significant recent programme has been the replacement of the APCP by the Agricultural Policy Reform Programme. This began in 1995 and is expected to cost $245 million. It is intended to remove any remaining policy barriers to private enterprise, and the release of cash transfers supporting the agricultural sector will be linked to GoE performance towards established policy reform benchmarks. These benchmarks are reforms of price and marketing policies in cotton, rice, sugarcane, livestock, and fertilisers; privatisation of marketing, processing, and distribution; increased public investment in research and improvement of sustainability of agricultural investment; removal of general consumer subsidies; the development of a targeted food security programme; and a reduction of the negative environmental impact of agricultural growth (USAID 1998b:2). Other USAID programmes include a planned $45-million expenditure on technical assistance for policy reform begun in 1995; $60 million for agricultural technology utilisation and transfer, also begun in 1995, involving the promotion of cash crop production for export; and, the tiny by comparison, farmer-to-farmer support, $3.5 million initiated in 1994. This latter involves U.S. private voluntary organisations, through Agricultural Co-operative Development International, promoting the sharing of knowledge relating to technical assistance, especially in the main areas of fruits and vegetables.

In promoting the above reforms, the MALR has argued consistently for the liberalisation of rural markets; the releasing of landowners from the constraints of tenancy agreements, because "free land markets promote efficiency by adding flexibility to production"; and the development of a competitive marketing system.

Characterising the Agricultural Crisis

Now that we have a clear idea about some of the actual reforms that have been put in place, we can indicate what the characterisation of Egypt's agricultural crises has been by the IFIs and in academic circles. We can also build on the role the GoE has played in promoting rural transformation in the contentious area of land reform. It is important to look at the ways problems are defined and described by policymakers because of the significant implications for the policy recommendations that are proffered. The characterisation of Egypt's rural crises has major implications for the well-being of the country's farmers and also for the relations between the countryside and the towns, labour migration, urban growth, and employment opportunities—or the lack of them.

The World Bank and USAID

There is now a growing consensus between the international agencies and many academic commentators on the type of adjustment necessary to avert continued crisis in Egypt's agricultural sector (World Bank 1992a; USAID 1990, 1992b). It is possible to trace a more-or-less continuous thread in the strategy shared by the agencies since the early World Bank report on "economic management in Egypt during a period of transition," written in 1978 (Ikram 1980). According to the World Bank's chief of agricultural operations, the decline in the growth rate of Egyptian agriculture is the result of "extensive Government intervention, the implicit taxation of the sector, and the low productivity of the reclaimed lands" (Okonjo-Iweala 1992:2).

Building on a critique of the 1980s, the World Bank and USAID argue that there are four main obstacles to agricultural growth in Egypt: the legacy of inappropriate pricing policies; the anticompetitive statist institutional framework; the need for technological innovation; and the more efficient and effective management of land and water resources. An additional worry is the size of Egypt's population and the pressure that its growth adds to a limited resource base. As I will show, the main vehicle advocated by the agencies for reforming Egypt's ailing agricultural sector is the application of a neoliberal market policy to reduce state interference in the allocation of resources. Coupled with this is the prescription for an export-oriented strategy for agricultural growth to yield maximum comparative advantage from horticulture and high-value cash crops. USAID seems to adopt a more aggressive stance than the World Bank. USAID also pays less lip service than does the World Bank to the likely effects of disruption to the lives of the poor in the countryside resulting from the adjustment policies being pursued.

Underpinning Egypt's agricultural crisis for the agencies is the excessive interventionist role that the state has played in allocating rural resources. Both USAID and the World Bank call for the state to stop interfering in commodity pricing so that the sector can be fully liberalised (World Bank 1992a:14). The World Bank calls for the complete liberalisation of cotton production, export, and marketing and the introduction of a cotton exchange where private companies can compete on an equal competitive footing. The World Bank has also called for a careful appraisal of the comparative advantage of Egyptian sugarcane production. It argues that because of the high use of water, sugarcane production is not the most efficient allocation of domestic resources. At the policy level, the World Bank requires the GoE to be less interventionist, "In order to complete the ongoing process of agricultural price liberalization, farm input subsidies dealing with fertilizers and pesticides should be removed, which should go hand in hand with the process of Government divestiture and liberalization of marketing" (World Bank 1992a:15).

USAID shares the World Bank's view that government pricing policies, planting controls, and delivery quotas on most crops, lead to a "predictable decline in per capita production, soaring subsidy costs, declining exports, rising imports of basic foods and animal feeds, and lagging resource productivity" (USAID 1992b:5). Recognition of these dimensions to the crisis, argues USAID, led the MALR after 1986 to embark on a programme of policy reform.

A further major obstacle to the growth of the agricultural sector identified by USAID has been the inefficient statist framework and the restrictions that this has placed on private competition. USAID noted: "Public enterprises are generally inefficient, are usually subsidized by the Treasury, and, therefore, unfairly compete with private investors. Public institutions are characterized by redundant employment, poor management practices, and absence of appropriate employee incentives. Public investment lacks suitable economic criteria. Food subsidies distort consumer decisions and contribute to false price signals to producers" (USAID 1992b:7).

While calling for a reduction in state intervention in all economic activities, the World Bank has also called for improved coordination between government ministries dealing with agriculture to improve the efficiency of the allocation of resources. Yet it remains unhappy at the pace of reform. In particular it has criticised the speed with which PBDAC has failed to relinquish its role in providing inputs and in marketing. The World Bank is unhappy at the persistent constraints on the development of a viable agribusiness subsector, which despite many years of liberalisation in agriculture is still seen to compete at a disadvantage with public enterprise (World Bank 1992a:15–16).

A further major obstacle to agricultural growth that the agencies identify is the failure of Egyptian agriculture to have access to appropriate
new technologies that would increase yields. This failure, the World Bank
argues, is related to the persistent and inefficient intervention by the state
in the countryside. The state has proved itself unable to disseminate technology to potential users because of poorly organised agricultural research and extension. Responsibility for this important area has been too
dispersed according to the World Bank. The result has been the duplica-
tion of efforts and the waste of resources. This failure has had repercussions across the agricultural sector. Research has not adequately advanced the use and development of new high-yielding and short-duration
seeds, and there has been a failure to develop "on-site adaptation and
dissemination of relevant technologies for the new lands" (World Bank
1992a:15). That has also restricted the potential growth and development
of export crops, upon which the IFIs place much importance. As the
World Bank argued, "There is considerable potential for increasing agricultural value added from increasing yields in the old lands through the
wider adoption of improved technologies and cultural practices; this
needs more focused research efforts and improved extension and other
support services" (World Bank 1992a:13).

Technological innovation has also restricted the efficiency of postharvest activities, notably in storage, processing, and marketing. According
to a survey conducted by the Egyptian Agricultural Research Center,
postharvest losses at the point of harvesting and in the wholesale and re-
tail markets for fruits and vegetables average close to 20 percent (quoted
in USAID 1992a:8). Both the World Bank and USAID want better opportunities for private sector research and for the state to provide incentives
for this by protecting intellectual property resulting from work with
biotechnology and genetic engineering.

USAID recognises that there is a difficulty with believing that technological innovation will raise productivity easily. Egyptian agriculture has
some of the world's highest crop yields that result from favourable climate and high rates of fertiliser application. Yet USAID thinks that new
technology will be relatively well received by Egyptian farmers because
of the low-risk conditions of universal access to perennial irrigation.

The final major obstacle to agricultural growth in Egypt for the IFIs is
the availability of land and water. Egypt's present area of cultivable land
is one of the lowest by international comparison at 0.13 *feddans* per head.
In addition, the fertile areas of the Nile Valley and Delta are being eroded
as population pressure and urbanisation increase. One estimate is that
about 30,000 acres are lost to these pressures each year. Both the World
Bank and USAID see potential in raising the efficiency of land and water
use to increase yields. And the World Bank concedes that although "the

overall efficiency of water use from the river Nile is quite high, there is potential for better managing this valuable resource through appropriate conservation and water management measures, thereby increasing overall water resource availability" (World Bank 1992a:13).

USAID argues that "water is *the* constraint for the further expansion of the land area under cultivation," and that it shapes the possibilities of expanding into the new lands (USAID 1992a:10). The Nile supplies 95 percent of Egypt's water requirements, and there appear only limited possibilities for exploiting new groundwater sites. Increasing the efficiency of water use is therefore seen to be critical for the expansion of agriculture.

Understanding the Rural Economy. World Bank and USAID identification of the obstacles to growth in Egypt's agricultural sector have been informed by their characterisation of Egypt's rural economy. The strategy for adjustment that they have pursued with the GoE relates to that characterisation. Yet as I argue in Chapters 4 and 5, the (mis)understanding of the Egyptian countryside promoted by the World Bank and USAID is at odds with the reality of uneven access to land and household organisation of production. How then should the strategy promoted by the IFIs and the GoE be understood? Is it a deliberate attempt to exacerbate rural inequality and limited access to resources under the pretext of creating a drive for betterment?

Two points need to be made here. The first is that where the World Bank characterisations of the Egyptian countryside appear to superficially approximate an accurate assessment of what is actually happening, it only takes on a rhetorical *policy* concern with issues of equity and the position of women and the landless. Nevertheless, at least the World Bank includes these issues in its reports and in theory recognises the sensitivity of these themes for the GoE; USAID seems more reluctant to recognise their importance.

The second point is that the characterisation of the Egyptian countryside employed by both agencies is devoid of any comprehension of the *dynamics* underpinning the relations of power and politics and the issues that are currently affecting the rural poor during the period of adjustment (Bush 1995). In the words of the World Bank, "Various characteristics of the rural economy need to be taken into account" when considering a strategy to revitalise agriculture and to ensure "social and economic equilibrium" (World Bank 1992a:7). The first of these is the extent to which rural household income is dependent upon nonfarming activities, estimated at 38 percent. For the World Bank, this level of income generation based outside agriculture is a structural feature of the Egyptian countryside and "offers the possibility of more rapid development of private initiatives and investments" (World Bank 1992a:7). Second, the

TABLE 3.2   Distribution of Landholdings, 1989–1990

	No. of holdings	%	Holding Areas		
			F	Q	%
Less than 1 F	1,050,900	36.11	508,144	17	6.47
1 –	1,566,091	53.81	3,329,491	1	42.42
5 –	198,926	6.83	1,250,038	23	15.92
10 –	42,808	1.47	494,897	16	6.31
15 –	18,124	0.62	298,809	21	3.81
20 –	27,288	0.94	770,403	3	9.82
50 –	4,520	0.16	287,585	4	3.66
100 +	1,622	0.6	909,803	4	11.59
Total	2,910,279	100	7,849,173	17	100

SOURCE: Ministry of Agriculture and Land Reclamation (1989–1990), p. 15.

World Bank notes that "women are prominent in the agricultural development process and because of high levels of male outmigration women make a lot of decisions alone" (World Bank 1992a:8). Third, the Bank recognises that farm size must be taken into account when designing agricultural policy. As indicated in Table 3.2, farm size is small. The accuracy of the data is questionable in terms of the contrasts between Centre for Public Mobilisation and Statistics (CAPMAS) figures and Institute of National Planning statistics, but Table 3.2 indicates that 36 percent of landholdings are of less than 1 *feddan* in size. Figures for landholdings of up to 5 *feddans* reveal approximately 90 percent of holdings covering almost half of Egypt's cultivated area—and about half of 1 percent of landholders account for 11 percent of the cultivated area. Table 3.3 confirms the heavily skewed ownership patterns, where almost 96 percent of landowners have holdings of less than 5 *feddans* covering 56 percent of the cultivated area with average holdings of less than 1 *feddan*. At the other end of the scale, 8.5 percent of the area is owned by just 0.1 percent

TABLE 3.3   Distribution of Landownership, 1990

Feddans	% of holders	% of area	Average holding
Less than 5	95.8	56.3	0.88
5	2.3	9.7	6.35
10	1.1	9.8	12.98
20	0.5	9.2	26.18
50	0.2	6.5	51.63
100	0.1	8.5	212.49
Total	100	100	1,49

SOURCE: CAPMAS (1991).

of holders, with an average holding size of 212 *feddans*. The structure of landownership is a crucial determinant of rural poverty. As Egypt's 1996 Human Development Report noted, "The uneven distribution of this principle asset [land], coupled with the prevailing farm sizes which are mostly far below an economic size for modernized agriculture, helps accentuate the problem of poverty in rural Egypt" (Institute of National Planning 1996:40).

In detailing its aims and objectives for adjustment in agriculture, the World Bank raises few hopes for those people it includes briefly in its map of the countryside—which incidentally also tends to neglect completely those not resident in the Nile Valley or in the Delta. For although the World Bank carefully stresses the concerns of equity and social justice as we will now see, the policies of reform that the agencies advocate are likely to intensify rather than ameliorate rural poverty.

Aims and Objectives of Economic Reform

The World Bank argues that "the agriculture sector has the potential for being the engine for rural economic growth" and that the main objective for the strategy in the 1990s "is to increase agricultural productivity per unit of land and water, through a more efficient use of these limited resources." This is achievable by reducing unit costs of production and in so doing increasing national output and farmer incomes (World Bank 1992a:10). This also meets the strategic objective of USAID: to increase productivity, production, and incomes in the sector and to raise its rate of growth from its historical level of just under 2–4 percent (USAID 1992b:14).

The key to the World Bank's strategy is the emphasis "on using free market considerations, in particular the promotion of the private sector, in resource allocations" (World Bank 1992a:iii). That requires a major divestiture of the state's responsibilities in providing the range of inputs and marketing that has been largely the role of PBDAC. Yet the World Bank is also concerned that although the public sector "should refrain from direct intervention in marketing," it should retain a "catalytic role in encouraging private sector participation"—although just how is not fully spelled out (World Bank 1992a:xii).

Liberalisation and privatisation are the hallmarks of the agricultural reform strategy. In the words of USAID:

Freeing prices will encourage farmers, buyers and processors of agricultural commodities to invest in productivity enhancing capital and technological improvements, and over time should shift the sector toward the production of commodities for which Egypt has a comparative advantage. Increases in

income in the agricultural sector will provide a significant and broad-based
contribution to the enhancement of Egypt's long-term prosperity. (USAID
1992b:15)

There are three crucial policy themes for the World Bank and USAID
that stem from liberalisation and privatisation. These are cost recovery
programmes, export-led growth, and land tenure arrangements. I deal
with the last of these when I assess the GoE characterisation of Egypt's
agricultural crisis. It is noteworthy, as we will see below, that these
themes are also the preoccupation of many academic specialists who are
trying to address their perception of agricultural decline.

Export-Led Growth.   Export-led growth is the major objective towards which the policies of agricultural reform are directed. It also provides the theoretical gloss of comparative advantage to the policies advocated by the agencies. The spokes of price incentives, technological
innovation (especially green revolution technology), and private capitalist investment are intended to provide the strength and support for the
hub of liberalisation and the opening of the Egyptian economy to the international market. Agency discussion of export-led growth also provides an insight into what the World Bank and USAID mean by "food
security."

According to USAID the shift towards the production of high-value,
low-nutrition foodstuffs for especially the European market—strawberries, fine green beans, peppers, and tomatoes, as well as grapes, peaches,
and other citrus crops—could yield as much as $100–$150 million a year
(USAID 1992b:2–3; interviews with USAID, January and April 1994). According to the World Bank, "In the new liberalized environment, farmers
are expected to follow market signals that would lead them toward production of those crops in which Egypt has a comparative advantage"
(World Bank 1992a:39). And for both the agencies, the drive for export-
led growth must come from changes in cropping patterns that have historically been shaped by government intervention rather than free choice
of farmers responding to market signals.

Dependence upon imports of agricultural commodities began in 1974.
In that year, the value of agricultural imports was greater than exports
for the first time. That gap has widened since the mid-1970s, and the cost
of food imports rose from $2.5 billion per annum in the early 1990s to al-
most $3 billion in 1997. About 50 percent of this cost is accounted for by
wheat, corn, vegetable oil, and red meat, and food imports accounted for
29 percent of imports in 1992, up from 23 percent in 1970 (World Bank
1994c). The value of agricultural exports in 1990 was $434 million—just
20 percent of the value of food imports. Between 1965 and 1991 the dol-

lar value of agricultural exports fell from about $267.5 million to $504,000 (Baroudi 1993:64).

The main items of agricultural export are cotton, rice, fruit, and vegetables, which in 1995 accounted for about 70 percent of the total agricultural export. Most land in Egypt is used for growing wheat, berseem, and maize. Most water is used for growing rice, maize, and sugarcane, and the World Bank stresses in relation to the resource use that cotton; wheat, and vegetables make a bigger economic contribution. Egypt has a clear comparative advantage in horticulture, fruit and vegetables, cotton, and wheat, and that advantage could be greater for cotton if the yields of the 1980s were re-created. In the new lands, in contrast, the advantage exists for horticulture and not for the traditional crops of berseem, wheat, maize, and beans. This evidence encourages the World Bank to promote changes in cropping patterns by moving producers away from the production of rice and sugarcane towards cotton, sugar beet, and vegetables and by reducing the area given to berseem in favour of wheat. This will only be possible if the price incentives are right and the distortions of allocating land and water are reduced.

One immediate difficulty with these suggestions for changing cropping patterns is the call to reduce the production of berseem. This is a main fodder crop and accounts for more than 20 percent of the cropped area. There is a higher livestock density on small farms, an average of 0.86 cattle, buffalo, and cow animal units per *feddan* compared with 0.38 for larger farms (Löfgren 1993:244). The production of berseem has historically been encouraged despite its low farm gate price because of the protection of livestock prices and import restrictions on livestock products. The increased planting of berseem became a strategy for coping with low farm gate prices on government crops, and raising cattle provided a way of gaining access to red meat. The lifting of these restrictions by 1994 had already led to a reduction in the cropping of berseem, but it still remains important in crop rotation with cotton and provides summer feed. Berseem also has valuable nitrogen-fixing qualities, and although this is recognised by the World Bank, it advocates substitution with other, nontraditional fodder—adding presumably to the import bill—and substitution with the cropping of more wheat to enhance food security and improve value added (World Bank 1992a:41).

An important caveat, too, in arguing for the reduction in the level of berseem production is the likely short-term reduction in the holding of livestock it would create and its impact on the position of women. It is women who are mostly involved with livestock production, and the World Bank's belief that the GoE can ensure its replacement by fish and poultry as a more efficient and healthy source of protein is misplaced.

The World Bank argues that Egypt should pursue its comparative advantage in a "dynamic sense" with new technologies and lower costs of production that would generate new opportunities in the agricultural sector. If cotton is to recapture its importance as an export crop, the World Bank argues for the increased opportunity for the private sector and the liberalisation of imports to meet domestic demand. It also notes the declining importance of the former Soviet Union as a market for Egypt's citrus—in the 1980s the USSR accounted for 60 percent of Egypt's market share of exports.

For USAID the biggest market potential for horticulture is the European Union (EU). The EU imports 35 percent of Egypt's cotton, 50 percent of its rice, 45 percent of its vegetables, and 2.5 percent of its fruits. Five crops have been identified for export expansion: asparagus, green beans, sweet peppers, garlic, and mango. Although the World Bank seems more circumspect about the EU export market—it notes that although Egypt may have advantages of location and climate, "it has no unique claim to any export markets" (World Bank 1992a:45)—USAID argues that Egypt can be "one of the lowest cost suppliers for all five products"(USAID 1998a:1). But even USAID understands that if "theoretical export opportunities" are to be realised considerable progress would have to be made on issues like quality control, postharvest technology, and management practices. It also needs noting, as I do in more detail in Chapter 4, that although Egypt exported mainly oil products worth $1.7 billion in 1996–1997, or about 35 percent of total exports, imports from the EU, notably foodstuffs, chemicals, and machinery, totalled $6 billion (Economist Intelligence Unit 1998).

Cost Recovery.   The second dimension to more efficient resource use called for by the agencies is greater attention to cost recovery techniques applied to irrigation water provision. Although both agencies recognise the political sensitivity of this issue, particularly in the old lands, the implementation of operation and maintenance costs (O&M) is seen as necessary to improve water use efficiency.

It is estimated that in 1990, water resources available to Egypt totalled 63.5 billion cubic metres (55.5 from the River Nile, 0.5 from deep groundwater, 2.6 from Nile Valley and Delta groundwater, 4.7 from agricultural drainage water, and 0.2 from treated sewage). The estimated demand in the same year was 59.7 billion cubic metres (49.7 for agriculture, 3.1 for municipal water, 4.6 for industrial, and 1.8 navigation). In theory, this left enough water for an additional 860,000 acres of new land. It is also assumed by USAID (1992b:10;1992e) that by the year 2025, improved irrigation efficiency, agricultural water reuse, and the completion of the Jonglei Canal in Sudan—currently halted by civil war—will increase the flow of water through that swampy area into Lake Nasser and will increase the available water resource to 71.6 billion cubic metres. Expected demand for water in 2025 is 67.7 billion cubic metres, and the balance of 13.9 cubic metres could enable an additional 2.38 million acres of new land to be cultivated.

These projections do not consider the implications of the Tushka project—dealt with in Chapter 6. Moreover, the above projections could be a reality for the agencies only if an irrigation cost recovery programme was introduced ensuring that the value of water became a more obvious factor in crop choice. These calculations are also dependent upon upstream developments in neighbouring African states, and none of these is currently optimistic in facilitating an increased supply of Nile water to Egypt. The MALR, moreover, appears adamant that cost recovery will not be implemented. The World Bank argues that a fee covering present O&M costs would imply an annual payment, "for representative farms of 3.5 and 2.2 *feddans* in the Delta and Upper Egypt respectively, equivalent to only 1–2 percent of gross farm revenue and 3–4 percent of total cost" (World Bank 1992a:20). This is seen to be a bearable cost for farmers given that real farm incomes have risen by about 40 percent since 1984. Yet it says little about those farmers who are not seen by the World Bank as representative—those with landholdings of 1 *feddan* and less than 1 *feddan*, who constitute 90 percent of landholders (see Table 3.2). And it fails to also take note of the World Bank's own recognition that there has been a steep fall in agricultural wages since 1985, which has had the effect of shifting income towards larger landholders and reducing the income of small landholders and the near-landless, impacting on their ability to cope with O&M charges (World Bank 1992a:20).

The GoE has accepted cost recovery in the new lands, and the World Bank argues that it is crucial for the cost recovery to be generalised. This will serve, they argue, to improve water resource management by encouraging the development of water-saving irrigation, improved on-farm water management, and the development eventually of price incentives for more efficient use. One way in which the GoE is trying to avoid the implementation of O&M cost recovery is to stress its initiatives in improving on-farm management, and in substituting high-water-use crops and varieties with those that are water-saving. The World Bank sees these policies as useful but also a prevarication: Nonimplementation frustrates the push for liberalisation. The World Bank views the state provision of irrigation and drainage infrastructure as a subsidy to the farmer. Moreover, "in the new liberalized environment, where farmers can independently take decisions on cropping patterns, the absence of a proper valuation of water creates a distortion in the decision making process, leading to decisions which in the long run would reduce national welfare" (World Bank 1992a:27).

The Government of Egypt

We have already noted that agricultural reform predated ERSAP. Agriculture may have been the arena in which to test the waters of reform in a sector the GoE considered easier to liberalise, where relaxation of government controls would be widely welcomed and where any opposition from poorer farmers could be more easily controlled. So although market liberalisation in pricing, inputs, and marketing have been introduced since the mid-1980s, it is very significant that the GoE has also driven a reform of landlord-tenant relations. This reform, as we will see, has been a long time coming and reflects the increased confidence and ability of the GoE to implement a measure that has been muted since the 1970s.

The World Bank has long argued, in Egypt and elsewhere, that for returns from land to be maximised, tenure rules must be revised, and that is precisely what the GoE has done. Rent for Egypt's tenants was fixed until 1992 at seven times the land tax, revised every ten years, and has been on average LE20 per *feddan*. The heirs of tenants had de facto rights of inheritance, and the contract was valid in perpetuity. Law 96 of 1992, which replaced Nasser's Agrarian Reform Law No. 178 of 1952, has changed that. The new law had a transition period of five years up to 1997, during which the rent was revised to twenty-two times the land tax, and owners have been allowed to buy back the contract from the tenant.[1] Since October 1997, land rents have been determined by the market, tenancy agreements are renewed for just twelve months, and owners have the legal right to end existing contracts. Conflicts over land rents after 1997 are settled by civil law, which stipulates that farmers who cannot meet their rental obligations can be removed from the land by force. There has also been an establishment of reconciliation committees, to assess conflicts between landowners and tenants, but these have mostly been convened by governorate or security officials, who are perceived by tenants to act at the behest of landowners; their adjudication is not viewed as impartial. There is also provision for compensation of displaced farmers and a government commitment that they may be moved to new, probably reclaimed, land. But as the GoE only belatedly recognised this need, and because it allocated in 1997 only something like $33.3 million for this purpose—when land cost about $35,000 an acre—billions of dollars are needed for effective compensation and capital building costs on new lands.

The Shura Council estimates that there are about 2.5 million land tenants, of whom 93 percent rent 5 *feddans* or less. Following the increase in the land tax, total rents paid to landowners in 1993 equalled about LE279 million, an average of LE460 per *feddan*, and an annual average rent of LE660. In 1994, however, the estimated annual crop return per *feddan* was LE500, which meant that the average tenant farmer paid rent of LE160 above the land's net return (*Al-Ahram Weekly* 3–9 March 1994). Although many tenants may also have had their own land in addition to that which they rented, it was clear as early as 1994 that tenants were beginning to feel the financial pinch of changes in the landlord-tenant relationship.

In promoting changes in tenant-owner relations, President Mubarak has continued a trend in the commoditisation of land evident from the 1970s. The new land act is probably the most fundamental piece of legislation since Nasser that has undermined the shift in the social relations of production that he had tried to invoke. The reform of Nasser's legislation that had provided security of tenure for farmers was initiated by collusion between rich landowning interests and former President Sadat. In the 1960s rich peasants often rented land from relatively poor peasants, those with less than 3 *feddans*—the poorer peasants gained valuable access to cash from rent and could work elsewhere. During the oil boom years of the 1970s, richer farmers often surrendered land to poorer farmers who had benefited from labour migrant remittances and who accessed cheap household labour. This did not reduce the power of rich farmers; they shifted capital into areas like machinery and commerce, but richer peasants were seen then to have become the "victims" rather than the beneficiaries of rent control.

This initiated the debate about the need to revise Nasser's legislation. Richer peasants had an ally in Sadat. From the early 1970s he began revising laws affecting rent control and strengthened the hands of landlords. Yet a policy measure initiated in the early 1970s was not translated into a revised (and diluted) land tenancy law until 1992. The hesitancy about reforming the tenancy arrangements might have reflected the inability of the "soft state" to make a bold decision regarding reform, in whatever direction: It failed to base any formulation of proposed law on an informed understanding of the dynamics of rural conditions, and it failed to take up (for understandable party political reasons) the option of directly choosing between titleholders and lessees promoted by the Wafd and Tagamu Parties.[2] (Sadowski 1991:301–307).

This failure reflected the power of rich landed interests in keeping the issue on the political agenda throughout the 1980s and state bureaucratic indecision and concern about competing elite interests. It arguably undermined any residual respect and legitimacy that bureaucrats had during the 1980s to come to terms with worsening agricultural terms of trade and increasing dependency upon food imports. It also raised the serious question about adjustment initiatives: no matter how readily the state might accept the need to reform, the ability to implement reform was problematic.

Reforming the landlord-tenant relationship is in many ways the key to Egyptian policy reforms. It accompanied the thrust by the agencies to promote monetary incentive as the underlying raison d'être for agricultural growth. It also became the underlying basis for targeting what the World Bank calls "progressive farmers" (World Bank 1992a:35). Although the attributes of this group are not spelled out, it is clear they are those with landholdings of more than 5 *feddans*. These are the middle or kulak class and those farmers with larger holdings that form the minority of landowners in whom both hope and resources have been invested during adjustment. Higher rents and security of private tenure are the means by which the World Bank has seen scarce resources of land and water, and therefore of the environment, being protected.

The Academic Consensus

With only a few notable exceptions, there is an academic consensus that the structural problems that confront Egypt's economy and agriculture derive from inefficiencies of the state-led protected pattern of development largely followed since 1952. (Two of the most rigorous exceptions are Mitchell 1998 and Fergany 1998.) The critique of the Nasserist model is that from 1967 on, and especially from 1973 on, it proved unworkable, and that *infitah* was too hesitant to overcome the years of bureaucratic state failure (Holt and Roe 1993; Handoussa and El-Din 1995; Richards 1991b, 1993a; Waterbury 1992, 1994).

For most academic specialists the reasons underpinning Egypt's agricultural crisis and the strategies suggested to address it mirror the views of the international agencies. That is not surprising. There is a big crossover between academia and international agency discourse, as evidenced in one recent publication that was the outcome of a conference in Alexandria to discuss the "ongoing efforts in the public and private sectors in Egypt to achieve sustainability in agriculture in the 1990s" (Faris and Khan 1993:5). The academic consensus characterising rural crisis emphasises the constraints of limited arable land and water and population pressure conceived of in a crude Malthusian way affecting scarce finite resources and aggravated by, if not the result of, excessive state intervention in pricing, subsidies, and controls on marketing (Harris 1988; Craig 1993; York 1993; Biswas 1993; Abu-Zeid 1993; El-Serafi 1993). One commentator noted:

> Agricultural productivity has barely managed to keep pace with population growth, but the increase in productivity has not resulted in significant increases in real income for the rural people. In the last 10 years per capita food production has increased by 23 percent whereas total food production

has increased by almost 60 percent. Thus, the Egyptian system of government intervention and management of agriculture failed to achieve the dramatic growth in productivity seen in some other areas of the world with favourable conditions, for example the Indian Punjab. Part of this failure can be attributed to the government's pricing and marketing system that has distorted farmers' incentives to produce. In addition, the government's management of the input distribution system failed in certain cases to provide the technology needed by farmers. (Antle 1993:176)

For Richards (1991b, 1993a) Egypt has three main problems. These are (1) the need to generate employment for a rapidly growing and young population; (2) the need to generate export earnings in order to pay for food imports, given the ecological and demographic constraints on agricultural production; and (3) the need to attract local savings into investment by securing property rights and controlling inflation. Richards argued that food security for a country like Egypt should not be confused with food self-sufficiency (an unrealisable goal) and that increased openness to the international economy is the only solution: "Food security (which increasingly means foreign exchange security) and job creation must be the centerpiece of any strategy for a sustainable national economy" (Richards 1993a:244).

Liberalisation. Market liberalisation for academic commentators is the vehicle to raise agricultural productivity by releasing pressures to increase farmer incentives. Market liberalisation will be possible, they argue, only if the state relinquishes its interventionist role and grasps the nettle of economic reform. The reason why structural adjustment has been so necessary for academic observers is that the two main areas of job creation in the Egyptian economy, government employment and labour migration, are unsustainable.

Paradoxically a major difficulty facing Egyptian agriculture is that by international comparison, it has sustained relatively high levels of productivity. Average crop yields compare favourably with production levels in the United States and other industrialised countries (York 1993:17). Yet, despite this record, Egypt imports two-thirds of its wheat and vegetable oils and one-third of its corn. Under these circumstances just how does most of the academic commentary on Egypt envisage increasing agricultural productivity?

The short answer is by promoting opportunities for market competition and privatisation. State intervention in the Egyptian agricultural sector is seen to have stifled growth, restricted private competition, and taxed agriculture to benefit urban and industrial development. Although input subsidies, for example, were introduced to compensate for low producer prices, there remained a transfer from the agricultural to the nonagricultural sector. One commentator has noted that in 1980 "the net burden on the agricultural sector was about LE580 million and the input subsidies compensated for only 41 percent of the 'tax' imposed on agriculture through price policy" (Bishay 1993:239).

Although there is increasing unanimity on the need to roll back the state from intervening in agriculture, there is less agreement on or real discussion of actual policies that the state might promote to extricate itself from this sector of the economy. Moreover, according to one of the leading advocates of economic liberalisation, the size and nature of state activity after privatisation is unclear. The agencies seem to call for a unilaterally reduced role for government, but Richards has conceded, that what is needed is not a weaker but a stronger public sector: "The government of Egypt needs to stop doing things that the private sector can do better. In this way the government can focus more clearly on performing those functions that it alone can fulfil" (Richards 1993a:244), and "Sustainability requires that the government should stop doing some things, start doing others, and do still other things better. . . . Continued government involvement in any productive activity which could become reasonably competitive in private hands is indefensible" (Richards 1993a:250).

In promoting the need to create a liberalised market economy, Richards argued that the prospects for sustaining economic liberalisation will need two processes. The first is greater participation—political reform to run alongside economic changes, something about which the international agencies are quiet. This is needed because the short-run losers in a real devaluation, which should accompany adjustment, will be the poor and those with access to only small areas of land. Thus it is necessary to secure a political constituency persuaded of the necessity of the pain of reform: "To the extent that they participate in the decision making process, they share the responsibility for the outcome" (Richards 1993a:250). Yet there is little practical suggestion to help promote empowerment and democratisation in authoritarian Egypt.

The second process that needs to be incorporated for Richards is increased provision of property rights. This is intended to provide the incentive structure for private participation in investment, which includes security of land tenure. This seems a departure from Richards's earlier discussion of land tenure and incentive structures as policy measures to generate agricultural growth. He previously argued that "it is easy to exaggerate the potential supply response which might result from a shift from a 'low' to a 'high' price policy for agriculture" (Richards 1986b:12). He continued, in his previous observations about possible policy changes to increase agricultural productivity:

> There are . . . some surprises in a country like Egypt awaiting those who believe that the problems of food dependency can be solved simply by "getting the prices right." Researchers . . . have calculated that if all Egyptian farm prices moved to international levels, Egypt would actually grow less wheat than at present, simply because the country obviously lacks a comparative advantage in this "land using" crop.(Richards 1986b:12)

In promoting these two themes, Richards expressed the view that a market economy can work efficiently only if there is a good flow of information to those in the marketplace and that a safety net for the poor is crucial for political sustainability of adjustment (Richards 1993a:251). Yet his notion that the Social Fund for Development could be a vehicle for ameliorating the effects of adjustment is misplaced. The Social Fund, as we have already noted, is underfunded for the task of employment creation. Moreover, the much-heralded view of GoE "ownership" of the adjustment programme directs opposition at its deleterious effects on Egypt's majority away from the agencies that are the main protagonists of such a policy.

Liberalisation of the agricultural sector will endanger the living standards of poor farmers and landless rural dwellers. Commentators seem agreed that this is a consequence worth accepting as long as the adjustment programme can be sustained. In one econometric study of Minoufia governorate in the southern Delta, it is asserted that liberalisation would increase farm incomes while increasing inequality, even if animal fodder is made available for poorer farmers (Löfgren 1993). Yet there also remain the dissenters critical of the impact that adjustment is having on poverty and levels of nutrition.(Nassar 1992; Korayem 1991a, 1994).

Cost Recovery. The availability of water is increasingly seen as the major constraining factor in increasing the productivity of agriculture (Bentley 1993; Okonjo-Iweala and Fuleihan 1993; Abu-Zeid 1993). And although there are significant political and cultural barriers to water pricing, the recovery of O&M costs is seen as a prerequisite to improved demand management (Richards 1993a; Biswas 1993; Bentley 1993).

The introduction of water pricing is an important corollary to the broader introduction of market principles in agriculture and the development of private investment. As one commentator noted, "As part of structural adjustment, water must be priced rationally for all its users, in harmony with the trend in other prices. This would limit its use in the aggregate and direct it to those uses that are most valuable to society" (El-Serafi 1993:149).

Water pricing is also necessary, many commentators note, because without it, and as a result of incentives following the increase in farm gate prices, there may be the increased cultivation of water-intensive crops like cotton, rice, and sugarcane, which would raise the demand for irrigation water (Okonjo-Iweala and Fuleihan 1993:138 of Hopkins 1999). Richards nevertheless argued that if water pricing was operative, the onus on efficiency gains would lie with the user, which would counteract World Bank fears regarding continued overuse.

The thrust of those who argue for water charges is that the system of allocating water should shift from one driven by supply (i.e., central government making decisions about the volume and timing of delivery) to a system where farmers make decisions about actual need. Water charges are critical not only to ensure the long-term sustainability of the irrigation and drainage infrastructure, but also to provide an incentive for a more efficient allocation of scarce water supplies. Liberalisation in agriculture means that farmers are increasingly free to make rational choices regarding crops and rotations (Okonjo-Iweala and Fuleihan 1993:137–138). Egyptian farmers currently pay only nominal charges for the delivery of water through Egypt's intricate system of irrigation and drainage. Farmers on the old lands are required to pay only the capital costs of tile drainage, which are spread over a twenty-year period.

The application of market orthodoxy to agriculture seems inextricably to lead to the introduction of water charges:

> The needed rate and amount of increase in irrigation water-use efficiency will not and cannot be achieved without introduction in the near future of universal and substantial charges for water. . . . appropriate water charges for all other users should also become universal simultaneously, along with high additional charges on those who pollute water. In view of the increasing scarcity of irrigation water, the introduction of universal charges for water should be a high priority for Egypt. (Bentley 1993:28)

Export-Led Growth. Government and academic commentators have stressed in recent years that increasing the country's exports of cotton and horticultural produce (Baroudi 1993; El-Serafy 1993) can ameliorate Egypt's agricultural crisis. The need to boost Egypt's agricultural exports has been a recurrent theme in the characterisation of the sectors crisis and strategies to reduce it. In the early 1980s, conclusions from a major conference on the development of Egyptian agriculture argued that the country should use its "considerable natural advantage" in the greater promotion of nontraditional exports like vegetables and fruit. And they went further, suggesting that the "new strategy for achieving food security in Egypt should be based on the promotion of agricultural exports rather than that of self sufficiency" (El-Shennawy 1982:4). The rationale for this argument was that the move from traditional crops to horticulture would reduce the food gap by raising the value of domestic food output and would generate foreign exchange earnings (see also *Al-Ahram Weekly*, 18–24 June 1992).

For Baroudi (1993) the freeing of the agricultural sector both in terms of pricing and in relation to government restrictions on exports would resolve problems in this area. He argued that if this strategy had been put in place to encourage a fairly large number of

> competitive private farmers and firms to dominate all aspects of production and export, success in the export sphere might have followed. . . . Such a policy would have promoted the entry of new private capital and talent into agricultural production and exports and hastened the exit of inefficient producers and exporters who failed both to minimize the size of their lost output and to supply markets with consistently high-quality commodities at competitive prices and in sufficient quantities. (Baroudi 1993:64)

One of the main areas omitted by Baroudi and other academic commentators is the neglect of important political reforms to facilitate a sustained growth in agricultural output. They also ignore issues of rural social differentiation, and of the way in which political and economic power in the countryside may affect levels of productivity.

Economic Reforms—An Early Success?

By examining the aggregate data used by the protagonists of reform, it is possible to assess the success of the reforms based on the criteria by which the reformers themselves define success. And because agricultural reforms began in 1986, it is possible to begin to see what the success of the programmes has been. Moreover, since 1991 the reforms have been part of the broader ERSAP, which has promoted some positive results. There remains, however, enormously high unemployment and poor economic growth.

According to the MALR, the "remarkable progress in implementing a macro-economic reform program has been reflected in the reduction of food subsidy from about 17 percent of total budget public expenditure in the mid-80s to about 2 percent in 1990" (Nassar 1993). By 1994, almost all subsidies for fertilisers, seeds, and pesticides had been removed. Almost all crops had government controls removed by 1996 except for sugarcane, which is grown on at least 15 percent of cultivable land in Upper Egypt and for which there was still no alternative to the public sector for marketing.

Early evidence on cropping patterns reinforces the GoE position that economic reforms have promoted increases in levels of production. Table

TABLE 3.4   Cropping Patterns for 1985 and 1992 (000s *feddans*)

	1985		1992		
Crops	Area	%	Area	%	Change %
Long berseem	1,923	17.21	1,969	13.36	13.21
Wheat	1,186	10.61	2,092	16.75	67.39
Barley	125	1.11	248	1.98	98.4
Broad beans	329	2.94	425	3.40	29.18
Lentils	20	0.18	15	0.12	(25)
Flax	39	0.35	29	0.23	(25.64)
Onions	26	0.23	32	0.25	23.08
Vegetables	377	3.37	455	3.64	20.69
Total winter	4,192	37.5	5,086	40.72	21.33
Rice	925	8.28	1,216	9.73	31.46
Maize	1,914	17.13	1,967	15.74	2.77
Sorghum	340	3.04	355	2.84	4.41
Peanuts	28	0.20	54	0.43	45.45
Soybean	119	1.06	52	0.41	(56.30)
Vegetables	712	6.37	643	5.14	(9.69)
Other crops	218	1.95	330	2.64	51.38
Total Nile and Summer	4,278	38.28	4,648	37.21	8.65
Cotton	1,081	9.67	840	6.72	(22.29)
Sugarcane	250	2.24	271	2:16	8.4
Orchard	457	4.09	907	7.26	98.47
Cropping area[a]	11,175	100	12,489	100	11.76

[a]Cropping area included area cultivated with short berseem.
SOURCE: Ministry of Agriculture and Land Reclamation (1994).

3.4, for example, indicates a positive shift in cropping in the seven years between 1985 and 1992.

Changes in cropping patterns and productivity per *feddan* as well as farm gate prices highlight interesting evidence. Egypt's cultivated area increased from 6.2 million *feddans* in 1981 to 7.6 million *feddans* in 1993. Total production of the main strategic food crops—wheat, maize, and rice—also increased. The total production of cereals increased from 8 million tons in 1981 to 15 million tons in 1992; the area cultivated with wheat, barley, broad beans, winter onions, and vegetable crops also increased significantly. Productivity per *feddan* improved for the main agricultural crops from 1985 to 1992, except for barley, broad beans, onions, and soybeans. Increases in rice, wheat, and maize led to a reduction in imports and were the result, according to the MALR, of improved technology and seed varieties (Nassar 1993 and interview with Nassar, April 1994).

A joint appraisal of the entire reform package since 1980, conducted by the MALR and USAID in the mid-1990s, confirmed for the authors the view that market liberalisation has had a high economic payoff. Increases in yields were attributed to increased farm gate prices, but cotton failed to respond significantly, and there was a fall in the area planted. That was explained by the MALR and USAID as being the result of uncertainty in world market trends (MALR and USAID 1995a). The same review conceded that liberalisation and the resulting increase in the prices of inputs and food prices may have a deleterious impact upon the poor. In response, a system of targeted food aid was thought possibly to be important in the medium term and could cost about one-third of the existing food subsidy bill. In the long run, it was felt that improved marketing and production efficiency would increase farm income and lower the real costs of food to urban consumers (Ministry of Agriculture and Land Reclamation and USAID 1995a, 1995b): no mention was made of rural hardship.

The MALR and USAID argued that the reform process has led to greater crop prices relative to input prices, and this situation has stimulated farmers to adopt new technologies, better management techniques, and high-yielding varieties. One example, indicated in Table 3.4, is the increase in the production of wheat by 44 percent between 1980–1986 and 1987–1992. In assembling their data, USAID used a proxy measure of gross farm income less costs of purchased inputs to simulate changes in producer surplus associated with policy change. The average value of this measure, for the eleven major crops on the old lands, they argued, deflated by a GDP deflator, was LE4.7 billion for the prereform period, 1980–1986, and LE5.8 billion for the reform period 1987–1992: an increase of 23 percent. Yet they also conceded that for the period 1991–1992, resource income dropped significantly, despite (because of?) further policy reforms, including the devaluation of the exchange rate and the increased procurement price of cotton. The explanation for this decline in rural income was that the international prices for wheat, rice, maize, and cotton (which accounted for 50 percent of the value of production) fell by about 15 percent between 1990 and 1993.

Overall, the joint review estimated that the programme of policy reforms had benefits that were bigger than their expected costs. This was because the economic rate of return to investment exceeded 75 percent, and the principle costs of restructuring labour, GoE support to the emerging free market, and other costs of privatisation were estimated at LE300 million per annum, whereas the benefits were seen to exceed LE4 billion per annum.

Economic Reforms—Still Not Successful Enough

Six issues need to be raised when appraising the evidence used by the advocates of agricultural reform. The first of these is to question at the outset the evidentiary base used by reformers, that is, to question the accuracy of their data and the usefulness of aggregate economic data for doing anything other than providing "guestimates" of rates of growth and economic activity. The accuracy of national accounts is an issue for policymakers in all developing countries (and in developed countries, too) and has recently been reiterated in Egypt in a dispute between the IFIs and the GoE. The GoE was accused by the IFIs of having overstated Egypt's rates of growth for the late 1980s and early 1990s. We will see in a moment when examining the debate about levels of poverty that a far more useful indicator of the impact of economic reform would be to look, for example, at detailed accounts of levels of income and expenditure in the countryside and also levels of employment and opportunities for long-term job creation—not to mention standards of health and education provision.

The second issue is to note that most of the arguments used by the advocates of reform relate to the *early* evidence of increases in output and changes in cropping patterns, particularly in the period between 1986 and 1992 (see Tables 3.4 and 3.5). Yet there is little evidence that early improvements in productivity have been sustained at a rate of growth envisaged by the supporters of reform. And of course, it is perfectly reasonable to assume that increases in productivity for certain crops would seem to emerge after years of intervention that had undervalued farm gate prices.

The case of wheat is an important illustration often used by the GoE to support the argument favouring liberalisation. Up to 1986, production seemed fixed at around 2 million metric tons. Yet by the early 1990s, it was 4.5 million metric tons. This "evidence" is used by the international agencies to demonstrate the success of economic reforms, but the assertions need clarifying. Although it is clear that there has been an increase in recorded wheat production, it is uncertain that it is either, first, as great as suggested or, second, the result solely of changes in farm gate prices. One commentator, for instance, has reminded us that because of extensive government intervention before 1986, many small farmers were disinclined to reveal to MALR officials the extent of their wheat or sugarcane and other quota crops. Farmers simply had

> good reason to divert part of their land to crops they could eat themselves, including wheat. At the very least they would ensure that any particularly poor soil was allocated to government crops, not those consumed at home.

TABLE 3.5   Crop Area, Yield, and Production Growth Rates (percentage per year)

Crop	Pre-reform Period, 1980–1986			Reform Period, 1987–1993		
	Area	Yield	Production	Area	Yield	Production
Wheat	−2.8	2.9	0.1	5.6	3.5	9.1
Maize	−2.7	2.3	−0.4	0.7	5.5	6.2
Rice	0.0	0.2	0.2	5.8	5.2	11.0
Cotton	−2.7	−1.6	−4.3	−3.0	5.2	2.2
Barley	6.1	0.9	6.9	−8.2	3.2	−5.0
Berseem (long)	1.9	0.6	2.5	0.1	−0.4	−0.3
Berseem (short)	−2.5	1.1	−1.3	−2.1	2.9	0.8
Broad bean	2.3	3.5	5.9	−2.9	−5.4	−8.2
Chickpea	2.6	1.0	3.6	−1.0	1.2	0.2
Flax	−7.4	0.6	−6.8	−4.1	0.2	−3.9
Garlic	−12.6	0.0	−12.6	−0.8	4.0	3.1
Groundnut	−3.2	−2.0	−5.2	2.3	3.8	6.1
Lentil	8.6	8.9	17.5	−5.6	−0.7	−6.2
Lupin	5.6	0.5	6.0	−3.0	0.9	−2.1
Fenugreek	4.9	0.9	5.8	−9.3	0.6	−8.7
Onion	6.2	2.7	8.9	−0.4	3.8	3.3
Potato	0.9	2.4	3.3	−7.0	3.8	−3.2
Sesame	−12.6	0.8	−11.8	14.3	2.4	16.7
Sorghum	−2.6	0.5	−2.1	2.0	4.0	6.1
Soybean	3.1	0.8	3.9	−15.8	0.6	−15.2
Sugarbeet	22.7	4.2	26.9	−2.0	3.7	1.7
Sugarcane	0.2	3.1	3.3	0.2	1.8	2.0
Tomato	2.3	7.2	9.5	−3.6	4.0	0.4

SOURCE: Reproduced with permission from Lehman B. Fletcher, ed., *Egypt's Agriculture in a Reform Era* (Ames: Iowa State University Press, 1996), p. 92.

. . . The stagnant yields of the years before 1987, which according to the official view made necessary the shift to an unregulated market, may in fact reflect, in whole or in part, the small holders' unreported diversion of land and crops to better serve their own needs. (Mitchell 1998:23)

Mitchell was led to the conclusion that "the impact of the free-market reforms may have been greater on the statistics published by the state than on what farmers actually grow" (Mitchell 1998:23). It is also odd, as Mitchell notes, that the advocates of economic reform use as an example that best demonstrates the efficacy of reform farmers' having moved *away* from the market towards enhanced self-provisioning. There is insufficient evidence to indicate that market deregulation per se has led to significant and sustained increases in high-value export crops. The years

TABLE 3.6   Agricultural Production (000 tonnes)

	1993–1994	1994–1995	1995–1996	1996–1997
Wheat	4,437	5,722	5,735	5,249
Corn	5,044	5,550	5,178	5,830
Rice	4,662	4,585	4,789	4,892
Beans	317	393	492	476
Cotton	1,083	681	610	977
Sugarcane	12,412	13,822	11,648	11,700
Vegetables	13,634	13,664	15,007	15,674
Fruits	5,146	5,480	6,243	6,380

SOURCE: © The Economist Intelligence Unit Ltd. Reproduced by permission of the Economist Intelligence Unit Ltd.

between 1986 and 1992 indicate a decline in the area planted to cotton and vegetables and an increase in the areas for crops used for household consumption like wheat and rice.

The third point is that the increases in productivity that have been heralded by the IFIs as resulting from liberalisation do not seem to have been sustained and, at about 3 percent per annum in agriculture, are below the levels predicted by the IFIs and the GoE. The 4.3 percent growth of production in 1996–1997 seems largely to have been assisted by good weather conditions, and Egypt remains one of the world's largest food importers. Table 3.6 indicates a levelling out of agricultural production and a decline for cotton. Cotton is the largest agricultural export, but a fall in subsidies increased the costs of production from an estimated LE595 per *feddan* in 1987–1988 to LE1,386 in the mid-1990s. Poor productivity led the GoE to reintroduce subsidies for cotton in 1996–1997 at a cost of $212 million.

Table 3.6 also indicates a decline for sugarcane in 1996–1997 compared with 1993–1995, as well as the obvious failure of vegetable and fruit production to take off and launch agricultural exports in a way that the IFIs indicated as both desirable and possible.

Fourth, although the GoE makes a repeated statement concerning promoting agricultural exports, any increase has been surpassed by an increase in major agricultural imports. Table 3.7 indicates that most Egyptian agricultural imports include commodities characterised by low elasticity of demand, like wheat, sugar, and edible oils. In contrast, most of Egypt's exports are marked by elasticity. Agricultural exports fell from $615.5 million in 1994–1995 to $320.7 million in 1995–1996, and imports of live animals, animal products, vegetables, food, and drink for the same period increased from $2,513 million to $2,898 million. This 1995–1996 figure of $2,898 million was up from $1,878 in 1992–1993.

TABLE 3.7   Major Agricultural Imports (000 tonnes unless otherwise indicated)

	1990	1991	1992	1993	1994
Wheat and flour	5,732	5,953	5,705	5,073	6,650
U.S.	1,938	3,400	4,055	2,520	5,207
Australia	1,633	1,633	1,200	n/a	n/a
EC/EU	1,937	620	300	n/a	n/a
Maize	1,874	1,315	1,380	1,820	2,021
U.S.	1,774	1,075	1,020	1,660	1,601
Vegetable oil	700	700	690	700	222
U.S.	15	48	38	n/a	7
South America	280	280	240	n/a	n/a
Southeast Asia	367	367	350	n/a	n/a
Beef and veal	120	115	130	217	171
Butter and butter oil	80	35	35	45	52
Cheese	30	25	27	15	21
Forest products (000 cu. metres)	2,400	1,700	1,600	1,650	1[a]
Soymeal	260	230	280	310	474
Sugar	595	500	570	550	550
Cotton	n/a	62	70	18	13

[a]000 tonnes.

SOURCE: © The Economist Intelligence Unit Ltd. Reproduced by permission of the Economist Intelligence Unit Ltd.

The fifth issue that needs to be questioned when examining the impact of economic reform is employment. According to the Egyptian Labour Force Sample Survey for the period 1990–1995, agriculture accounted for 37 percent of employment, services 24 percent, manufacturing 14 percent, and trade 10 percent. Construction and transport each accounted for about 6 percent of employment (Fergany 1998:52). In fact, the majority of employment was in rural Egypt because in addition to accounting for 37 percent of total national employment, rural employment was also large in services, the government sector, and private employment, ensuring that rural employment accounted for about 58 percent of the total (Fergany 1998:54). There is dispute in Egypt regarding the actual level of unemployment. Official figures put it at 9.4 percent for 1996–1997. It is more accurately closer to 20 percent, with an additional 20 percent being underemployed and a further 20–30 percent scratching a living below the poverty line (*Financial Times*, 22 April 1994).

One of Egypt's most acute problems is that each year there are at least 450,000 new entrants into the job market, and if any proper headway is made in reducing the existing number of unemployed, an additional 250,000 jobs will need to be created to reduce the numbers who will be out of work before 2010. But that would mean creating close to 700,000 jobs a year, dependent upon an unrealistic rate of growth of GDP. (Fergany 1998:61; see also Assaad 1997). The implications for agriculture are dramatic: economic reform in this sector is premised upon high levels of national economic growth to create urban jobs to absorb displaced rural labour and upon these jobs' being created by the private sector. There is little evidence of either. According to Fergany, the period 1990–1995 was one of employment havoc, especially for the countryside and especially for female labour. Agriculture lost about 700,000 jobs in this period, and women lost more jobs than men. Indeed, these traumatic effects of economic reform were noted in late 1996 by a Shura Council Report expressing alarm that structural adjustment policies between 1990 and 1995 slowed economic growth and raised unemployment because of layoffs resulting from liberalisation (*Al-Ahram Weekly* 19–25 December 1996).

The sixth and final area that I want to look at briefly in assessing the data presented by the advocates of economic reform is poverty. Clearly one set of aggregate data that the deregulators need to have on their side when they want to argue the positive impact of economic reform is the decline in levels of poverty that their policies are meant to promote. The GoE is immensely sensitive to this type of data. None are recorded in the World Bank World Development Reports, and Egypt is not alone in this shyness. It seems that in 1998 a major report on poverty was essentially quashed by the GoE because the figures compiled by researchers painted too gloomy a picture: the report's authors were asked by government if they had any other figures that could be used. Yet the GoE's own data leave little room to doubt the deleterious impact of economic reform on poverty. The government's statistical service (CAPMAS) released in 1998 results of its Household Income and Expenditure Survey (HIES) for 1995–1996. The data have completely undermined any optimism about earlier government figures on growth in the early 1990s.

Household income and expenditure data are a more appropriate set of indicators to gauge the impact of economic reform than bland macroeconomic indices of productivity and cropping. Income and expenditure data are a more accurate record of economic reform than general macroeconomic data because they relate to a more direct impact on respondents' standards of living. The economic reform programme has generated price rises for transport, petroleum, and cigarettes, and although the price of the essential bread loaf has been largely unaffected, its size has been reduced. In 1990, 40 percent of the total expenditure of poor families was on subsidised foods, and the price index for food rose by more than 52 percent for controlled food and 686 percent for decontrolled food over the period 1990–1993. A consumer price bulletin issued by CAPMAS put interim price rises for 1992 as averaging 15.7 percent on food and drink,

22.5 percent on transportation, and 32.4 percent on rents, electricity, and fuel. There have been additional price increases across the range of essential items that constitute the basket of commodities for the majority of Egyptians since 1992.

The latest HIES indicates that the level of poverty has more than doubled in Egypt between 1990–1991 and 1995–1996 from 21 percent to 44 percent. The criterion is a poverty line defined by the cost of a minimum basket of nutrition. But if the more widespread criterion is used—namely, for the purposes of international comparison, a minimum of $1 per person per day, and we assume that LE500 is necessary for a family of five per month—the extent of poverty is far worse. By this measure, more than 80 percent of Egyptians are poor.

Real incomes in Egypt have fallen by an average of 14 percent in the cities and 20 percent in the rural areas. Average income per income earner in the household fell by 19 percent in the cities and 32 percent in the rural areas. Average income per capita in the countryside was LE982 for 1990–1991 compared with LE724 per capita expenditure. As Fergany noted, "These figures simply mean that a larger number of household members has to earn an income, *at a lower rate per person*, in order to maintain the level of real income of the early 1990s; an attempt that has, on average failed, especially in rural areas! This is a very powerful sign of impoverishment" (Fergany 1998:69, emphasis in original).

Fergany reinforced his argument about the intensification of rural poverty by highlighting the decline in real per capita expenditure on food and the increased incidence of stunting and wasting in Egyptian children. He concluded, "To sum up, indicators derived from the recent HIES document a *fast deterioration in the standard of living since the official structural adjustment programme started. 'Reform' has considerably impoverished the people and the countryside has paid a heavier price*" (Fergany 1998:70, emphasis in original).

Conclusion

This chapter has stressed the similarity in the views expressed by the GoE, the IFIs, and many academic commentators on the causes of Egypt's economic and agricultural crisis. The consensus has stressed the nonsustainability of Egypt's recent economic structure, which depended heavily upon rents and the ineffective organisation of commodity-producing sectors. Yet it remains uncertain that the market orientation of reforms will structurally transform the economy so that there will no longer be a need for the continuation of significant, albeit reformed, state intervention. That is because, among other things, the ERSAP will not serve to bolster, but in all probability will rather undermine agriculture, and it will marginalise manufacturing industry. The export-generated growth from an agricultural sector intended to be shaped more by market power than state power has not materialised.

The essential weakness of the Egyptian economic reforms is that they have failed to generate economic growth, employment, and an entrepreneurial class willing to engage in activity from which the state has been encouraged to withdraw. The reforms have exacerbated levels of poverty that showed little signs either of being adequately addressed by the GoE or of being transitory. On the contrary, structural poverty that predated reforms has got worse, and new dimensions of poverty have emerged. Nowhere has this been more the case than in the agricultural sector. One of the reasons for these difficulties has been the way in which the GoE and the IFIs have characterised the weaknesses of the Egyptian economy. The prevailing view of Egypt's problems, as this chapter has demonstrated, has been the oversimplified view that the state has historically been the root cause of all the country's ills. What has followed from that oversimplification has been a set of policies that has sought to extricate government from economic activity. There has been a policy, moreover, that has pronounced the importance of the market's driving economic rejuvenation. And there has been the heroic assumption that the GoE will be willing to implement reforms at a pace and with the gusto the international agencies think is necessary to produce economic growth. Finally, there has been the view that the policies promoted will generate the growth necessary to transform the economy; this simply has not happened.

This chapter has assessed the policies of economic reform by setting the reformers' own assertions about the needs for reform against the evidence of the impact of reform. I now want to establish the broader lines of my critique. I begin in the next chapter by detailing my view of the macroeconomic consequences of structural adjustment in agriculture, and in Chapter 5, I set this view alongside the farmer responses to reform in examples from the Delta.

Notes

1. The finest account of the Introduction of Law 96 of 1992 is by Saad (1999).

2. The New Wafd was created after Sadat's provision for political parties was announced in 1977. It is the main opposition party. It is on the centre right and was formed by members of the original Wafd. The Wafd was founded in 1918, largely by the landed elite, to promote independence. It was outlawed by Nasser in 1952. The New Wafd now promotes the interests of professionals, the private sector, and greater political liberalisation. The Tagamu Party, or National Progressive Unionist Party, has its roots in the Arab Socialist Union and at different times has tried to defend its Nasserist roots. Its support comes from intellectuals, workers, and peasants.

4

Agricultural Modernisation and the Egyptian Countryside

A Critique of Structural Adjustment

My critique of the current agricultural strategy has four elements. The first is a criticism of comparative advantage and the role of markets and power in agency prescriptions for economic reform. It is very noticeable in exploring this theme, especially where expectations for reform are not met, that the IFIs explain problems by reference to the transition from state-led to market economies. It will become clear in my critique that the problems I will document, exemplified by the fertiliser sector, are not "teething" problems of transition but are structural problems inherent in policies of economic reform. The second area that I criticise in this chapter is the IFIs' and the GoE's placement of too great an emphasis in the role that the state has played in agricultural modernisation. The third is the agencies' use of only a partial and incomplete view of agricultural modernisation. It is a view that, along with other omissions, seldom includes the importance of women and labour migrancy in its understanding of Egypt's agriculture. Finally, this chapter briefly examines the relationships between farmers, politics, and the state. My critique is that the agencies and the GoE have misunderstood local politics and the policy reform process. They are reluctant to examine the nature of rural politics and the different roles that peasants and farmers have taken in Egypt.

These four themes lead to the importance of building an alternative agricultural strategy around the small farmer. I now trace the background to my argument that it is especially important in understanding the outcome of economic reforms to recognise the *dynamics* of the countryside that sustain and transform the rural economy. This chapter provides the necessary context within which Chapters 5 and 6 confirm the

importance of understanding the ways in which households in rural
Egypt have made decisions about coping and managing livelihoods during the era of reform. These are areas where there are enormous gaps in
the policy pronouncements of the international agencies and the GoE.

Comparative Advantage and
Tyranny of the Market

Comparative Advantage

There is now an extensive and critical literature on the character and impact of IFI strategies (Mosley, Harrigan, and Toye 1991; Gibbon, Havnevik,
and Hermele 1993; Engberg-Pedersen et al. 1996; Bromley 1995; Oxfam
1994). Criticism has been at two levels. The first is a critique of the policies
advocated by the agencies and the failures that have ensued. These criti-
cisms have been around such issues as the inability of devaluation to promote export-led growth, especially in raw materials or primary products,
which are often precontracted and relatively price-inelastic—the result
often being a fall in earnings.

Second, adjustment policies have seldom led to an increase in direct
foreign investment by multinational companies, which have been reluctant to locate in much of Africa and the Near East unless in primary export enclaves. Third, where multinational companies do locate, they tend
to "crowd out" local competition, as much as the state is seen to do, and
therefore frustrate the development of an indigenous capitalist class.
Fourth, structural adjustment lending tends to impose draconian cuts on
social investment, thereby affecting the development of the next generation of producers and consumers. Finally, perhaps the main intention of
structural adjustment is to promote debt servicing rather than repayment, with the added concern of integrating the adjusting country into
global and not local markets.

In promoting the view that export-driven growth from the agricultural
sector is possible, by encouraging the development of high-value low-
nutrition foodstuffs for the European market and the regeneration of the
cotton industry, the agencies have promoted comparative advantage: the
view that Egypt can find and keep its niche in the world market for many
of its agricultural products. Yet the agencies have tended to neglect the
fact that the overhead costs of developing export horticulture still seem
beyond the capacity of the Egyptian state (Sadowski 1991:270). There
have been repeated statements by government officials regarding the efficacy of new productive techniques for horticultural crops such as fruits,
vegetables, ornamental plants, and flowers. Yet there seems to have been
very little recognition of the problems involved in these crops entering

markets dominated by competitors that are more efficient. Seifeddin Abu Bakr, for example, of the Horticultural Research Institute noted in January 1997 that Egypt was introducing new farming techniques and crops like apples, which are not indigenous to Egypt but which compare favourably in price with U.S. or Lebanese imports—LE2 per kilo against LE10. Yet there remained three difficult issues. The first, expressed by the Horticultural Research Institute's fruit-handling department was that exporters "do not know what standards of quality are demanded by the country to which they wish to export." Second, there is little attention to good transportation networks and refrigeration to preserve perishable crops. And third, the European market is dominated by countries with similar climates to Egypt, and therefore new markets need to be expanded in eastern Europe. More assistance was identified in providing for available markets, yet freight charges often reached "50 percent of the value of the product itself" (*Al-Ahram* 9–15 January 1997).

Arguing the case for comparative advantage in agricultural export markets is very difficult in the light of this evidence. Comparative advantage, moreover, is used by the agencies in a very static way. Despite World Bank claims that it is arguing for a dynamic position for Egypt in the world economy, the agency and GoE positions adopted with regard to comparative advantage locate its agricultural expansion in products that are the object of fierce competition from neighbouring countries. In addition, raising cotton primarily for export, rather than for local industrial development, denies Egypt the greater value added by national processing and finishing. The question is whether Egypt can compete with the technologically more advanced Japanese cotton industry. Japanese industry now produces finer yarn from lower-count raw cotton, but locally generated investment for indigenous industry may ultimately be more advantageous than wedding Egypt to the vagaries of the international market and international traders.

It is also questionable whether short-staple cotton varieties should be substituted for longer-staple varieties. That would seem merely to lock Egypt into the production of low-quality fabrics instead of the traditionally high-quality finished garments normally linked to Egyptian cotton. Moreover, the development of a national cotton exchange that USAID has promoted (shipping in representatives from the New York exchange in early 1994 to show Egyptians how they operate) is more than likely to work against the interests of raising the levels of revenue from cotton sales, largely because of the power that international buyers have in precontracting raw cotton. A central cotton exchange would also not preclude the dominance of local cartels in buying local raw cotton for delivering to the exchange. There were, in addition, signs in 1993 and later that expatriate Egyptian business interests were getting ready to swoop down on the spoils by asset-stripping the aging cotton industry. This did not take place through open, transparent, and free competition, as the reformers argued would be the case under the aegis of the marketplace. It took place instead through a network of patronage and clientelist politics. Finally, it is highly questionable, as I have already intimated, that price incentives will sustain increased production. One prominent World Bank observer noted, commentating on Africa more widely, that changing farm gate prices for cotton is only a "once and for all phenomenon" (Lele, quoted in Gibbon et al. 1993:15).

Similar caution needs to be expressed about the possibility of Egypt's capturing the international or regional market for sales of fruit and vegetables. The agencies recognise the problems linked to generating local infrastructure and storage and marketing facilities to transport strawberries and similar items to European tables—Egypt was glutted with strawberries unable or unfit to be transported to Europe in 1994. Yet there is the additional problem of local competition for Europe's markets. There are already more advanced producers in the market competing with Egypt, namely, Israel, Turkey, Jordan, and Palestine.

Serious questions need to be raised about the agency prescriptions of export-led growth based upon comparative advantage. There is the problem of the "fallacy of composition": the agencies neglect the effect of falling prices of commodities that receive a boost in production following an increase in farm gate price or devaluation. Export-led growth based on comparative advantage is thus unlikely to achieve sustained growth and revenue for future investment. In fact, emphasis on attempting to generate export-led growth is more likely to reimpose the limitations of primary production upon Egypt. Promoting such a strategy fails to recognise that all the evidence from the newly industrialising countries is that development needs not less state intervention to compete in the world market, but a strong, active state. This is not the strong state that some have called for (Richards 1993a; World Bank 1997) that simply acts to subsidise private capital by providing infrastructure and possibilities for securing the interests of capital in general. It is a strong state that can make strategic decisions that redirect internal economic activity and redefine the position of economies in the global economy.

Wade highlighted this position when discussing the East Asian experience (Wade 1990; see also Barratt Brown and Tiffen 1992). Wade argued that developmental states have ensured that local capital is internally competitive and that foreign capital must serve the interests of national export-earning targets. Developmental states, moreover, must ensure that the bank-based financial system is under close state control and oriented towards clearly defined national goals. Liberalisation must be gradual and progressive (not the short, sharp shock sometimes advocated by the agencies), and growth must again be directed into strategically identified sectors. Growth, moreover, cannot simply be left to notions of inward investment's resolving problems of national capital accumulation. I will return below to the local political difficulties that confront Egypt and that reduce the chances of promoting such a strategy. It is worth recording here, however, that this view of developmental states contrasts with the views expressed in Egypt by the increasingly influential think tank called the Economic Research Forum for the Arab Countries, Iran and Turkey (see its recent, optimistic collection on the new trade agenda for the Middle East; Safadi 1998).

There are no iron laws that the Egyptian state can follow to ensure sustained agricultural and industrial development. Yet it is clear that the broad themes which Wade and others have identified, in either describing the experiences of East Asia or criticising adjustment policies, raise crucial questions about the character of the market that the agencies have reified. How a market is organised and structured, for example, is not simply an expression of abstract principles of rationality and efficiency. Markets embody concrete configurations of power. Indeed, markets are *determinations* of power relations, and they express relations of domination and subordination within the global order (Bush and Szeftel 1994:155). These questions regarding the East Asian "miracles" are the more relevant in the late 1990s following the financial crises and the massive IFI bailout of most of the "newly industrialised countries" in 1997–1999—models that Egypt has been encouraged to emulate. It is because the effect of adjustment may be to wed Egypt, as it has other developing countries, to the vagaries of the global market, by resurrecting patterns of primary product exports and failing to promote autonomous and sustainable growth, that commentators have been so critical of structural adjustment.

Tyranny of the Market

A further issue to explore is whether the market will act as an efficient and effective conduit to facilitate agricultural growth. A major difficulty with the view that it can is that the IFIs do not say what market forces represent and why they should ipso facto raise productivity—apart from a notion of increasing incentives—and they say nothing about which social class will replace, and with what effect, the state or parastatal authorities in providing the necessary agricultural inputs and marketing after the state has relinquished its position.

The World Bank continues, despite its rhetoric to the contrary, a neoliberal ideology that Polanyi more than forty years ago called "the economistic fallacy," that is, the false notion that people make decisions based constantly upon what they perceive their (economic) ideal interests to be

TABLE 4.1   Ex-Factory Prices for Nitrogenous Fertilisers Produced by Different Factories, 1988–1997 (LE per tonne)

	Urea	Ammonium nitrate	Ammonium sulphate
Average 1988/89–1990/91	234	198	207
Average 1991/92–1994/95	433	359	305
Average 1995/96–1996/97	483	392	345

SOURCE: Table compiled from data in Magdy El Guindy, Ibrahim Sidik, and Edgar Ariza-Nino (1997), p. 72.

and that economic beings are able to make decisions isolated from their position in society (Polanyi 1957). The World Bank also extends the belief of what Bryceson called "the ubiquity of entrepreneurial behaviour," the hope that the erosion of the state in food production and marketing will automatically be replaced by efficient and non-rent-seeking economic actors (Bryceson 1993, 1994:145). Bryceson's study of liberalisation in Tanzania offers interesting insight into the geographical circumstances of Egypt, even though they are very different. She argued that the liberalisation of Tanzanian grain markets revealed its unevenness, and that the *process* of rolling back the state-generated contradictions demonstrating liberalisation is not the outcome of decree but is instead "moulded by the interaction of policy-makers, traders and consumers" (Bryceson 1994:150). The outcome of market liberalisation is clearly the result of a number of different class struggles in and around the state and in the countryside; it is not simply the outcome of state edict.

The role of private companies in the supply of fertiliser in Egypt's agricultural sector illustrates graphically both a problem of rent seeking and the reluctance of the country's entrepreneurs to increase the efficiency of domestic resource allocation. Contrary to the design and intention of the reform programme, liberalisation of fertiliser production between 1995 and 1996 away from the PBDAC monopoly failed to improve efficiency within the domestic market. Indeed liberalisation and the emergence of three oligopolistic producers had three serious adverse effects on the local supply of fertiliser. The first impact was a dramatic increase in the domestic price of fertiliser from LE21 to LE90 a packet between 1994 and 1996. That led to estimated falls in agricultural yields by ten tonne per *feddan* in the case of sugarcane in Upper Egypt. There were also long-term price increases that had serious implications for offsetting any farmer gains from increases in farm gate prices. Table 4.1 indicates the increases in the three main fertilisers per tonne between 1988 and 1997.

A second consequence of the liberalisation and the emergence of three oligopolistic producers was that private fertiliser producers preferred to export their production, benefiting from an export price of LE800 per tonne compared with the local delivery price of LE450 per tonne. This rush to export led to serious local supply difficulties in 1994 and acute ones in 1995 (Abdel Aal 1998). It is difficult to estimate exactly the loss in agricultural production resulting from this fall in domestic supply.

The third consequence was that the PBDAC was allowed to reconvene the organisation of public sector fertiliser provision in 1995.

Public outcry over the fertiliser debacle promoted a seemingly un-precedented debate in the Peoples Assembly forcing Kamal El-Shazli, the Minister of State for Parliamentary Affairs, to approve a commission of enquiry in February 1996 to investigate the difficulties that the liberalisa-tion of fertiliser production had generated. The crisis of private sector fertiliser provision led to a severe shortage of 750,000 tonnes in 1995 and became a major source of criticism for Egyptian commentators on the ad-justment strategy. And the issue refused to go away even after the Peo-ples Assembly (Lower House of the Egyptian Parliament) debated the issue at the end of 1998. In February 1999 the Agricultural Co-operatives Union debated the issue for four hours, noting constant farmer com-plaints that a new "mafia" was bleeding the agricultural sector dry be-cause of high fertiliser prices. Although the prime minister announced a LE250-million fund to prevent any significant distortion in the price of agricultural products, dissatisfaction continued over what was labelled market chaos. The head of the parliament's agricultural committee noted the new fund was "a mere ink on paper," and Saad Hagras in the (con-sultative) Shura Council explained how farmers were in trouble market-ing their crops because of high farming costs (*Egyptian Gazette*, 2 Febru-ary 1999). Market failure in the fertiliser sector following liberalisation highlighted private sector interests in maximising company profits. It has also highlighted the failure of liberalisation to deliver an essential com-modity of high quality at prices affordable by the majority of farmers. As one farmer noted, "The spiralling prices of fertilisers are unaffordable. They come to add to our problems which make it extremely difficult for anyone of us to repay his debts, let alone secure satisfactory profits from his farming activities" (quoted in *Egyptian Gazette*, 2 February 1999).

The a priori assumption about the efficacy of market liberalisation also lay at the heart of the false hopes that the World Bank extended in dis-cussions about the privatisation of land tenure and the principle that those with security of title would invest in their land and protect it as a resource. Authors of a World Bank examination of agricultural decline in sub-Saharan Africa argued that private individualised tenure is desir-able: "Individual land ownership does provide an incentive to develop and maintain the land" (Cleaver and Schreiber 1994:59). And although there is the concession that privatisation can lead to problems of land grab, concentration of ownership, and landlessness, these problems—and others, too, like changes in the farming system, crop mix, access to inputs, and social differentiation—are invariably seen only as problems of transition. They are not seen to be problems inherent in the strategy of agricultural modernisation itself. Indeed the neoliberal strategy of agricultural modernisation is promised to yield higher agricultural returns, thereby simultaneously raising rural incomes, reducing poverty, and providing export crops that will generate foreign exchange and sustain the interests of a new agrarian bourgeoisie. That is the characterisation of agrarian reform detailed in the collaborative project between the Egyptian Ministry of Agriculture and Land Reclamation and USAID Cairo (Fletcher 1996).

The State and Agricultural Modernisation

For many years, blaming governments for poor economic performance has been part of the World Bank's ideological assault on developing countries. It provides the rationale for liberalising markets and encouraging private investment. Yet it is not enough to assert simply that rolling back the state will *necessarily* improve efficiency and the productive allocation of resources. For this view of the state assumes more than it demonstrates. It assumes, for instance, that the Egyptian state—or the states of most other developing countries, for that matter—is strong, efficient, well maintained and staffed, and able to do what states in capitalist societies do well, namely, sustain the economic interests of the dominant capitalist class within the shell of liberal social democracy. Of course, this exercise of class dominance is problematic. There is working-class opposition and conflict within and between national and international capitalist interests, but Western liberal democratic states (mostly) combine the reproduction of dominant economic interests with political legitimacy or hegemony (Gramsci 1971).

The simplistic view of the state expressed by the IFIs also assumes that there is a strong and vibrant bourgeoisie available and *willing* to fulfill functions vacated by the state (Giugale and Mobarak 1996). The IFI perspective, in short, makes assumptions about the Egyptian state that are ill founded. As recently noted, the position of the Arab state has been "overstated" (Ayubi 1995b). It is true that the Arab state is a "fierce state" (some are clearly more fierce than others) and often resorts to violence. Since 1991, in its total war against Islamists, Egypt is nevertheless not a "strong state" (Hansen 1991). Its infrastructural power is weak. It has difficulty collecting revenue like income tax, and it has failed to establish government by ruling through a bloc of social classes that govern with *legitimacy* and where elections may lead to regime replacement without the use of violence (Ayubi 1995b; Beetham 1994). Indeed, it seems the contrary is the case. There has been a considerable degree of deliberalisation since the early 1990s. There have been amendments to the penal code that have tightened patterns of repression and amendments to the ways in which professional syndicates and trade unions are allowed to organise. And there has been extensive electoral fraud, the undermining of political representation and participation that makes any notion of a transition to democracy in Egypt look baseless (Kienle 1998).[1]

Two further issues need to be considered with specific reference to agricultural development. The first has been well documented in a recent assessment of the processes of agricultural modernisation in sub-Saharan Africa, and the argument is useful for better understanding the assumptions of IFI strategy in Egypt (Berry 1993).

Sara Berry argued that "the rural consequences of state intervention are neither determined by nor limited to the stated aims of rural development policy". In other words, although the "presence of the state in rural communities is palpable," it is also "unpredictable" (Berry 1993:46). This point has been made in response to three commonly held views on Africa's agricultural crisis, and these can be extended to a characterisation of the agricultural crisis in Egypt. These views are, first, that government policy can have very little impact in the countryside because peasants escape government controls (Hyden 1980, 1983). In Egypt, for example, many peasants refused to grow cotton in cotton-designated areas after the 1960s and instead grew more financially rewarding crops. They managed to do that by bribing agricultural extension officers or by simple defiance. That defiance can be traced back to the very introduction of cotton by Mohamed Ali, when cotton seedlings would often be lifted from the ground just enough to ensure they did not grow (Schulze 1991:179). Opposition to cotton production, especially when the farm gate price was much less than the border price, continued during both the British presence at the turn of the nineteenth century and later, during the Nasser period. It has also been documented that after World War 1, when rents increased along with instruments of state control, resistance took the form of rural banditry. That banditry, moreover, seems to have been less a form of nationalist revolt against the colonial state and more an opposition to the colonialisation of rural life (Schulze 1991:189).

The second commonly held view that offers an explanation for agricultural crisis is that government policies are inappropriate for rural interests because politicians are more concerned with lining their own pockets (Bates 1981, 1983). In Egypt, concerns with generating agricultural surplus for industrial development and producing cheap food for a rapidly growing working class have at different times sustained the political power of the ruling party. The third most commonly held view to explain agricultural crisis in Africa has been the effect of the colonial legacy of neopatrimonial rule. In short, this refers to the use by politicians of public office for private gain, (corruption, or *el-fasad*), which undermines any attempt to develop agrarian strategies that might generate sustained growth (Sandbrook 1986; Berry 1993:43–45).

Not unsurprisingly, there are veils of secrecy in Egypt that make investigations of corruption difficult. Yet a report compiled by El-Mahroussa (1997) documented thirty-six recent press investigations of corruption. These had mainly been published in the opposition press, like *El-Gomhoriya, El Sha'ab, El-Ahali, Rosel-Youssef,* and *El Mossawer.* The major accusations related to the embezzlement of public funds and the use of public office for private gain; collusion between the public and private sector, which reduced the effect of market liberalisation; and instances of bribery. One such case was the issue of the leading figure of the public sector holding company, who had embezzled public funds and transferred money to a private Swiss account. Initially, in return for nonprosecution, he returned LE23 million to Egypt. That amount was only a proportion of the alleged sum that he had possibly embezzled, and he was eventually imprisoned for his wrongdoing. In another alleged case, two sons of a senior minister were accused of acquiring assets, including state land, to support a restaurant in Heliopolis that also had senior government officials on the company's board. In yet another case of fraudulent behaviour between the public and private sectors, an importer employed by the public company El Nasser was dismissed after allegations of losing the state company LE70 million. Clearly, these more publicised cases of the frailty of human behaviour in Egypt's business community raise questions about the vibrancy and effectiveness of unregulated liberalisation and the need for stronger government regulation.

Poor agricultural performance in the explanations that I have just reviewed call it the result either of the particular rationality of different class actors or of the structure and organisation of political institutions. In doing so, these formulations "tend to ignore the interplay between individual action and institutional structure, and both imply that rural development programs have definitive consequences which can be clearly labelled successes or failures" (Berry 1993:45). In the Egyptian context, the characterisation of rural violence during the Nasser period has tended to take two particular perspectives. The first has been to individualise it and to see it as episodic and personalised, conflict about familial assets or bad neighbourliness. Yet it is often the case that these types of conflicts have roots in the struggle for limited village resources and dissatisfaction with government policy. It is also the case that the outcome of farmer activity and government policy is inconclusive: It is simply impossible to identify clear winners and losers. It is more appropriate to try to situate the outcome of policy initiatives, and their rural impact, within the context of the nature of the particular economic and political struggles involved. In other words, the outcome of government rural development policy is not simply deducible from declared policy.

Yet, that is what the IFIs and the GoE seem to do. Moreover, at one level, the IFIs seem unconcerned with the effect of the removal of government from economic activity as long as market liberalisation is in place. The IFIs have shown little concern with the actual consequences of market-driven formulas for rural people's well-being, and more generally for the type of agricultural growth and the identity of the winners and losers that market-driven formulas create. The IFIs' rhetorical concern with the poor and the short-term losers from structural adjustment has become convenient camouflage for their ideological persistence with market-driven formulas and reinvigorated policies of comparative advantage, which have failed throughout the Middle East and Africa. It has become much clearer that the interests often served by the IFIs are those of the sanctity of free trade and therefore the defence of U.S. interests overseas. This was revealed very starkly recently in the remarkable conflict between Japan and the World Bank over the characterisation of the state's role in promoting economic growth in East and Southeast Asia (Wade 1996).

Government Neglect of Agriculture

In contrast to arguing that Africa's agricultural problems are the result of too much government intervention, it is more accurate to say that it is precisely government *neglect* of agriculture that has aggravated food security. Agricultural budgets across the African continent and the Middle East have declined; rural investment in facilitating effective rural infrastructure, including health and education, have not kept pace with urban demands on national exchequers after independence, and the budgets plummeted during the lost development decade of the 1980s, resulting from the debt crisis, and in the 1990s from policies of structural adjustment. It is also noteworthy that the World Development Report of 1991 includes China and Egypt among the better-performing countries, where agricultural yield per hectare was more than 2.5 percent in the years 1960–1988, and where average nonagricultural growth was more than 4 percent. These two economies were fuelled by extensive state provision—now criticised by the World Bank as detrimental to the growth that it previously applauded. For although the World Bank in Washington, with the publication of the World Development Report of 1997, sought to distance itself from some of its previously cruder neoclassical formulations regarding the state, it is unlikely to moderate its stance in Egypt.

Certainly, there is little evidence of moderation regarding the size and extent of government intervention.

It is too simplistic to argue that state intervention has on its own undermined private initiative in agriculture. This argument presents a static and patronising view of peasant farming and is not supported by the historical evidence. Lucie Wood Saunders and Soheir Mehanna, for example, documented the emergence, causes, and impact of entrepreneurship in an Egyptian village during the twentieth century. They showed that the growth of entrepreneurs in a particular village was dependent upon a mix of factors and not only the outcome of state policy. They demonstrated how "national conditions and community or familial resources constrained or facilitated different kinds of entrepreneurial activity with different impacts on the village over time" (Saunders and Mehanna 1986:75). They also demonstrated that pressures on farmers were promoting the use of land for more capital-intensive farming. This took the form of livestock and chicken farming as well as investment in higher-yielding and more profitable grains and speciality crops like sesame. That research was conducted in the early 1960s, and it is a pattern that has been confirmed by Hopkins (1993) and Glavanis and Glavanis (1983). It again demonstrates the varied and uneven nature of agricultural modernisation, its dynamic impact on social differentiation, and the need to build these processes into the equation when assessing Egyptian agricultural transformation.

It may well be a counterfactual question whether the state has undermined agricultural production or not, but it is important to note that for many years, the state has overseen a fall in the share of agriculture in public investment. In the period 1960–1980, moreover, in comparative productive terms, "Heavily regulated Egyptian farmers [did as well as] free wheeling, largely unregulated Turkish farmers" (Hansen 1991:475). In the 1960s, public investment constituted 94 percent of agricultural investment, but this had fallen to 6.3 percent by the end of the 1980s.

As G. A. Amin (n.d.) noted, the 1970s and 1980s were periods of "absolute negligence" in agriculture. And private investment, too, neglected agriculture, as more profitable pickings were to be had in services, construction, and tourism during *infitah*. Amin continued his observation of agricultural stagnation, to argue that many government controls, which have been seen to stymie growth, were seldom adhered to and in many cases were ignored. This partly accounts for the evidence I found in the two villages Kafr Tasfa and Kafr Saad (documented in Chapter 5) of creeping urbanisation and loss of agricultural land, which has taken place *despite* formal government restrictions outlawing it. Amin therefore noted:

> It might have been more useful for the Egyptian agriculture not to lessen the government intervention, but rather to apply more effective intervention. Such intervention might have included the more strict implementation of specific laws that aim at the protection of this sector, as well as the increase, instead of decreasing the size of public investment in developing the basic infrastructure of agriculture. (Amin n.d.)

Rather than a blanket withdrawal of the state from agricultural activities, government intervention has a continued place and role, but greater thought and efficiency are required in identifying what it does (for a discussion against state minimalism, see Streeten 1993). There has been little evidence of an indigenous bourgeoisie that has interests in developing the agricultural sector beyond quick returns from agribusiness ventures. The withdrawal of government from the high-value agricultural sector leaves room for short-term mining of Egypt's already marginal soils by investors seeking quick returns from speculation and asset stripping.

One of the repeated ways in which policymakers view the Egyptian countryside has been expressed in the way the state is seen as an effective tool in the management of agricultural resources. Whether efficient or not, and whether active or not, the state has been viewed as a major actor capable of intervening in and shaping the lives of the fellahin. The actual efficacy of that intervention historically can be questioned as I have indicated. The questioning leads to a discussion that does not seem to have taken place within the Egyptian polity about what type of intervention is necessary in the contemporary period, what social forces will replace the state, and whether they are more desirable than, or simply different from, the interests promoted by the state since before the Nasserist revolution?

It is one of the ironies—or more accurately, contradictions—of the period of structural adjustment that the withdrawal of the state from participation in the agricultural sector (and therefore a presumed reduction in state rent seeking) is likely to lead to the *continuation* of rent seeking by the same social forces that have been linked to the state. The difference will be that the rent seekers during the period of adjustment will be seen by the IFIs as legitimate: rent seeking will be part of the market economy (or at least the attempt to construct one), and in the short term, at least (whatever that means), it is viewed as an inevitable transaction cost. Just which social groups will have to bear that cost, however, is not made clear, and neither is the way in which the state is suddenly meant to become efficient and to shed rent seeking. This point has been made elsewhere. Noting the consequences of economic reforms on agriculture and politics in sub-Saharan Africa, where simplistic notions of state withdrawal have been promoted by the World Bank, Gibbon et al. commented, "Replacing exploitative forms of state regulation by a regime of non-regulation allows the state bourgeoisie to legally 'privatise' its interests without transforming its essentially parasitic form of economic operation" (Gibbon et al. 1993:147).

One of the consequences of viewing the state as a major actor in agricultural development has been a preoccupation among policymakers in government, and with the IFIs, that remedies for agricultural decline should focus on supply-side issues. The IFIs, for instance, focus attention on issues of environmental accounting, pricing of environmental assets, reforming landlord-tenant relations, and promoting the liberalisation of markets. These concerns largely ignore issues that underpin the *demand* for agricultural assets and that ensure viable production. This preoccupation is not accompanied by an understanding of people's choices and expectations. Poor household concerns with collective or communal action, revealed later in my case study material, is undermined (ignored) by market-oriented formula. That is because many poor people's incorporation into the market is marginal or uneven and is either not recognised by policymakers or not viewed as equally important alongside more powerful (economically stronger) market participants.

The agency and GoE strategy for reforming the agricultural sector advances a particular view of agricultural modernisation. It represents the need for increased application of technology to increase growth underpinned by the need to accelerate the pattern of commoditisation: the development of commodity production, rural markets, and division of labour. It is a view that argues for improved technical efficiency reflected by concern with high-input and high-output farming and improved allocation of resources through competition: "the operation of demand and supply transmitted by market prices which determine (optimal) ways of producing agricultural commodities" (Bernstein 1990:6).

In general terms, the World Bank has used a model "that is simultaneously an abstract and idealised representation of the development of capitalist agriculture in the West, *and* the inspiration of policies to 'modernise' agriculture in Africa and other parts of the Third World" (Bernstein 1990:7). It is a view of modernisation that includes a process of commoditisation requiring specialisation and the drive to standardise technical conditions of production to "reduce the variations, obstacles and *unpredictability* of natural environments" (Bernstein 1990:6–7).

The conception of agricultural "modernisation" thus produces two (associated) processes: (i) satisfying the conditions of economies of scale, technical efficiency, market competitiveness, specialisation, and standardisation *at the level of the unit of production* for yields that are as predictable, as well as large, as possible. . . .(ii) integrating farming units (whether "family farms" or capitalist enterprises) so that the above conditions and effects are satisfied *at the level of the agricultural sector and its linkages as a whole.* (Bernstein 1990:7, emphasis in original)

Both the agencies and the GoE promote this model. In pursuing it, they have failed to recognise the character of existing relations of production and reproduction in Egypt's countryside. The logic of agricultural modernisation pursued is to blame existing agricultural crises upon the inefficiency of state policies and also on the ineffectiveness of small farming units. These shortcomings in the organisation of Egyptian agriculture are seen by the IFIs and the GoE to inhibit the development of the necessary conditions for boosting productivity of high-yield crops.

Underpinning the agency and reformers' characterisation of the way in which agricultural production is organised is the misconceived view of the farm unit as a single economic actor that performs the role of allocating its resources for goal maximisation. For although especially the World Bank has been keen to declare its interest in the importance of understanding issues like the persistence and dominance of labour migrancy, the role of women in production, and problems of rural inequality, the implication and the importance of these themes for agricultural reform either is not properly grasped or seems to be included merely to appease reformers who may have a more differentiated view of Egypt's countryside.

Understanding the Countryside

The Agrarian Question

The main source of agricultural production in Egypt is the small farmer. And it is the dynamism and the dynamics of small-scale household production that prescriptions for agricultural reform fail to consider—except by undermining them. I now want to indicate where the *strategy* for agricultural modernisation is at odds with the character of the way in which agricultural *production* is organised.

There is little evidence that agency and Egyptian policy reformer claims that they are concerned with the plight of Egyptian small-scale producers are being translated into policy. My critique is based on evidence that suggests policies of agricultural modernisation will erode the security of small-scale rural producers—those with landholdings of less than 5 *feddans.* The land tenure act will also have the effect of dispossessing many small farmers, reducing the size of holdings of others, and generally reducing guarantees of tenure rights. And there will be insufficient industrial or urban economic growth to absorb numbers of rural landless and unemployed.

The debate about the nature of agricultural modernisation in Egypt is not new, and it has inevitably been informed by the more general debate about the "agrarian question." This is essentially the debate about whether rural inequalities have led to a process of rural class polarisation and what the consequences of agricultural modernisation have been for the character of rural social relationships.

The argument about the polarisation and eventual disappearance of the peasantry relates to Lenin's characterisation and understanding of the likely impact that capitalist penetration would have in the countryside. Lenin's view was that rural social structure would take the form of five social classes: landlords; rich, middle, and poor peasants; and landless workers. He argued that there was a long-run tendency for that class structure to become increasingly polarised into landlords (capitalist farmers) and landless labourers. That analysis was based on a view that precapitalist agrarian structures were undifferentiated and that the major criterion of differentiation was landownership (Lenin 1964).

Parallels have been drawn between Lenin's analysis and the historical development of capitalism in Egypt's countryside. Abdel Fadil (1975), for example, assembled data for the period 1952–1970 on the dimensions of rural inequality using the criteria of landholding, access to agricultural machinery, and reliance upon the market. In contrast to his position, which suggested that class inequality based upon uneven access was accelerating despite the land reforms of the Nasser period, a persistent current in the debates about agrarian change in Egypt is the view that the agrarian transition posited by Lenin has been frustrated. Since 1952, farms of less than 5 *feddans* account for more than half the country's cultivated area; holdings of less than 1 *feddan* increased the most.

Debate about the agrarian question in Egypt has centred around the extent to which class polarisation in the countryside has been stalled and frustrated by the persistence of middle-ranking rural social classes (Abdel Fadil 1975; Radwan and Lee 1986; Adams 1986b; Hopkins 1988; Glavanis and Glavanis 1983; Seddon 1986). Debate about why proletarianisation has been stalled has ranged from, first, seeing the rural bourgeoisie as frustrating the transfer of rural surplus to the industrial sector, ensuring its continued existence and the preservation of existing rural class structure and, second, excessive state intervention, which has blocked class polarisation (compare Abdel Fadil 1975 and Adams 1986b).

Another explanation for the resistance to modernisation, or the failure of the universal and even spread of capitalist relations of production, has been the persistence of peasant household producers. It is important to note that in contrast to Lenin's view of peasant social differentiation, Chayanov (1966) argued that there was not a tendency "to create increasing groups of rich and poor or landless peasants with a more and more unstable group of middle peasants in between. The village was an overwhelmingly homogeneous community, able to reproduce itself both economically and socially" (Harrison 1982:264).

Chayanov envisaged the modernisation of the peasant sector without it necessarily following a capitalist or socialist path. Peasant producers were capable of adopting new technological means of production through agricultural extension and cooperative organisation while simultaneously keeping peasant institutions and small landholding farms. There was also the importance for Chayanov of the life cycle of the peasant household. The relationship between hands to work and mouths to feed sustained the persistence of family nonwage labour and production organised around the household.

Two major positions seem to exist in Egypt to explain the persistence of household peasant production. Hopkins (1988, 1993) expresses the first. He has argued that although a sixfold process of "depeasantisation" has taken place in the last 150 years, the vitality and vibrancy of the Egyptian household as an economic unit, "based on people who in various ways live, produce and consume together," have continued (Hopkins 1993:186). According to Hopkins, the process of depeasantisation has resulted from the following trends: the emergence of capitalist farmers; the increasingly common presence of agricultural machinery; a large rural population of free wage labour; the continued presence of the household as an organiser of labour, which is perceived as a "block" to agrarian transition; the village being "largely dominated" by outside forces like the state and market but retaining many autonomous social processes; and education and migration as ways in which peasants can generate income to extricate themselves from rural poverty (Hopkins 1988:27).

Hopkins's characterisation of the reasons for the persistence of small-scale production is very useful. It describes many processes that have taken place in recent years, and it reminds observers of the importance of what he called "the labour process model." For him the "analytical starting point is the commodity-producing household operating in the context of the village or other rural community and in conjunction with the state" (Hopkins 1993:190). Hopkins argued that focusing on the way in which production is organised takes attention away from "static class analysis." In the process, he tended to reify the organisation of production rather than the interrelationship between households, village structures, the state, and the world economy. Hopkins is nevertheless almost alone among commentators focussing on the character of households and the *dynamics* within them and the necessary importance of including, rather than excluding, peasant producers in debates about agricultural transformation (see also Adams 1986a, 1985; Weyland 1993).

The second explanation for the persistence of peasant agriculture has in many ways redressed the balance away from reifying the household to include a fuller treatment of its relation with capitalist encroachment. Glavanis and Glavanis (1986) noted the continuing importance of non-capitalist forms of household production, notably in dairy produce. They argued that this was not simply a persistent precapitalist form but the product of the articulation of household survival strategies and the character of capitalist encroachment. The persistent importance of noncapitalist relations of production and the dynamism of the way in which they interact is best summarised as follows:

> Within the reproduction cycle of the small peasant household in Egypt there has been considerable development and intensification of commodity relations over the last two and a half decades. However, it is likewise evident that non-commodity relations are essential to the reproduction of the peasant household and remnants of the past but have emerged out of a given conjuncture of new forces, e.g. the phenomenon of *tabadul* (exchange). (Glavanis and Glavanis 1986:191)

Glavanis and Glavanis conducted their fieldwork in the mid-1970s. Since then there has been an increase in the way in which household activities have been mediated by the market. Yet although the market has become increasingly important in providing opportunities for peasant access to farm implements, tools, livestock, food, credit, and labour, the market has not been, nor is it now, always central to that process of acquiring access to means of production and social reproduction. As Glavanis and Glavanis noted, in some cases, nonmarket transactions—payments in kind for services like the provision of farm implements, impregnation of *gamusa* (water buffalo), sharing of livestock—might coexist alongside market transactions. There has nevertheless been the erosion of the relative autonomy of noncapitalist household production since the 1970s. The incursion of the demands of the market especially in areas of dairy production and in the acquisition of farm implements is taking place, and the household has developed means of coping with the needs of the cash economy by developing, among other things, sales of household goods like milk and cheese and baskets.

Debate about Egypt's agrarian question focuses attention on the continuation of the household as the unit of production. Household agricultural production may well be under threat, and the way in which it survives is constantly being transformed, but the *izba* system still holds the key to any successful agricultural reform. It remains the case that "the peasant household still organises reproduction autonomously to a considerable extent while at the same time a large part of its agricultural produce is diverted to exterior markets" (Weyland 1993:101). The household is essentially organised around a nuclear family of parents and children that may be accompanied by new children and previous-generation parents or other relatives. In addition to the nuclear family there is also the extended version, which includes married sons and their families. It is this system of production that is threatened by the economic reform programme.

These categories are ideal types of family economic and social organisation, and they mask complex (inter)relationships within and between families, with the division of labour and the social reproduction of relations within households. It is tempting, as the World Bank and other agencies have done, to see these households merely as rational economic actors making decisions about the optimal allocation of resources. Yet as Hopkins has declared, "The Egyptian village is not a *tabula rasa* on to which one can impress whatever one's ideology prefers" (Hopkins 1993:186). He continued to make the point that choices made by individuals are structured in ways that make sense to them without the inevitability of the economically active and rational actor so loved by the agencies; "Choices are not made by hypothetical (economics) men and women, responding to economic and financial incentives in disregard of social values and cultural concerns. Rather they represent the outcome of people operating in an institutional (social and cultural) context" (Hopkins 1993:186).

The point is that households follow very different, varied, and complex strategies for production and reproduction and to cope with economic and environmental forms of crisis during periods of stress. These patterns of survival relate to different social relations of production within the household and village and in relation to local markets and interaction with the state—previously with marketing and cooperative organisations. They also relate to the differential access to resources and means of production between households—the village class structure. And patterns of survival relate to shifts in the character of national economic crises that in turn are inextricably linked to global capitalist crises and restructuring—most recently with adjustment policies.

The ways in which those policies affect producers and peasant abilities to respond and transform their conditions of existence, and entitlements to food and the environment, will depend upon the historical way in which commodity markets have developed in their location and beyond. Variation in patterns of commoditisation, as well as environmental differences even within what is seen as the more-or-less homogenous Delta region, will generate an uneven impact of adjustment. Yet agency and GoE policy does not take note of regional or household differences and dynamics. The Minister of Agriculture and deputy prime minister, Yusuf

Wali, it seems, in fact refused the offer of an assessment of the economic and social impact of adjustment that was proposed in 1997 by USAID.

Women and Labour Migrancy

One household dynamic not grasped by reformers is the nature of women's labour and the gender division of labour. There has been a mushrooming of debate in recent years regarding the gender division of labour in developing countries including Egypt, yet the agricultural reformers seem to be impervious to it (on the Middle East, see Keddie and Baron 1991; Ahmed 1992; on Egypt, see Weyland 1993; Toth 1991; Karam 1998; Ali 1998). Much of the early general criticism of the World Bank's agricultural modernising strategies was that women and gender issues were neglected in the promotion of project and development assistance. Criticism more recently has focused upon the way in which women have been incorporated into the development process and the deleterious effects that strategies of agricultural modernisation have had on them (Boserup 1970; Elson 1991; Young et al. 1981; Moser 1993; Bakker 1994; Sparr 1994).

Many rural women in Egypt have responded to changes in the macroeconomic conditions of the countryside, in employment opportunities, in prices, and in local services, by increasing the range of opportunities for income earning by consolidating animal husbandry and engaging in petty commodity production like basket weaving. These strategies for coping with poor agricultural wage rates for women and children, compared with those for men, have generated the view that Egyptian agriculture is presided over by a part-time labour force: women securing their survival within and beyond the household with income generating opportunities that are not dependent upon the sale of labour power in agriculture, and men working a combination of on- and off-farm employment, often in neighbouring countries.

In the few pages that the World Bank gives to the role of women in Egypt's agriculture (1992a:68–71), planners concede that Egyptian women play an important yet, they argue, under-researched role. In fact an estimated 47 percent of the total active female population is engaged in agricultural work, and because of outmigration, notably during the oil boom years of the 1970s and early 1980s, women became very often de facto heads of households. Richards (1991a) estimated that one-third of all crop labour was carried out by women, and for the first time in 1983, the national labour force sample survey tried to include the amount of family labour in the rearing of livestock; it estimated 40 percent of the work was done by women (Badran 1993:203). Women are engaged in most agricultural work and animal husbandry. Many also engage in petty commodity production of handicraft and basket and carpet weaving.

It is tempting to be persuaded by a popular and mistaken view that the gender division of labour is rigid and shaped by simple practices of custom, purdah, and Islam. This might be easier to do in the case of women in Upper Egypt, yet even there it is a misrepresentation of actual social practice and dynamics of the household. In short, men seem to perform the hardest agricultural tasks of land preparation, plowing, hoeing, thinning, and irrigating, and women tend to engage in somewhat lighter physical tasks—although that is not universally the case. Women are not just relegated to animal husbandry, however; they also engage in labouring in the cultivation of wheat, cotton, and rice (Toth 1991:219), and all this in addition to household work of cooking and caring for children and the elderly. It would also be mistaken to continue a view of gender relations in Egypt that view rural households where women are oppressed, in uncaring relationships, and subject to crude notions of powerlessness. Although all these aspects of relationships, and the gender division of labour, may indeed be true for some women, it would be mistaken to merely reiterate what have been crude expressions by commentators of "orientalism"(see the interesting discussion in Ali 1998).

The World Bank recognises the importance of targeting women with "new techniques and methods'" that might help reduce postharvest losses. More attention, they concede, also needs to be paid to women's literacy, high fertility, high maternal and child mortality, and poor village extension services. Egypt's record on each of these is poor. Average maternal mortality in Egypt is 320 per 100,000. This compares with the average ratio of 27 in Bahrain and 6 in Kuwait. Moreover, 67 percent of babies have low birth weight compared with 8 percent in Turkey and 9 for Iraq (before the post–Gulf War sanctions). And the illiteracy rate for rural women is 76 percent (Badran 1993:201) although as with all such figures there is the need for caution in relation to their accuracy.

Women's participation in farming has had a crucial effect on national economic performance and in shaping the way in which production is organised in the countryside. Toth (1991) has argued that the demand for women's labour, in the crucial cotton-harvesting month of September, coincided in 1961 with increased demand for male migration, as it did repeatedly in the 1980s following the oil boom. Female labour was demanded because of the differential gender wage rate: as much as LE1–2 per day. Consequently many cotton producers were unable to get access to adequate supplies of labour, and income from cotton sales reduced the GoE ability to promote desired strategies for economic development—Nasser's first five-year plan in 1961.

This was a labour constraint in a country where labour supply is not seen as a restraint to agricultural production by the international agencies. The increased evidence of women and children in agricultural work in the 1980s followed from increased male labour migration and increased mechanisation that allowed women to engage in heavier work. In the 1960s, female participation rates were more explicable because of male resistance to engaging in cotton picking and their preference for higher-paid casual *(tarahil)* labour.

Women receive a lower wage rate for agricultural work. The frequent explanation for this is the greater physical strength that men possess, but this is less sustainable as an excuse for employers with increased mechanisation. Patriarchy and seclusion also explain women's nonparticipation in some farming activities, yet this cannot account for why, when women's labour becomes crucial as a source of work, purdah becomes unenforceable (Toth 1991:215–216). A more accurate explanation of why women engage in the way they do in farm and off-farm income activities relates to women's ability to secure the conditions around them for the reproduction (renewal and maintenance) of themselves and the household. As Toth has noted:

> The cultural definition of women as dominated, docile, and servile serves mainly to obscure the true relations of production and to strengthen their exploitation. [Yet] men lose out, too, when the stridencies of their efforts are diluted. Men reject this manipulation by turning to *tarahil* labor, and women escape from it by turning inward to home-based labor activities. (Toth 1991:230)

Chapter 5 indicates the responses and initiatives of women and other rural producers to economic adjustment. The pressures of economic hardship and environmental crisis need to be put much more centre stage in the way agricultural reform is viewed. Unless planners incorporate the actual dynamics underpinning decisionmaking in the household relating to women they will fail to recognise one of the most powerful promoters for transforming rural relations of production and reproduction. It is clear, for instance, that women are taking much of the strain of the economic reform process in the countryside and not necessarily, as Toth has indicated, escaping inward to home-based labour activities. Table 4.2 indicates a summary of survival and livelihood strategies engaged in by respondents in two villages in Daqahliya and Giza in the early 1990s. These villages were chosen for their representativeness as a periurban location near Cairo and a "traditional" Delta village. An unstructured sample of twenty households and detailed case histories of women and women-headed households generated important indicative evidence at the beginning of the adjustment programme in the early 1990s (for a detailed discussion, see Bush 1995).

TABLE 4.2   Summary of Survival and Livelihood Strategies in Two Villages in Daqahliya and Giza Governorates

Strategies for increasing resources	Strategies for increasing the efficiency of current resources
Intensification of the labour process	Change in diets that may involve changes in the preparation of food
Greater participation of women in labour process	Fewer visits to health services and reduction in numbers of children receiving education
Increased petty-commodity production	Change in overall consumption patterns and reduction in cultural association
Migration—local and international	Increased pressure on women's labour time
Asset sales	
Theft	

SOURCE: Adapted from Cornia (1987).

My evidence indicated six survival and livelihood strategies for coping with economic crisis. All of them impacted on women. For example, households during crisis have changed diets. It has been much discussed in the literature on rural survival strategies that households may, in the early stages of economic crisis, prioritise the security of assets that guarantee future survival rather than increase current food consumption levels (Corbett 1988; De Waal 1989). Wherever possible, rural households make rational decisions about what is likely to best provide for their social reproduction. In my sample, there were a number of strategies that were promoted to cope with worsening rural conditions and that did not directly result in an increase in household food consumption. Nevertheless, richer households seemed not to change their dietary intake, whereas poorer respondents did report a change, notably a reduction in the consumption of protein—especially meat, poultry, and eggs—and an increase in household consumption of carbohydrates. Meat tended to be eaten in poorer households once every two weeks rather than twice a week, and in four households, meat was consumed just once a month. Diets became heavily dependent upon consumption of bread, cheese, and pickles. Even the consumption of macaroni declined in the poorer "traditional" Delta village. And in the Giza village, of the seven respondents that reported a decline in the consumption of meat, two noted a total absence of vegetables and fruit from the household diet.

The impact of economic crisis on changes in dietary consumption has been reported before in Egypt, and of particular concern has been the purchase, during lean years, of cheaper commodities without regard for nutritive value (Galal and Amina 1984; Hussein 1989). Although this switch in diets has been attributed to a "deficient knowledge about nutrition" (Hussein 1989:11), it is also the outcome of family budget constraints and decisions taken by women to cope with economic crisis. Here, women make decisions about shifting household consumption patterns in line with the new economic realities.

The second major way in which households in these two villages coped with a mounting crisis of access to resources and depletion in the values of the income that they had been able to earn since adjustment, was for those with work in urban areas to intensify the labour process and for those without access to such wage employment to try and migrate—at a time when opportunities for work had fallen. Yet it was clear that the strategy of working longer hours, for example, or of finding different work to supplement agricultural labour was realistically only a strategy for *men* who could work in nearby urban centres. Farmers did try to find opportunities for work in their villages, but economic crisis had reduced the outlets or employment entitlements. In addition, women experienced the most intensification of their labour time. They spent longer in the souk finding substitute foodstuffs for the more protein-rich meat, chicken, and eggs that since, economic liberalisation, had become less common in household diets. Women also spent more time in health centres, which were threatened with reduced funding and the erosion of service provision. Respondents also noted that women were more and more being drawn into longer working days in the fields, weeding and harvesting family and other people's land. Moreover, the sale of handicrafts had become a major source of income for more than 50 percent of households. It was the women in the households who both made items like baskets and rope and were responsible for selling them in the market.

Women stressed in both villages that there were increased pressures on their time. These included household responsibilities of preparing food and caring for children and also the demands on them to generate an income by selling either handicrafts or their labour time as agricultural labourers. In both villages it was clear that the women respondents' time was demanded increasingly, both in the household and in generating income outside the family home. As I have noted, agricultural labour is not new for women in Egyptian villages. What is perhaps new is the centrality of it in providing a necessary element of survival in coping with rural crises and mounting costs of services, especially for their children's health and education. Yet GoE and IFI proposals for reforming the agricultural sector are gender-blind.

Women expressed a feeling of increased isolation following the intensification of their labour processes. That isolation was reported in terms of less social contact with their neighbours and the reduction in celebrations like weddings because of their increased costs.

Nowhere is this isolation felt more than in the way in which women have engaged in different forms of agricultural work during the periods of their husbands' labour migration. Although labour migration received a severe blow during and in the aftermath of the Gulf War, many migrants have reengaged with work outside the village, and the responses of women to those conditions is essential in understanding the changing features of the countryside and how best to mobilise female labour and ensure the survival of the village. Recent discussions of women as heads of household describe the vitality and vibrancy of women as de facto heads, and decisionmakers for a range of economic and social issues and the process of empowerment that has often followed the absence of men (Weyland 1993; Bach 1998).

There are two important points here. The first relates to decisionmaking structures within households that are a source of labour migrancy, and the second is the role that women play. Current strategies of agricultural modernisation are likely to undermine considerable strides that women have made in shaping their conditions of existence. This will happen if patterns of transformation are set in motion that alter labour migration and female employment opportunities. It will also happen where the reforms jeopardise households that engage in more than one economic activity to survive and the resilience of the household depends upon the combination of several, and often changing, income-generating activities. Continuing labour migration, moreover, whether to neighbouring countries or locally, generates the persistence (and transformation) of the village and the household within the context of national and global capitalist relations of production. Labour migrancy generates many benefits for capital in general. The costs of reproducing labour are carried by the household and notably the women within it, whereas the employer only has to cover the costs of maintaining a single labourer—rather than consider the cost of a "family wage" rate. This split cost to capital has served the interests of regional (and local) employers. And it remains possible for capitalist interests to benefit from this process if peasant labour power is generated in a "household which is still organised as a unit of production for consumption" (Weyland 1993:133; and for labour migrancy in other contexts, see Meillassoux 1981; Burawoy 1985).

Although policy planners note the role of labour migrancy and of women, the consequences of agricultural modernisation on these two themes appear not to have been adequately thought through. It follows, for instance, that if the status of most small landholding households changed, following policies that might accelerate primitive accumulation, like changes in access to credit, removing the tenants' security of tenure, and increasing landlessness, it is unlikely that those same house-holds would be able to continue (and expand?) the production of cash crops. Such a pattern of primitive accumulation would seem likely to also undermine the way in which labour migrancy is sustained within the household and the benefits to employers accruing from that practice of splitting the sites of maintaining and renewing labour power.

I detail more on the position of women in Chapter 5, but to reinforce the argument here it is crucial to note that in times of rural economic and social crisis there appears to be a disproportionately greater impact on the position of women than on men. Of course, that impact varies be-tween women of different social classes, but it is clear from even indica-tive evidence that women's labour time increases within the household and beyond it when there are economic constraints to the way in which families generate income.

Peasants, Politics, and the State

My final critique of the proposals for reforming agriculture relates to the failure of the agencies to grasp the way in which politics is conducted in Egypt. Here I am concerned with two particular issues, although there are many more that might be considered. The first is at the level of the state, and the second relates to the way in which the peasantry and the countryside are viewed.

One characterisation of the Egyptian polity is to view the state as "soft"—unable to take decisions quickly, especially when it involves an attack on or reduction of powerful sectional interests (Sadowski 1991). This view is at odds with the perspective expressed by the international agencies. They have argued since the early 1980s that the excessive, large (and strong) state needs to be pruned in order to enable the conditions of private capital accumulation to flourish. Yet it seems the agencies have very much mistaken the politics of the reform process, and they have el-evated policy reform above government action (Sadowski 1991:41,50). Moreover, despite the somewhat ambiguous and conceptually flawed terminology, it seems probable that the reform process will exacerbate the "softness" of the state rather than create the conditions for it to pro-mote its own demise (Sadowski 1991:315).

As the agencies seek to undermine what they perceive as the strength and interventionism of the state, in all avenues of life, and they especially seek to draw a line between the public and private sectors, they fail to understand the character of "crony capitalism" and the politics of rent seeking and clientalism that especially emerged during the Sadat period and that has not since been broken.

Crony capitalism has been defined as a political-economic system where businessmen and decisionmakers "ally in cabals to seek mutual benefit by influencing the pattern of state intervention in the economy. ... They do not peg the allocation of state-created rents to the performance of productivity of recipient enterprises, so the system augments personal profits and private power without promoting national economic development" (Sadowski 1991:140).

Crony capitalism therefore promotes widespread corruption—the use of public assets for private gain—and patronage politics: both became the hallmark of Sadat's regime. It was a regime that simultaneously promoted *infitah* and engaged particular entrepreneurs to promote government projects: the state effectively became the source of private rents. This was so pervasive by 1980 that "state created rents ... touched the operations of nearly every business" (Sadowski 1991:118). Sadowski referred to different levels of rent seeking, ranging from the use by companies of subsidised electricity to light offices and the ability to pay a workforce less because of subsidised food, to the allocation of contracts for construction and land reclamation. His critique goes much further than commenting on what many may see as legitimate government activity, namely, state support to initiate and protect local and national business and to protect labour. Most pernicious of all for Sadowski, and what in many ways shaped the fundamental nature of politics in Sadat's regime and since, is the way in which state contracts are used to create and sustain patronage. As he noted, "The key to successful rent seeking is to build some form of political influence that can be translated into economic privilege" (Sadowski 1991:119). And although this may have always been evident throughout Egypt's recent history, Sadowski noted that the possibilities for rent seeking grew during Sadat's period. They grew because of increased overseas rents and remittances and the growth of state resources: Sadat used the distribution of increased largesse to consolidate his authority.

Mubarak succeeded Sadat, as we noted in Chapter 2, with a declared commitment to rid government of corruption. His attempts were short-lived. It seems that rather than simply co-opting large businessmen at important times for particular tasks, whether economic or political, Mubarak has tried to ensure that the ruling National Democratic Party (NDP) becomes the conduit through which business interests are expressed and mediated. This has certainly been the case in relation to agricultural business interests, and Minister Wali has been active since 1985 in encouraging the NDP to liberalise the agricultural sector as a means to generate rural support.

On the surface, the growth of business lobbies and organisations under Mubarak's presidency might seem to indicate a freer civil society, a growth of the plurality of private sector representation, and a block to patronage. There may well have emerged an increased autonomy of business organisations under Mubarak. Nevertheless, there has also simultaneously been the increased co-optation of businessmen and their lobbies into government and parliamentary committees. One consequence of this is that decisionmaking, especially around issues of liberalisation, often remains frustrated by vested "interests in both public and private sectors which have combined to stall policy change" (Kerr 1994:877).

The role the state plays in Egypt in its ability to make decisions, to refer to business and other interests, and to reflect with some independence on information that its bureaucrats receive seems to be misunderstood by the protagonists of the reform process:

> Just as the development community often overestimates the power of the state, it has failed to appreciate the influence of the private sector in Egypt's economy. . . . Over the last twenty years the formulation and execution of government policy have increasingly been shaped by businessmen. But Cairo's business community does not consist of the market-oriented entrepreneurs envisaged in neo-classical economics. Egyptian businessmen pursue profits as eagerly as their counterparts elsewhere in the world, but they have learned that lobbying the state for various forms of rent may be a sounder way to do this than risking their capital in a volatile market-place. Cabals that ally businessmen and bureaucrats often determine the operation of economic policy in Egypt today. The weakness of the state and the strength of social forces, contrary to the expectations of the development community, played an important role in retarding economic growth in Egypt. (Sadowski 1991:12)

The characterisation of the soft Egyptian state does have much to commend it. Not least, any visitor to Egypt could identify with it. She or he would not experience strong, robust, and efficient institutions but overstaffed and underfunded administrative systems. The corollary to this view about the Egyptian state is that Egypt has strong and robust social classes in business, in the countryside, and within the state apparatus itself, which frustrate the halfhearted attempts at reform emanating from bureaucrats who are trying to show the IFIs that the state really is serious about reform.

But there are problems with this view of the state, too. It is a view that is theoretically weak, and it seems to be ahistorical. And the clashes of class and elite interests often render the uses of the terms *hard* and *soft* meaningless. This view is nevertheless helpful in indicating the final area of criticism regarding the reform process in agriculture that I want to explore: both state officeholders and international agencies have little idea about what is actually happening in the countryside. They seem to share ignorance about the political economy of the Egyptian countryside. The problem with the way in which Sadowski and others have formulated this observation, however, is that they see politics and political change as emanating from the state. There has been very little consideration of the local character of politics and the way in which power relations are exercised in the village or even what villagers recognise to be their main concerns and anxieties. It is one thing to promote strategies of agricultural modernisation that support the interests of large landholders, and it is quite something else to imagine that these strategies will provide for sustainable long-term expansion of rural forces of production. The latter will only be sustainable if rural social and economic cleavages are recognised and the conflicts over village access to resources are addressed. Without an understanding of the ways in which power is articulated in the countryside, it is probable that antagonism derived from the impact of economic reforms will hinder the major agricultural transformation that is currently under way.

It is only recently that there has been a historiography that locates the importance of the politics of resistance and opposition in rural Egypt in different dimensions of state and elite policy (see Mitchell 1991b; Schulze 1991; Brown 1990, 1991; Kazemi and Waterbury 1991; Cuno 1992). It is possible, to see a continuum in the writings of commentators on agrarian issues in Egypt between British colonial and Egyptian views regarding the ignorance and backwardness of Egyptian peasants. As Brown has noted talking about the colonial period and criticising the persistence of such a view in the work of Hinnebusch (Brown 1991), "Because peasants would not cooperate with officials, felt no loyalty to the state, and seemed impervious to reform, they were routinely branded as ignorant and inscrutable. They were denounced as ignorant largely because their political outlook differed from that of their rulers and as inscrutable largely because few observers sought to discover the nature of their outlook" (p. 204).

It is not surprising for Brown that peasants have been reluctant to accept openly the changes in policy promoted by the colonial authorities or the successive Cairo regimes since 1952. Colonial projects were viewed with suspicion because they were intended to initiate increases in agricultural production while "the condition of the peasantry was incidental. It was the land, not necessarily the population, that was to be enriched" (Brown 1991:218; see also Warriner 1948). It is possible to make similar conclusions about reform programmes since the 1930s. Although there may have been an increase in the interests among Egyptian planners regarding the health and conditions of the peasantry, it was usually related to how poverty affected issues of crime and levels of productivity.

The Critique: Bringing the Fellahin Back In

My critique of the economic reform programme has examined problems associated with agency promotion of comparative advantage in agriculture and the tyranny of the market that has began to engulf Egypt's farmers. I have argued that one of Egypt's main agricultural difficulties has been the *type* of attention it has received from government rather than the extent of state intervention. And I have linked this latter argument to the misconceptions agencies and the GoE have regarding the effectiveness of state intervention and the poor knowledge about the ways in which Egypt's countryside operates.

There is still very little activity within the agencies or the GoE that examines the character of rural political and economic living standards: agricultural modernisation is still perceived by farmers as "either a substitution of new burdens for old or frequently ineffectual attempts to improve standards of living" (Brown 1991:218). There is also a more serious indictment of policymakers. This refers to the way in which the peasantry is viewed and the persistence of a modernisation view of agricultural change that is teleological, is devoid of local class actors and action, and is reduced to the effects of central state authority—or the lack of it.

Contemporary state and agency prescriptions for agricultural change conjure up a rural vacuum that can be easily filled by government policy and political practice if only the bureaucracy could be more effective and efficient. This is a false picture of a countryside without conflict and social actors that view the state and its agents as regulators of coercion and extortion, in the late 1990s because of changes in the tenancy law. It is a view that has little recognition of local political struggles that help decide and shape the rural political economy. This critique has been exemplified recently by Brown:

> The narrative of change, focusing on initiatives from the center and abstracting them into a story of development, inevitably tends to overlook the concrete political struggles in which political and economic control is contested or reaffirmed, as well as the forms of coercion and violence such struggles involve. Power is not simply a centralized force seeking local allies as it extends out from the political center but is constructed locally whatever the wider connections involved. (Brown 1991:237)

I have argued that adherence to market principles promoted by the adjustment programme ignores the character of the way in which production is organised in the countryside. Structural adjustment in agriculture has not been informed by a nuanced or clearheaded understanding of what life in rural Egypt is like. And where knowledge of rural production relations is indicated by agency and government reports, it shows a flagrant disdain for the majority of Egypt's peasantry. We can now begin to look in more detail at some of the probable consequences of agricultural reform by examining two case studies of villages in the Delta.

Notes

1. There was much reforming rhetoric by the ruling party and Hosni Mubarak in the buildup to the presidential referendum on 26 September 1999 that confirmed the only candidate for a fourth term of office. Yet there was no evidence why political liberalisation would suddenly emerge during the president's fourth term. Indeed, hopes of promoting a stronger civil society were dashed during the rhetoric as the Council of Ministers approved the Non Governmental Organisations and Societies Law No. 153 of 1999. This law tightened state control of NGOS, seemed to give stronger power to the Ministry of Interior over the Ministry of Social Affairs, and seemed intent on scuppering any autonomous action by NGOS.

5

Views from the Village

This chapter views the impact of the economic reforms on two villages. The perceptions of villagers serve to highlight the empirical and methodological failings of structural adjustment policies in agriculture that I have already dealt with. The first of the two villages is in Qalyubiya governorate, and it is called Kafr Tasfa. The second is in Dumyat governorate and is called Kafr Saad (see Map 5.1). I first describe the character of village and household access to resources and examine the various and multifaceted ways in which livelihoods are sustained and reproduced in the two villages. I concentrate on the uneven access to resources, land and inputs for production, access to markets, and the major problems that the villagers have targeted as requiring urgent action. These latter include a range of environmental and economic issues, not least the consequences of changes in the land tenure law that have generated considerable disquiet and opposition in the countryside, not only in the Delta but also throughout Egypt. My argument is that the strategies for economic reform in Egypt fail to embrace the dynamism of change and transformation in the countryside. Moreover, the priority to change farm gate prices, which has been central in the adjustment package, overlooks many local problems and initiatives with which the fellahin are grappling with seemingly little support from outside their communities.

In summary, the structural adjustment programme in agriculture has promoted market liberalisation, "getting the prices right," changes in land tenure, promotion of cash crop production, and the general neglect of the interests of peasants who have access to less than 5 *feddans* of land. That package of reforms is promoting a process of modernisation in agriculture that seeks to specialise crop production, standardise technical conditions of production, and integrate farming units. This chapter argues that the social conditions of existence in Kafr Tasfa and Kafr Saad, and by extension throughout much of the Delta, reflect a very uneven access to village and household resources. And unless policymakers recog-

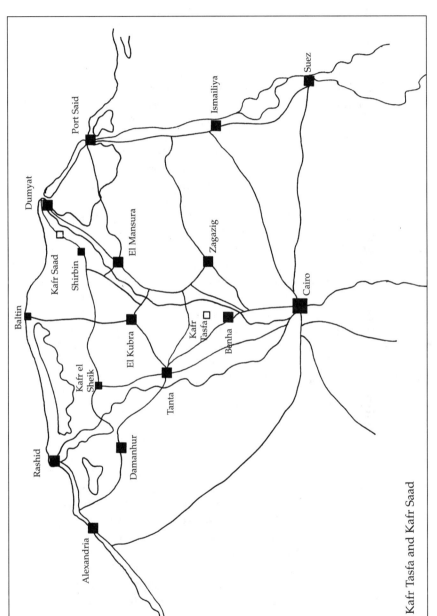

Map 5.1   Kafr Tasfa and Kafr Saad

nise this and act on it to support the interests of small landholders, government reforms threaten the integrity and vibrancy of the Egyptian
countryside. Village and household poverty, defined by the relationship
between the number of household members and household access to
land, livestock, and cash income, indicates that the package of reforms
promoted by the state and the IFIs does not address the problems of the
majority of households. These are especially households with less than 1
feddan of land, either rented or owned, and where there is little or no livestock ownership or access to farm implements (El-Bendary 1994).

Poverty in Egypt's countryside is clearly not solely attributable to economic reform. Yet, as I discussed in Chapter 3, when referring to the
1995–1996 Household Income and Expenditure Survey, there is considerable evidence linking the impact of economic reforms with increases in
incidences and intensity of poverty, especially in the countryside. I do not
here attempt to make a direct causal link from the evidence that I have
assembled, although many respondents have indeed done so. I am concerned instead to raise questions about the *probable* effect of an agricultural strategy that concentrates attention, and resources, upon peasants
with more than 5 *feddans* of landholding, and upon owners rather than
tenants. That strategy flies in the teeth of the fact that at very approximate estimates in 1987, there were 2.5 million landless families and 13.5
million Egyptians with access to less than 5 *feddans*. Five *feddans* in one
estimate is calculated to generate an average net return of the common
crops and rotations of $440 per hectare per annum. Five *feddans* is 2.1
hectares and could return crops in the value of about $924 per annum. If
an average family of five could also generate an additional income of
$600 a year, then the annual income per family member would still be
less than $300. This means that 90 percent of total landholders in Egypt
are really poor (Kishk 1994:55).[1]

Other calculations suggest that a minimum landholding of 2.43 *feddans*
is necessary to avoid the poverty line, but many suggestions using the
most productive and profitable rotations seem to require larger holdings.
My argument is that the current strategy for agricultural modernisation
is likely to undermine the conditions of production and household reproduction for the majority of village dwellers. The majority already in
many circumstances have began to cut their consumption of proteins in
family diets, as a mechanism to reduce weekly expenditure, and are increasingly dependent upon the women in the household to spend longer
periods of time searching for cheaper commodities in the souk, and to
spend longer periods of time in the health centre (as its service deterio-
rates) and if possible in wage labour.

Crucial to any meaningful understanding of Egypt's countryside,
therefore, must be a recognition of its uneven development. Where the

policymakers concede this, it is to view it as a virtue to be accelerated in the name of modernisation. Little is said about the effects of the strategy on Egypt's small landholders, who produce the bulk of Egypt's food and cash crops, and many of whom have experience of some kind of integration into a market system for exchange, but one that may tend to marginalise them compared with larger landholders. Little is also said about the rural poor, the landless and near-landless, and the need to provide rural (and urban) employment for them and to absorb the displaced peasants that will result from accelerated rural differentiation. Little again is discussed about the particular effect agricultural modernisation may have on women's labour. That labour is involved in both the "productive economy" of tradable and exchange activities and in the "reproductive economy" of health care and provision of nutrition, education, and child care—areas under threat by economic reform.

Definitions of poverty are fraught with difficulties. The starting point, in terms of landholding, is important. It represents access to a means of production that historically has been a crucial, although not the sole, criterion for income. It is also the case that family size and the household life cycle—the relationship between mouths to feed and hands to work—is important. The gender mix and age profile of households also need to be considered in decisions regarding the ways in which fellahin cope with their economic and social crises. For instance, families will tend to be wealthier if they can draw on remittances from an economically active son or access to labour power from a large family that might bring in cash with which to rent land.

Conventional assessments of rural poverty tend to focus on observations regarding access to land and income, but this does not adequately capture the difficulties of the poorest. Although access to land remains a crucial indicator of inequality, it is also clear from the evidence here, and referred to in Chapter 4, that there are, and have been for many years, multiple strategies for managing households confronted by economic transformation. These strategies relate to more than just access to land. They relate to the entire world of work, within and beyond the village, and to the demographic stage of the household. For strategies for coping with crises to be effective, moreover, especially for the poorest without land or with the barest minimum of less than a *feddan*, the poor need to be able to use their limited asset base effectively. This means that constraints on asset use—like access to water, health and hygeine, education, regulated markets, transportation, information, and political representation—need to be built into assessments of rural inequality. The worry in Egypt's countryside must be that years of mounting crisis threaten the livelihoods of poor farmers and the landless so much that opportunities to recover, even to precrisis levels, look remote.[2]

These issues of what constitutes poverty, and also the ability of households to survive go to the heart of what the impact of the economic reform strategy has been and farmers' perceptions of it. This chapter indicates that the strategy is at odds with what is actually happening. It also raises questions about what rural peoples themselves are saying and thinking about their own predicaments and what they see is imposed upon them. There has for a long time been a view of the Egyptian peasantry as passive, ignorant, and unchanging. Commentators who share that view may be surprised by the findings reported here. There is an anger, expressed by peasants, at the pace of change and its direction. There is also an anger at the persistent lack of consultation between policymakers and rural people. And central to this anger is the continued arrogance of policymakers who assume the interests of either the country ("nation") or the fellahin.

It is now a commonplace conclusion in the literature on rural development that if peasants are not consulted, policies tend to be ineffective and reforms frustrated by rural intransigence and opposition. At the heart of the issue in Egypt is a fundamental question. It relates to the "integrity of local knowledge systems and the ability of rural people to effectively communicate their strategies and goals through the plethora of existing development institutions" (Redclift 1992a:256). For a rural development strategy to be effective, people must be included in setting the agenda as well as implementing it. A strategy must also recognise the differential access to resources between and within communities. And of course, what then follows from that recognition (depending on the balance of political forces) is the need to begin to redress the levels of inequality, resource access, and landholdings, to redistribute rural income. Egyptian policymakers have chosen to ensure that income distribution further bolsters the interests of large landholders, and this is done under the guise of agricultural modernisation. In doing so, policymakers fail to recognise the elementary fact that when people are excluded from decisionmaking and management of their local environment, they cease to be seen as stewards and become known as poachers (Redclift 1992). That perception views poor farmers as a threat to stability and order that further promotes their exclusion from decisionmaking.

Kafr Tasfa and Kafr Saad

The village of Kafr Tasfa lies towards the east of the Nile Delta 70 kilometres from Cairo (see Map 5.2). It is one of the villages in the Kafr Shukr district, or *markaz*, and is situated in the northeastern part of the governorate of Qalyubiya. The village is about 5 kilometres from Kafr Shukr, and 18 kilometres from Banha, the capital of the governorate.

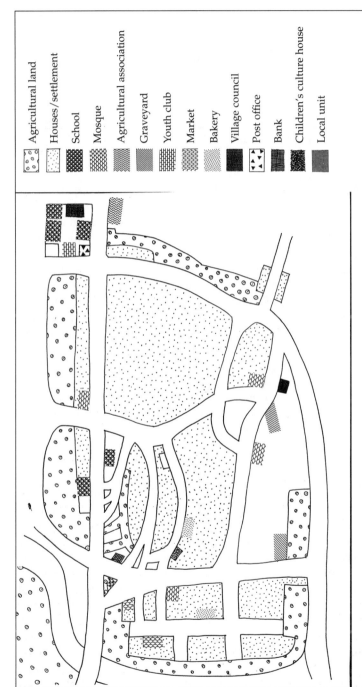

Legend:
- Agricultural land
- Houses/settlement
- School
- Mosque
- Agricultural association
- Graveyard
- Youth club
- Market
- Bakery
- Village council
- Post office
- Bank
- Children's culture house
- Local unit

Kafr Tasfa

Map 5.2

TABLE 5.1   Cropping Patterns in Kafr Tasfa (*feddans*)

Summer 1993/1994		Winter 1994/1995	
Cotton	50	Vegetables	5
Wheat	120	Beans (balady)	10
Maize	255	Garlic	1
Rice	10	Barseem	137
Vegetables	11	Wheat	195
Barseem	135		

SOURCE: Agricultural Co-operative, 1994

The parliamentary members in 1999 were Khalid Mohi el-Din, the long-standing national general secretary from the Tagamu, and Samir Noseer for the ruling NDP, who is also a large landowner from a village subordinate to Kafr Shukr. Two members of the Shura Council represented the NDP. They were in 1999 Gamal Mahdi, an agronomist, and Mohemad Husein Al-Ashhab, who was head of the board of directors for the public sector bus company. Most of the senior village figures, the *omda* and president of the local council, supported the ruling party, although the Tagamu did have support from a large landowner with about 10 *feddans* who was also head of the peasant unit of the party in the village. There seemed little support in the village for the Labour Party.

The total area of the village is about 850 *feddans*, of which cooperative records indicate 798 *feddans* are cultivated. The land is divided between 448 *feddans* for citrus production and 377 *feddans* for other crop production. Table 5.1 indicates the area devoted to crop production.

The village is relatively small by Egyptian standards, but if it includes surrounding villages, it accounts for between 30 and 35 percent of the population of the entire Kafr Shukr area. In 1986 CAPMAS estimated that the village population was 6,418: 3,338 men and 3,080 women. The number of people in Kafr Shukr district as a whole is approximately 103,000. The village has a reasonably good infrastructure, including 4 pharmacies, 61 licensed and 52 unlicensed shops, 2 blacksmiths, and 2 carpentry workshops. There are also 2 cement shops and 1 shop that sells gas pipes. The village received large amounts of remittances from migrant workers in the 1980s, a sum that was used for, among other things, house building and improvements to dwellings, including the development of blocks of flats for family dwellings and one large villa. The village also has nine schools, a veterinary office, and a telephone and post office centre, as well as a dairy, *masr el alban*, and it has its own local council. There are five mosques and six smaller *zawya*—places to pray. There is also relatively good access to agricultural services. There has been an agricultural cooperative and a local food cooperative, and there is a slaughterhouse. The village also has 5 agricultural tractors, 5 tractors for cleaning the irrigation and drainage canals, 84 irrigation machines, 8 machines for hoeing, and 5 for threshing.

Kafr Saad is the second village and lies within the administrative and geographical sphere of the Dumyat governorate, in the north of the Delta bordering the Mediterranean Sea. It is about 5 kilometres from the town and administrative centre of the same name, Kafr Saad (see Map 5.3).

It lies about 20 kilometres equidistant between the towns of Dumyat and Shirbeen, which are important trading centres for the surrounding villages. Kafr Saad is not a remote village. It is located on the main road connecting the town of El-Mansurah with Dumyat. Many of the people of Kafr Saad work in services and crafts production outside the village, particularly in carpentry, for which Dumyat is famous. Table 5.2 indicates the area devoted to crop production.

The two parliamentary representatives for this area, elected in 1995, are from the ruling NDP. Mohamed Shalpi Aashour, from Al-Rikabia, who owns 15 *feddans*, and Sourour Salem Shaheen from Meet Abu Ghaleb. Their rivals in 1995 were also from the ruling party and were all without land: Mahmoud Hamed Al-Shami, a government employee; Mohamed Hamed Aissa, who worked in the health administration; and Hassab Al-Dengawi. The NDP and the Wafd both had administrative offices in the village.

Agricultural production in Saad is mostly characterised by a tendency towards the production of "traditional" crops, and this has until recently followed the official regulations of the agricultural rotation cycle dictated by the government. The total population of Kafr Saad, including the villages attached to it, numbered 21,505 in 1992. The population of Kafr Saad alone was estimated to be 16,054 in 1993–1994, with a male population of 8,195 and a female population of 7,859.

Kafr Saad is a much larger village than Kafr Tasfa. It is the site of a number of official governmental institutions—education, health, and services. It has six large schools and a nursery, six mosques, two youth centres, an agricultural cooperative, a veterinary unit, a general hospital, an agricultural association, and a transport station. Figure 5.1 shows the number of households growing crops in each village.

Land and Markets

The bulk of the field research was conducted between 1994 and 1995, and there were return visits in 1998 and 1999. By means of local agricultural cooperative records, a structured sample of 80 households was taken in each village. There were considerable similarities in the characteristics of households between villages. In Tasfa there were 483 members in the

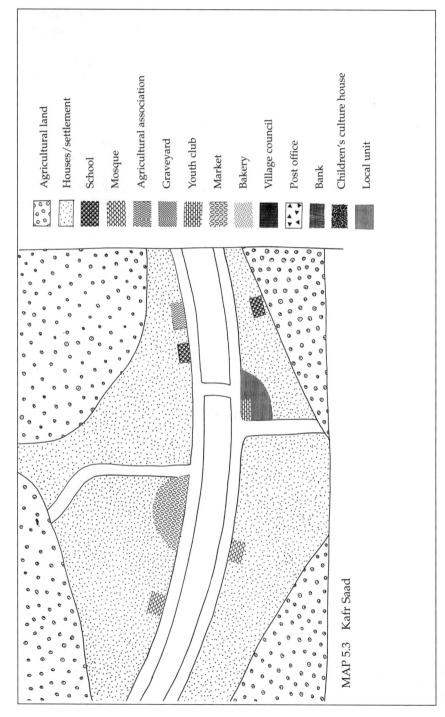

Agricultural land
Houses/settlement
School
Mosque
Agricultural association
Graveyard
Youth club
Market
Bakery
Village council
Post office
Bank
Children's culture house
Local unit

MAP 5.3   Kafr Saad

Map 5.3

TABLE 5.2   Cropping Patterns in Kafr Saad (by number of *feddan*)

Summer 1993–1994		Winter 1993–1994	
Cotton	516	Clover	450
Rice	1,200	Wheat	565
Vegetables	582	Beans (local)	156
Dura	305	Kittan	70
Soybeans	45	Berseem	1,406
Sunflower	21	Gardens	4
Gardens	0.1	Cane	17
Cane	1	Fallow	1
Fallow	3		
Total	2,674	Total	2,674

SOURCE: Agricultural co-operative.

households interviewed, and in Saad there were 448. The average age of our Tasfa sample was 23 years, 42 years for the head and 35 for the wife. For Saad the average age of the sample was 27 years, 46 years for the head and 39 years for the wife.

Questions were asked across a broad range of issues. Attention was especially given to developing household and village profiles relating wherever possible to changes over time. An assessment was made of shifts in household access to resources, changes in the gender division of labour, cropping patterns, and changes and problems in the community. A combination of interviewing techniques was used to elicit a mix of

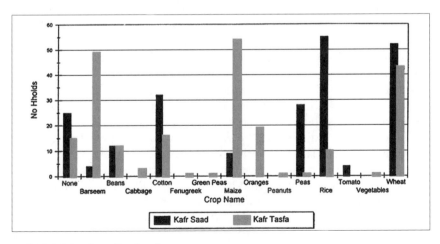

FIGURE 5.1   Crop Production

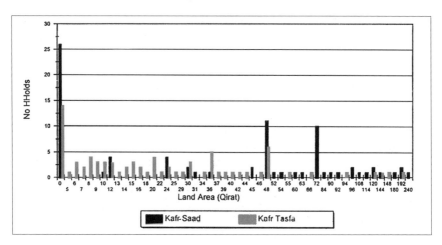

FIGURE 5.2   Land Distribution

qualitative and quantitative responses. A separate survey of 33 women in each village focused on changes in their work and consumption habits.

The village samples included a cross section of both landless (14 in Tasfa and 26 in Saad) and those who both owned and rented land. There were three large landholders in the Tasfa sample: two with approximately 6 *feddans* and one with 8 *feddans*. In Saad there were five large landholders: two households with 10 *feddans*, two with about 8 *feddans*, and one with 6 *feddans*. Only eleven households in the total sample (four in Tasfa and seven in Saad) had landholdings of 5 *feddans* or more (one measure, as I noted earlier, of what constitutes an economically viable holding to avoid poverty). Indeed, average landholding from the Tasfa sample was just 1.37 *feddans*, and it was 1.59 *feddans* for Saad—both less than the estimated national average of 2.5 *feddans*. Two households in Saad and twenty-five in Tasfa had landholdings of less than 12 *qirats* (half a *feddan*).

Land fragmentation was a more serious problem in Tasfa than in Saad. Figure 5.2 shows land distribution patterns, and Tables 5.3 and 5.4 show the landholding structure for the respondents.

There were two differences between the village respondents that are important to note. The first is that 21 households in Saad had access to land via a sharecropping arrangement. In every case this arrangement seemed to involve equal sharing between the landowner and the sharecropper of the costs and the output from the agricultural production. The cost of labour, however, and of cultivation and, wherever necessary, of hiring was borne by the sharecropper. In total, sharecropping accounted for just less than 24 *feddans* of the total landholding in the sample. Sec-

TABLE 5.3 Landholding Structure in Kafr Saad from Survey Sample (80 households)

Land size	Rent		Own		Sharecrop		Land reform	
	No. hh	Area	No. hh	Area	No. hh	Area	No. hh	Area
<5 qirat			1	4				
6–11 q			1	11				
12–23 q			7	30	1	12	2	32
1–5 F	4	117	24	498	19	414	5	190
>5 F			3	612	1	144		

TABLE 5.4 Landholding Structure in Kafr Tasfa from Survey Sample (80 households)

Land size	Rent		Own	
	No.	Area (q)	No.	Area (q)
<5 qirat	1	2	2	9
6–11 q	12	96	10	79
12–23 q	12	201	10	159
1–5 F	16	563	12	572
>5 F	1	144	2	340

ond, respondents from Tasfa seemed to have greater access to mechanised farm implements, notably tractors and threshers(see Figure 5.3), but all of these were rented rather than owned—as was also the case in Saad. Indeed in Tasfa only 14 households owned their own irrigation machine. Access to all farm implements, apart from the most rudimentary and those like irrigation pumps, which in the majority of cases had been in the family for ten to fifteen years, was dependent upon relations with merchants and larger farmers.

There were also similarities between our samples. Access to land was uneven and was fragmented often between two and sometimes three and four plots that varied in quality, distance from the family residence, and sources of water. Respondents in Saad noted that the highest-yielding land was controlled by two or three families, and that was land nearest the irrigation and drainage canals rather than on the desert perimeter. There was no sharecropping in Tasfa, but there was the mix of access between hereditary family ownership and land distributed and inherited from the Nasser land reforms.

Average household size from the Tasfa sample was 6.04, and it was 5.6 for Saad. Figure 5.4 shows the distribution of household size. For the poorest families at times of economic flux, and when the household age

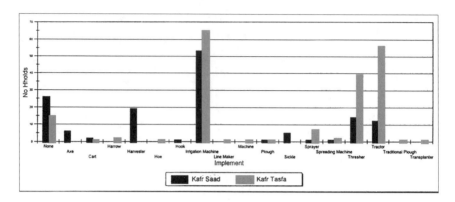

FIGURE 5.3   Access to Farm Implements

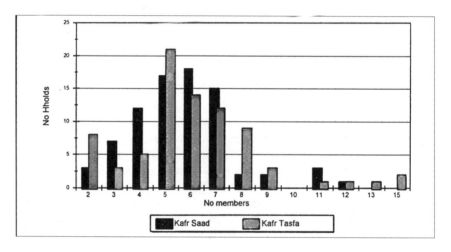

FIGURE 5.4   Household Size

structure prevented extra income being earned, family size placed an extra burden on household survival. There were other factors inhibiting large families from generating income from the extra hands they had at their disposal. There was a fall in the demand for labour, which inhibited households from generating income from agriculture or other activities to take them out of poverty. Landholdings alone were too small to generate sufficient income for family size, and there was insufficient income from other sources.

Fifty-one of the households in Tasfa (63 percent) and thirty five (43.7 percent) in Saad had access to livestock. Figure 5.5 illustrates the owner-

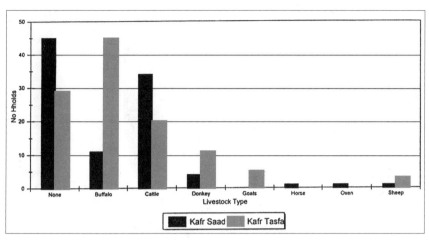

FIGURE 5.5   Livestock Ownership

ship of livestock by type. From the total sample, 53.7 percent had access to livestock of some kind. And it was the larger landholders who owned livestock. Average landholding size for all categories of livestock owners exceeded 3 *feddans*. The number of households, however, which owned and had income from livestock and crops was just two (4 percent) in Tasfa and twenty-one (60 percent) in Saad—only twenty-three for the total sample or 26.7 percent.

There are some general points that need to be made about the two villages and the sample before examining in detail the issues of social change and crises confronting households and how the years of economic reform, especially since 1991, have failed to address respondent concerns. The first point to make is the growing dependence many households seem to have upon the market for providing access to foodstuffs and inputs and for crop sales. Fifty-five households in Saad and forty-seven in Tasfa received income from crop sales. Yet respondents in both villages complained about the difficulty in providing enough food for household consumption from self-provisioning, a situation that has got worse with land fragmentation and declining yields often resulting from land degradation. Respondents also complained about the increasing pressure to find wage work within the village, or outside, to sustain household members.

Kafr Tasfa is a major citrus-growing area, and 18 of the village respondents sold oranges (see Figure 5.6). Other major crop sales included cotton (16 households), *berseem* (6 households), and wheat (4 households). Crops grown for sale in Saad included cotton (31 households) and peas (12 households) and other vegetables like beans (4 households), tomatoes

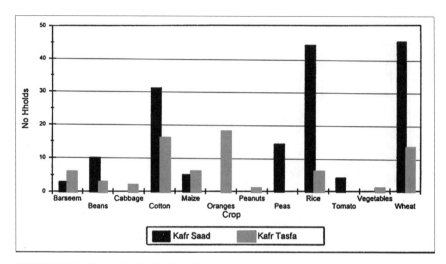

FIGURE 5.6   Households Selling Crops

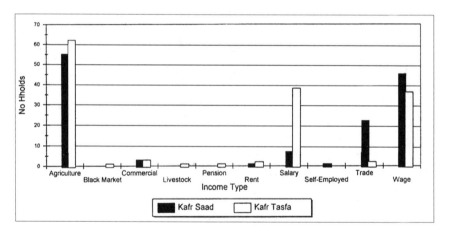

FIGURE 5.7   Income by Type

(4 households), and *berseem* (3 households). Crops were sold either in the village souk or to merchants, traders, or individuals. Only 13 of the households in Tasfa stored enough for consumption before they purchased in the market; only 8 households growing beans were self-sufficient; and 29 growing wheat and 34 that grew maize.

There was also a heavy dependence in both villages upon access to cash or wage work(see Figure 5.7). Only 20 respondents from Tasfa were

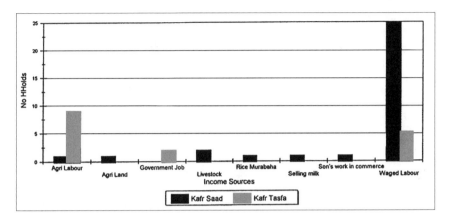

FIGURE 5.8   Income Sources of the Landless

reliant upon one source of income. Of the 14 landless households, 13 were solely dependent upon agricultural labour, and 1 worked in a government job for LE120 per month (see Figure 5.8). Agricultural labourers reported wages of LE5 a day and between LE600 and LE1,000 a year. Only 7 households from the total Tasfa sample were solely dependent upon agriculture for their livelihoods. All other respondents had more than one source of household income, usually from agriculture and salaried work of the head or son. It is also noteworthy that all of the 9 households in Tasfa that hired workers had paid employment themselves.

The dependence upon multiple sources of income was also very evident in Saad (see Figure 5.9). Only 23 households accrued income from agriculture in the form of crop sales or trade in livestock; 7 households were dependent upon crop sales alone for their income; and 16, on a mix of crop sales and livestock trade. The overwhelming majority of respondents mixed agricultural work with wage income from the household head or children: 58 households had income from wages supplementing agricultural income; 27 landless labourers earned income from agricultural and wage labour. Even 3 large landholders from both villages derived a part of their income, although a less significant part than the small landholders, from off-farm employment with the government (see Figure 5.10). In Saad, 39 households, compared with 9 in Tasfa, hired agricultural labour, although unlike in Tasfa, 11 of these 39 households were dependent upon their own income sources rather than working for others. The average landholding for the 9 households that employed labour in Tasfa was only nominally greater than the average for all land-

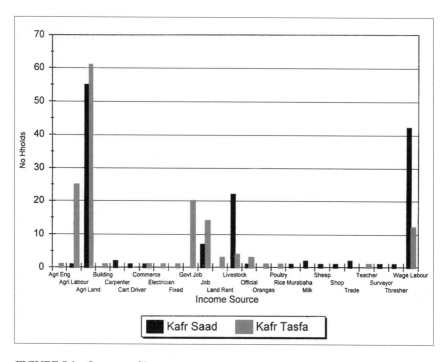

FIGURE 5.9   Sources of Income

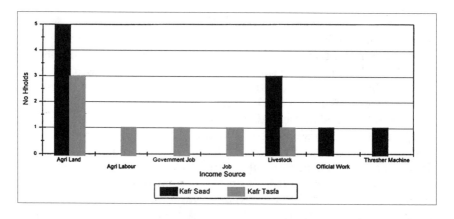

FIGURE 5.10   Income Sources for Households with More Than 5 *Feddans* of Land

holders, namely, 1.9 *feddans* compared with 1.3 *feddans*. The average size of landholding for the hirers of labour in Saad was 2.74 *feddans* compared with 1.59 *feddans* for all landholders.

These findings seem to confirm the view that where access to land is too small to provide for household needs, peasant producers engage in two strategies: in the market, generating cash for purchases, and in the village or elsewhere, seeking wage or salary employment. The importance of the need for varied employment opportunities implies that the peasant producer is both a worker and a producer of food, one who often retains access to land—a peasantariat perhaps—and that his or her perceptions of social change and politics will be affected by the mix of these experiences and circumstances. It also means, of course, that the fellahin has been increasingly involved in relations with merchants and traders not only in the village but also in nearby towns in the search for markets and employment.[3] This has accelerated since economic liberalisation. Policy reform has led to the decline in the activities of both PBDAC and the cooperative, and it has led to numerous complaints by farmers about merchants' monopoly power and their control of markets. It led many respondents to call for the reinstatement of a reinvigorated PBDAC (which did increase its activities, as I have discussed, in 1995–1996 because of "market failure" in fertiliser provision) and also the strengthening of village cooperatives, as suppliers of inputs and as marketing agencies. Farmer complaints were of two kinds: merchants were determining market prices, and the end of state activity in agricultural marketing and the supply of inputs generated farmers' uncertainty about their future. There was a real indication that the reality of market power confronting producers, and landless labourers, resulted from economic reforms from 1991 on, and market liberalisation was having a deleterious effect on household vulnerability to economic hardship.

Although respondents in Tasfa indicated a greater dependence upon markets for purchasing and selling goods than five years ago, the extent of the involvement was uneven (see Table 5.5). Only 46 households sold crops, and only 11 sold in either the town or village souk, yet 76 purchased goods in the village market, and 65 did so in the town. It was women, moreover, who dominated village market activity, and only the male household head declared that he alone went to town to buy and sell goods. Men in Saad did seem more active in the local market, buying and selling crops. Only 2 sold in the village and 2 in the town market, whereas 50 households went to purchase goods in the town market and 62 purchased supplies from the village souk.

Respondents noted the increased need to buy and sell goods in the marketplace rather than to rely on household self-provisioning. That view was confirmed by the introduction of new methods of food prepa-

TABLE 5.5   Household Market Activity

	Kafr Saad Households		*Kafr Tasfa Households*	
	Buy	*Sell*	*Buy*	*Sell*
Town	50	2	67	6
Village	62	2	78	7

ration, which involved the use of *butagas* instead of the traditional stove and the accompanying purchase of new food items. Increased dependence upon the market, and the accompanying market power of merchants, was also revealed by respondents when they indicated their source of fertiliser (see Figure 5.11). All purchased fertiliser in Tasfa was bought from merchants rather than a government outlet or PBDAC. The cost in Tasfa of a bag of fertiliser *(shiqara)* before liberalisation was between LE2 and LE4. By 1995 and the liberalisation of fertiliser production and distribution, the price had increased to between LE15 and LE20 a bag. It had also led, in one instance in Tasfa, to an increased usage of organic fertilisers. The cooperative in Saad still sold to eight households in 1995 but respondents in both villages commented on this input's higher cost and the lack of flexibility in credit terms or methods of payment. Merchants' power was also indicated in Saad by the way they tended to monopolise information regarding input and crop prices and the availability of land for sale.

Another area in which merchant power was being increasingly felt in both villages was in the limited access respondents had to credit. Only

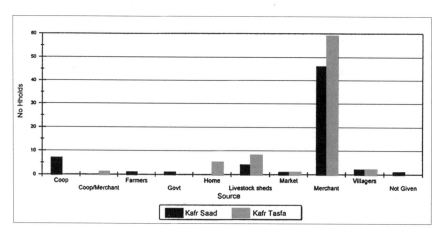

FIGURE 5.11   Sources of Fertiliser

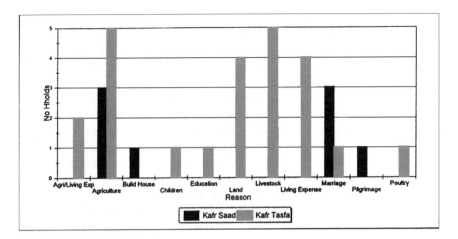

FIGURE 5.12   Reasons for Credit

eight households from our sample in Saad and twenty four in Tasfa had access to credit. The stated reasons for seeking credit are detailed in Figure 5.12.

Crisis in the Villages

Policymakers have failed to recognise the awareness shown by rural households, perceptions of their social and economic problems, and the changes experienced by farmers in their village communities. The fellahin, as I will indicate, are keen to embrace change and take initiatives to transform their livelihoods. Yet their initiatives and their *capabilities* are ignored by officialdom. There is also an enormous political awareness among the peasantry of the detrimental effects to their position following policies in the countryside that have been introduced by the state: liberalisation of markets and price increases. In particular, there is considerable resentment at the prospect of a completely free market in rents and the legal right of landowners to repossess land from tenants as a result of the new land law revising tenancy agreements.

Respondents noted that although there had been a general improvement in the quality of life in the two villages since the generation of their parents and grandparents, there was now a challenge to that prosperity. Availability of health care, schools, transportation, communications, and electrical and water services had improved since their grandparents. It was often noted, for example, in both villages, that their grandparents had lived under "feudal" conditions with little autonomy and much servitude. Yet, although the institutional provision of services had improved, there were also dimensions of crisis confronting households and the village as a whole. These crises were of two kinds: one was immediate and hard-felt; the other was longer-term and less acute but nevertheless seen as equally important.

The long-term crisis affecting both villages related to land fragmentation, pollution, and environmental decline. Respondents invariably had less land than their parents, as a result of fragmentation following inheritance divisions in the household. The market in land had declined, and the price had risen dramatically. In Saad, all respondents noted that there had been an approximate increase across the board in the price of land per *feddan* between roughly 1991 and 1995 of LE10,000: land that came on the market fetched between LE30,000 and LE40,000. Land values escalated because of urban encroachment and the use of land in house building. Land fragmentation also followed sales in Tasfa to pay off bank loans and land purchases by larger land owners—in one case, it seems the prime minister's brother purchased 36 *feddans* in three months in 1993.

The increase in the price of land in 1994–1995, the fall in opportunities for village migration, and declining available income led to a decline in land sales compared with 1993. It was also noted that the quality of the villages' environmental surroundings had declined. There was more pollution resulting from road construction, land taken for urban growth, and, especially in Tasfa, problems resulting from inadequate drainage. Maintaining land quality had also become more dependent upon greater application of fertiliser, and crop yields had required increased application of pesticides, despite the increase in market price for these two products. That was certainly the case in Saad, but in Tasfa one respondent noted angrily the increased cost of fertiliser per bag and commented that as a result of its 400 percent increase to LE20, he no longer applied seven or eight bags per *feddan* but three or four bags. Moreover, because of the increased cost of pesticides following market relaxation and the entry of private traders into pesticide distribution, he tended to use netting from the cooperative that had been impregnated with hormones for pest control rather than the more expensive chemical-based formulas. This respondent's strategy to combat increased costs of production did not seem to be very common in Tasfa and in Saad. All respondents commented on the *increased* application of chemical-based fertilisers and pesticides despite their increased costs. I return to this below.

The immediate crises affecting villages related to the perception that the improvement in village amenities was being undermined by recent neglect—declining budgets resulting in longer queues at the health centres and costs of education. There was also the perception that there had been, in the last five years especially, declining standards of living and changes in access to credit. There was also the very immediate problem of unemployment, which affected both the households and the village as a whole. That is not a new phenomenon in Egypt and especially in rural Egypt. Yet the burden was particularly felt with the short-term decline in remittances from the Gulf and returning migrants during the Gulf War in 1991. The demand for labour was also seen to have declined resulting from the increased use of machinery in agricultural production. It seems to have been the case that although male respondents reported that women's work in agriculture had fallen from eight to four or five hours a day, this stated decline was insufficient to provide increased employment opportunities for unemployed men. Female informants reported that they were working longer hours in family agriculture, and although there did seem to be a shift, in the period 1991–1995, in the supply of young girls working in agriculture (because of increased education opportunities), this decline was insufficient to provide work for the unemployed men.

There were exceptions in both villages in terms of the characterisation of whether livelihoods were improving or declining. It was noticeable that the more optimistic descriptions of changes in the household, village, and environment were made by larger landholders. They were especially looking forward to the free market in land, but across the sample, too, was the observation that some services, like local communications, were better than they had been. Respondents in Tasfa seemed to characterise their difficulties in stronger terms than respondents in Saad, yet the respondents from Saad seemed to have a greater recognition of the sources of decline in living standards—at least they saw the importance of government intervention and adjustment policies as undermining security of small landholder conditions of existence. In Tasfa, seventy-one respondents recorded that they had more difficulties than either their parents or their grandparents, and one of the remaining nine (who all had above average size landholdings) noted that things were *getting* worse.

The notion of a transformation, that life seemed to be getting worse, was also expressed by respondents in Saad. It was especially evident around the issue of changes in landlord-tenant relations. Reported changes in life chances mostly involved declining access to household resources: land and employment opportunities. This was uneven between households, and those with access to more than 2 *feddans* and other income-earning opportunities were able to purchase commodities in the souk without experiencing a deterioration in their living standards. It was also noted that village services in Tasfa had declined with the reduction in the activity of the cooperative, which had been replaced by merchant entrepreneurs.

Erosion of the activities of the cooperative were reported along with the decline in the efficiency of the health centre as two of the most important changes in the period 1991–1996 by respondents in Tasfa. Changes in the service provision of these two local institutions has been significantly shaped by the adjustment policy. The village cooperative was dramatically scaled down following market liberalisation and lack of government support for cooperative provision. The GoE and the World Bank reformers might express surprise at village dissatisfaction with the alternative merchant provision of agricultural inputs like farm machinery, fertiliser, pesticides, and seeds. Yet at least one-third of our respondents in Tasfa expressed the view that a new cooperative would be important that could more actively engage with farmer initiatives of decisionmaking and allocation of cooperative resources.

The old cooperative clearly came in for a lot of criticism. It had been poorly managed and was seen to be inefficient and subject to spoils politics, and respondents suggested that it had been manipulated in its service provision by larger landowners. Yet, in the teeth of the adjustment process, villagers in Tasfa were keen to preserve the role that a revamped cooperative could provide. Not surprisingly, respondents wanted subsidies to continue, along with controlled prices for inputs and greater involvement by peasants themselves in decisionmaking (see also Abdel Aal 1998). It was recognised that this would require an increased and improved rather than a reduced role for the state in the countryside. Larger landholders were more content with the liberalisation of prices and the activities of merchants with input provision: many large landholders were also merchants. This was the case, too, in Saad, where fourteen of the fifteen respondents who commented on the performance of the agricultural cooperative noted that it had improved. All but one of these fourteen respondents had above-average access to land, although they were not the largest landholders.

Although fifteen respondents in Tasfa, including a majority that were landless, noted an improvement in the services of the health centre, the overwhelming majority complained about its deterioration. The reason for this dissatisfaction was the attitude of doctors, who tried to see patients on a fee-paying basis only—LE5 for a consultation. Doctors implied that the only good service was one that was paid for. There had been a deterioration in the service, moreover, in the last two years, a reduction in surgery hours, absence of medication, and an increase in the cost of attendance. As we will see below, this particularly placed a burden on women in the village, who spent a longer time trying to get medical attention.

Socially, respondents in Tasfa noted a decline in opportunities for leisure because of its cost and the disappearance of communal work and economic relations between relatives. Each household was now increasingly chasing commodities and opportunities for their own immediate family, and this was becoming more difficult as living costs were increasing and income-earning opportunities were declining. Respondents noted the increased need to find cash income to pay for household expenses rather than rely or be seen to rely on contributions from others. This coupled with the increased supply of labour in Tasfa meant that in the last five to ten years, *mozamla* (communal labour) had all but disappeared—although it was still seen to be a very attractive option for respondents with smaller landholdings. Change was also noted in the diets households were now forced to follow: less meat and other protein-based foods and more carbohydrates.

Respondents in Saad, especially with smaller landholdings, also faced income constraints in participating in leisure activities. The majority nevertheless noted that there were improvements in opportunities for relaxation if they had the income to participate. These included drinking coffee in the café, watching television, or, in two cases, taking an actual vacation in Ras el Bar.

The Agrarian Reform Law

Probably the most dramatic change for the two villages in the recent past has been the consequences of Law 96 of 1992. This agrarian law has set in motion a fundamental transformation of landholdings in Egypt's countryside. Because access to land is one of the most significant influences in social standing and in shaping access to wealth and changes in the relationship between landowners and tenants, it is likely to have a significant impact on household livelihood strategies. Pressure on land was reflected in the fact that only ten of our respondents in Tasfa reported that they had more land than their parents. All noted an increase in the market for land in the last two years in Tasfa and an increase in landlessness in the village. This latter resulted from fragmentation of landholdings, as I reported earlier, as well as the early effects of the new land law.

Land rents have risen considerably since implementation of the land act. Before the law, legal rents were LE66 per *feddan* and about LE1,200 on the black market. Respondents also recorded paying rent of LE600 and LE616 in the transitional period, 1992–1997. After the land act, rents rose to between LE1,400 and LE1,800 per *feddan*, or between LE58 and LE75 per *qirat*. It seems that between 200 and 300 tenants were forced to leave their tenanted land in Tasfa after implementation of the act, although most then returned to take up tenancies with different landowners.

The relatively small number of displaced tenants may reflect the low number of tenants in Tasfa. About 120–150 *feddans* of land were returned to landowners after 1997, and at the end of the transitional period, landowners put tenants in a difficult situation. Tenants were asked to either remove their crops from the ground or pay an inflated rent until harvesttime. Five farmers abandoned their crops as their landlord hurried to take back their land.

Although large landowners in our sample reflected positively on the right to levy a higher rent and on the prospect of being legally able to dispossess tenants, most respondents were, as early as 1995, very alarmed at five important effects of the new land law. The first and most immediate was the increase in financial cost to tenants. Many reported that the increase in rent eroded what positive effects there had been over several years in their standards of living and especially in being able to afford to send children to school. The increase in rent was a "last straw" on top of other price increases that had made village life difficult for "tired villagers." The land law was now seen to be "destroying people's lives" as the poorest tenants were forced to sell land and in the process to become landless and unemployed. In Tasfa, six tenants were reported to have left the land during the transition period 1992–1997.

There was also a second and associated important impact of this new legislation: the denial of credit to tenants by the local bank. In 1994 it had been more than two years since the local village bank had loaned to legal tenants. That is because tenants were no longer seen to have collateral to repay their loan after the five-year transitional period, when they might be dispossessed. And this was at a time when a greater number of farmers were trying to get access to credit and when interest rates for those who had borrowed in 1992 had risen from 6–7 percent to 18–20 percent.

The third major effect of the land law was that tenants did not see much reason for trying to preserve the quality of the land that they were farming if it was likely that they might be dispossessed within two years. The farmers were, in their words, waiting to see what was going to happen, and they were unlikely and unwilling to invest in the land if they were no longer going to be guaranteed rights to it. That meant an obvious reluctance to invest in drainage and other environmentally important projects.

The fourth effect of the legislation was to generate uncertainty for the fellahin about their livelihood. Peasant producers noted fear about the future and fear of dispossession—six in Tasfa had already left the land. Loss of land would mean greater dependence upon the market for food purchases, and increased food prices. One household had already sold its only buffalo to pay for the increase in rent. And another household had sold some of its possessions to buy a small piece of land to avoid dispossession. Landowners reported that the change in legislation was long overdue, and that the effect would be to increase the pool of agricultural labourers at a cheaper cost (tenants who had lost their land, totalling about 22 *feddans* in 1997, had remained in the village), but the tenants were very angry and bitter at what was seen as a betrayal by the government and collusion with the landowners.

Households in both Tasfa and Saad seemed to understand very well that the new law was transforming rural relations of power. They seemed aware, too, that it had the potential to establish a new (reconfirmed) absentee landlord class and a reinvigorated local landowning class. In many ways this process may be under way in Tasfa. One landlord, for instance, had sold just over 22 *feddans* of land. That sale was divided between 12 *feddan* to a citrus merchant in a neighbouring village; 3 *feddans* to a cattle merchant (possibly interested in preserving access to fodder); 3 *feddans* to the village marriage recorder, or *mar'zoun*; 2 *feddans* to a local landowner (spoken of as a rich farmer); and 2 *feddans* to the tenant. By early 1999 there was little evidence of further land sales. All recent land sales had in fact taken place during the transition period, including a further 3 *feddans*. This suggests that landowners viewed revenue from increased rents as a more lucrative source of income than was possible from land sales, despite the fact that land values had risen from between LE2,000 and LE2,500 per *qirat* before 1997 to between LE3,000 and LE4,000 per *qirat*. Returns from rents after the act were about three times greater than they were before the act. Tenants reported in most cases that they were forced to pay the higher rents because they had no alternative and little training to do anything else. Yet they also admitted that the returns from the land barely covered cost. There had been no changes in cropping patterns despite the claim by policymakers to increases in cash crops. Land for vegetable cultivation, for example, remained small in 1998–1999.

Tenants at the end of 1998 did note that they had more actively sought wage work within the village and outside the village in nearby towns. Some of these tenants had a history of seeking work outside the village, but it seemed, following the increases in rents, that there was a more concerted effort to do so, and fathers more actively now encouraged their sons to look for off-farm work.

The fifth effect of the agrarian reform law was the increase in political consciousness of respondents. Almost all people questioned about the new law before 1997 were angry and questioned the legitimacy of the new legislation. Many tenants were clear that they would challenge any attempt to dispossess them of their tenancy agreements. One respondent noted that he would "shoot the owner when he comes to take his land." In three cases tenants said that the end of the transition period would culminate in violence and physical challenge to the government and landowners. This did not happen in Tasfa or Saad, but as I note in Chapter 6, it did happen in many villages elsewhere in the Delta and Upper Egypt. It is possible that this opposition to the land law could be galvanised if disquiet between villagers were built upon. Threats to tenant rights were increasingly being challenged throughout Egypt by landholders up to and following 1997.

These five consequences of the new land law were also evident in Saad. Owners had already increased rents from LE100 to LE600 per annum per *feddan* in the transition. After 1997 the lowest village rent was LE1,500 and the highest LE2,000. These rents were determined by land quality, distance from the main road, and distance between landholding and water sources. The rent was also shaped by the financial power of the landlord. Where he was wealthy, he tended to hold out for higher rents than where he was not.

Rents on sharecropped land were determined by the length of time crops took in the ground. For berseem, which lasted seven months, and local beans, the rent was LE1,200 for each planting. Rice lasted five months, and the rent was between LE700 and LE800; cotton, which lasts eight months but occupies the land effectively for twelve because of the necessary four fallow months, cost between LE1,800 and LE2,000 a season. Rent for tomatoes and black-eyed beans, which last from June to November, cost the same as maize, between LE800 and LE900.

According to the Agricultural Association, 162 tenants lost their land following implementation of the act in October 1997, and 337 *feddan* were returned to landowners. There were, however, approximately an additional 150 tenants who did not have registered agreements who also lost their tenancies. A similar amount of land, about 337 *feddans,* was returned to landowners who controlled these contracts. These unregistered agreements have been common throughout the countryside and operated according to the balance of market forces: rents were not shaped by previous legal arrangements, although this group of landowners took the opportunity of the new act to charge increased rents.

Some of the dispossessed tenants renewed contracts with different landowners. Others sought land in the new valley and in al-Farafra. Still others applied for land in Sinai, but it seems the majority of these at the end of 1998 were having great difficulty surviving on the new land: the returns of agriculture were reported to be very much less than the costs of production.

It seems that the majority of the landowners who refused to renew tenancy agreements chose to hire labour on their newly acquired land. Only about 9 *feddans* were rented out again by landowners. Dispossessed former tenants at the end of 1998 indicated that they had been forced to work as agricultural labourers at LE8 for a four-hour working day. Those former tenants who managed to arrange a new contract complained about the new rents, survived by selling livestock, and searched for wage work to supplement income from farming. Tenants also hoped that future agricultural returns would increase in value. They noted that more vegetables and beans were grown, although there was not an indication as to what happened to these crops, whether they were for self-provisioning or the market. They noted, too, that the productivity of rice and cotton declined since 1997—despite liberalisation the sale of these crops barely met production costs.

Respondents noted that although the consequences of the new legislation were not universal, they had a strong consciousness that the new law had had significant villagewide repercussions. These were being felt especially with an increase in rural unemployment resulting from dispossession. Respondents were very aware that it was most unlikely that there would be any growth in the village economy to absorb the dispossessed, and although there was some sympathy for landowners, especially among the landowners themselves, it was clear among the majority of respondents that the new legislation had increased the market and village power of the landowners. This happened through their power in the hiring of agricultural labourers and, for those that continued to rent out, in their levying of increased rent.

The anger as well as the political awareness of the consequences of the new land law was very well revealed by respondents during the transition period. Atif (a pseudonym)—a 55 year old tenant with three *feddans* expressed commonly held views very clearly. Speaking in 1994 he said that within two years, there would be big problems if the land owners tried to drive tenants away from the land. "I and my fellow *fellahin* who rent the land will not keep silent on the increase in the rate of land rent" which will be similar to prices prevailing in the black market, approximately LE1200 per *feddan* per annum. In fact, as we have noted he underestimated the actual increase in rents that followed October 1997 by between LE300–800. He continued that tenants would "not keep silent if [they] were driven out from the land. We may tolerate the rate of rent to be increased to LE800 per *feddan* a year, provided that we remain on the land. Our eviction from the land means that we will die of hunger we and our children. How can it be conceived that we and our like—at this stage of our age—will become agricultural labourers?!!"

Atif was also very pessimistic about the future because he said that conditions would become worse, and when they do there would occur organisations (congregations) and demonstrations. That, moreover, was not simply his own personal opinion but the opinion of his fellow fellahin. In fact while there were significant tenant objections to the land act being implemented in 1997 the protests in Saad or Tasfa were not as violent or as significant as elsewhere.

TABLE 5.6   Household Difficulties in Kafr Saad and Kafr Tasfa

Kafr Saad		Kafr Tasfa	
Difficulty	*No. households*	*Difficulty*	*No. households*
Childless	3	Agri expenses increase	1
Cost thresher	1	Agri input price increase	1
Disability	1	Education costs	17
Education costs	5	Education needs	2
Education needs	3	Fear land repossession	2
Failure in education	3	Health costs	1
Family planning	1	Illness	1
Few hospitals	1	Land rent increase	2
Fodder prices	2	Living conditions	1
Health	5	Living expenses	20
Housing incomplete	1	Low income	17
Illness	5	Marriage	2
Increased needs	1	No agricultural guidance	1
Inflation	7	No answer	1
Irrigation problems	1	No family support	1
Lack son's success	1	Price increases	15
Large family	3	Sharing house	1
Living expenses	3	Unawareness of wife	1
Low income	27	Unemployment	16
Marriage	12		
Unspecified needs	1		
Pollution	1		
Poverty	1		
Price increases	18		
School leaving	1		
Unable build flat for son	1		
Unable furnish house	1		
Unemployment	4		
Utility prices	2		

Village and Environmental Transformations

The main difficulties reported by respondents as confronting their household and their village are listed in Tables 5.6 and 5.7. The difficulties for households refer in the main to increased living expenses due to commodity and livestock price rises and falling real income to pay for necessities. In the case of one landless respondent in Tasfa, it was clear that he had considerable difficulty in meeting the family's weekly food bill LE50. Like other landless labourers, he received LE5 for work between 7 A.M. and midday, and he tried to find work in the afternoons, too. The prob-

TABLE 5.7   Village Difficulties in Kafr Saad and Kafr Tasfa

Kafr Saad		Kafr Tasfa	
Difficulty	No. households	Difficulty	No. households
Cleanliness	1	Agri input price increase	2
Crime	1	Bad cotton seeds	1
Diseases	2	Bad road conditions	1
Education costs	1	Bribes	1
Education needs	1	Consumer co-op	1
Electricity prices	4	Education costs	2
Few hospitals	5	Failure of co-op	1
Fodder prices	1	Fear land repossession 1	
Food pollution	1	Illiteracy	1
Health	1	Illiteracy increase	1
Health service	3	Illness	1
Ignorance	2	Inadequate drainage	55
Illiteracy	1	Land rent increase	2
Inadequate drainage	4	Living conditions	1
Inefficient govt. admin.	1	Living expenses	5
Inflation	6	Low income	5
Lack govt. response	2	New projects	1
Lack of roads	1	No agricultural guidance	1
Lack school places	1	Price increases	8
Lack schools	1	Project cancellation	1
Lack transportation	3	Religious institute	1
Lack youth movement	1	Shortage drinking water	2
Livestock diseases	2	Unemployment	16
Living expenses	3		
Low crop yields	1		
Low income	6		
Medicine prices	1		
Need for services	1		
New factories	1		
No solutions to problems	2		
Pollution	9		
Population increase	1		
Poverty	1		
Price increases	14		
Roads	3		
Shortage drinking water	1		
Transport costs	1		
Unemployment	9		
Useless cafés	1		
Utility prices	2		

lem was that he noted a decline in the demand for labour following increased mechanisation and a contraction of work opportunities as orchard owners and landowners replaced hired labour with their own family labour. This labourers' diet was typical of a poor agricultural worker: breakfast consisted of foul (beans), *ta'miyya*, and eggs. If a water buffalo was owned, there might be access to cheese. Dinner was rice, cheese, and, on a Thursday, occasionally meat. He had seen the price of meat increase between 1991 and 1994 from LE9 to LE14 per kilo, and the price of gas for cooking was LE8.25. Supper might include rice or potatoes and salad—perhaps also some macaroni.

Of particular importance to households were the increase in costs of schooling, the decline in agricultural income, and the increase in land rents. The increase in prices and increased cost of living were blamed on the government, as was the concern about unemployment and the lack of job opportunities for youth in the village. The government was indeed identified as failing in its responsibilities to provide for people's basic needs, for local infrastructure, and for corruption. The government was also accused of failing to meet its duty in averting the villagewide problem of environmental degradation.

While households reported that the cost of living and unemployment posed serious problems for the village as a whole, the biggest village problem was poor sanitation and drainage. Over several years, there had been an increase in the level of groundwater, which had undermined the foundations of houses and buildings and affected agricultural productivity. There was also a serious problem with the absence of satisfactory sanitation in the village. This had aggravated the view of government neglect and sense that the local surroundings were changing for the worse: agricultural land was becoming more polluted, and there had been a steady increase in the application of chemical fertilisers and pesticides and the dumping of waste materials that had contaminated irrigation canals. The government had been blamed for the general lack of environmental regulation.

There were several other environmental difficulties that confronted the village and that were probably aggravated by the adjustment package. The first of these related to the application of pesticides and fertilisers. The World Bank, as we have seen, promoted the view that the free market in the supply of these two agricultural inputs, following the removal of the state subsidy, would lead to a reduction in use and would offset detrimental environmental consequences of their asserted overuse. My evidence, however, suggests that the application of these two inputs has not uniformly declined and that the deterioration in their *quality* since liberalisation has meant that farmers have had to apply more of these chemically based compounds, with less effect on productivity and possibly more detrimental effect on the environment. Respondents noted the poorer quality of pesticides and fertilisers since liberalisation. They had increased in price but had not had the desired effects on productivity. Moreover, the suppliers of these products were accused of cheating: overcharging and undersupplying the declared weight.

Another area of villagers' environmental concern was the fluctuating level of irrigation water. This was the result of extra channels being dug for higher-lying ground resulting from land reclamation and from less water in the main canal. There had also been changes in the timing of irrigation, of which some respondents had obviously not been properly notified, and the quality of the irrigation water had deteriorated because of greater levels of salinity and pollution. That pollution was the result of poultry waste being dumped in the canals, and poor water quality resulted from the reduced flow of silt—something that followed the completion of the High Dam. But there was also a problem with covered drainage. The pipeways were often blocked, and there was an increase in groundwater level and salting.

These environmental crises in the village were having an effect on crop yields and agricultural productivity. Seventeen respondents noted that productivity had increased, but two of these noted that the costs had also increased—for one they were greater than the productivity gains from mechanisation. The other respondents noted the decline in crop yields for a variety of reasons. Soil and seed quality had got worse, land scarcity meant that there were no opportunities for fallowing, and there was for the poorer households a difficulty in affording improved mechanisation to raise productivity. Poor drainage resulting in salinity had also affected soil fertility. Only one respondent noted an increase in the fertility of the land. Other respondents argued that the fertility had declined because of the reduced use of indigenous fertiliser and manure and changes in the length of the growing season, which had been affected by a warmer climate and less rainfall.

All respondents commented on the decline in the access to village land. This had resulted from population pressure and fragmentation of land-holdings as I noted earlier, but it had also been the result of progressive use of agricultural land for urban expansion or house building. This is a problem across Egypt and has affected Kafr Tasfa especially in the last fifteen years. That coincided with returning migrants buying land for house building and marriage, and with the government building of schools.

These reported changes in the surroundings of the village are likely to have an effect on household access and ability to maintain and protect environmental entitlements: access to productive land and clean air and water. The GoE has said very little about an environmental dimension to agricultural adjustment, and the agencies are limited in the main to trying to attach a market price to nonmarket goods. It follows from the World Bank and USAID perspective that all individuals are seen to act as rational economic people operating in a self-interested and consistent manner. The rational villager is seen to operate in a competitive market way and will therefore ration his or her use of environmental entitlements if the use is priced by the market and not freely available.

In trying to assign market values to public goods, the World Bank and the IFIs argue that the environment has been undervalued in the past and that is why it is under threat now. The environment for policymakers is broken down into separate goods and services to be consumed by individuals. This framework fails to recognise that environmental "goods" are unlike actual commodities. They are public goods that cannot be given a *market* value, as they are not goods that are bought and sold in the market. Neoclassical economists have to assign a value imputed from what they think consumers are willing to pay (Jacobs 1994).

A major problem is also that monetary values cannot capture the value of the environment to different groups of people. Here again we are faced with the undifferentiated view of the agencies in prescribing universal market-oriented panaceas for a complex set of problems. Men and women, for example, value the environment differently because they seem to make different use of it. Women's use of the environment tends not to be revealed through tradable or market relationships per se. Yet we know that the work women do within and outside the household—collecting produce, water, and other items for daily self-provisioning—is crucial for most households, especially the poorest. It is unclear in this example how environmental accounting measures the real value of the environment to women when these use values are part of direct household provisioning?

Women and Coping with Economic Reform

Historically involved in a range of agricultural activities for the household and as wage labour, female respondents were reportedly involved less in paid work as male unemployed labour had increased and men preferred their wives and daughters to work on the family farm rather than for others. Women were also believed to be more reluctant to work in the fields because of improved educational standards and the demand for office workers. And women, as reported by male respondents, were seen to be less industrious than in the past, to have easier lives than before, and to have a stronger position within the household. Yet the decline in demand for women to work in the fields was not uniformly reported. Women's wage rates in agricultural labour were LE3–LE4 compared with LE5 paid to men for a five-hour day.

There are many reasons to explain participation rates for women and also the type of responses made by men about women. There seemed to be no restriction on the participation of young, unmarried girls in the agricultural labour force, especially during harvesting. Indeed, to assume that women were "taking it easy" was at odds with what was actually happening to women's work and livelihoods. Evidence from women indicated that their time spent in both the "productive economy"—agriculture or wage labour—and petty commodity production had *increased* and so, too, had their role in the "reproductive economy"—sustaining the household through domestic labour and promoting and protecting health, education, nutrition, and family skills of primary socialisation (Elson 1994a:42; Young, Wolkowitz, and McCullagh 1981; Joekes, Leach, and Green 1995). Women indicated that they were spending more time than two years before in the preparation of food, cooking, cleaning the house, and washing clothes and feeding the children. They were also spending more time in the souk, chasing food that was affordable and still relatively nutritious, especially when there were small children in the family (cf. Martelo 1996).

The women who were not spending more time in these activities tended to have children that had already reached an age at which they helped in the house and in agriculture. They were also women who were wives of men who had access to waged work that was relatively secure. Most women noted that they were tired and busier than two years before. Although this was often due to increased numbers of children to care for or changes in the household demographic cycle—as some members became more productive and others less so—women noted that they were engaged in labour-intensive activities linked with increased prices and higher cost of living: they took longer searching for food in the souk. Women noted a decline in visiting friends, attending festivities, and opportunities for leisure. All noted that expenditures had increased by between two and three times between 1991 and 1994 for items in the souk, education, health care, clothes, and farming inputs. Where an improvement in service provision was noted, the matching increase in cost outweighed any possible benefits.

In contrast with the neoclassical view of the economic individual, women in Egypt cannot enter freely into voluntary contracts for the purchase or sale of goods and services. In just one instance, the application for credit, women are restricted by their lack of rights to family assets. Women seldom have the legal right to sign contracts on their own without a male guarantor. And this raises a big question not only about the struggle that women have to engage in to make themselves heard, and the success that they do have in many cases (Weyland 1993; Ali 1998), but also about the persistent way in which orthodox economics of the World

Bank views individuals as fundamentally rational economic actors able to make rational choice decisions.

The failure to recognise that households are areas of conflict, which are themselves part of village, local, regional, and other economic and political conflicts and relations of power, is a failure to see that people cannot make decisions along the lines of a well-defined preference function. Instead people make decisions about access to resources in response to their particular relationship of subordination within the household. As Elson has commented, "Rather than the gender division of labour and income in the family being seen as the optimal outcome of free choices, it may be seen as the profoundly unequal accommodation reached between individuals who occupy very different social positions with very different degrees of social power" (Elson 1994a:38).

It is only possible to move away from a male bias in understanding the characterisation of the countryside and of relations between men and women by moving away from a neoclassical "choice theoretic" framework of analysis. We also need to examine how it is that social institutions and monetary relationships which may not be intrinsically "gendered" become bearers of gender. An intrinsically gendered role refers to a role that is gender-ascriptive—for example, to be a mother, a child bearer; to have particular kinship relations; and so on. Yet we also know that relationships that are not necessarily gendered *become* bearers of gender because of the way in which institutions are constructed between people (Elson and Pearson 1981; Pearson 1992). For example, monetary relations between buyers and sellers, the way in which markets operate, and the organization of companies and public utilities are informed and shaped by "gendered" structures. These are structured and shaped by men and exclude women, where organisation is hierarchical, and male bonding and cohesion marginalise initiatives by women.

Of course, the dominance of men is often explained in terms of indigenous and cultural mores and customs and in terms of women's having ways of operating and struggling to promote their own interests. That might be so, and I have referred to that debate briefly in Chapter 4, but it still has to be recognised that theoretically and methodologically planners must help in constructing an arena for development that is shaped by women for women. The reform process, as I have documented, has tried to reduce the role of the state, has transformed local institutions, and has liberalised markets. New institutions have started to replace the old, and unless thought is given to how the new agencies for marketing, entrepreneurship, and production are biased still towards the interests of men, women will continue to be marginalised. It must be put centre stage that the new monetary relationships supposedly released by market liberalisation, which the World Bank and the GoE have so much faith in, sustain and promote gender inequality.

As rural markets are disrupted and transformed by adjustment, so, too, are the areas of women's activity in the "reproductive economy." I have noted the increased burden experienced by women on their time and management skills, and it is likely that this will have repercussions for the productive economy, too—the flexibility that women have had in terms of the relationship between the household activities and agriculture and in their relationships with the market. Elson is one of the few writers who has begun to raise this point, and it is important to quote her at length:

> Current forms of economic policy reform that emphasise rolling back the state and liberating market forces give scant consideration to how this will impact on the "reproductive economy." There tends to be an implicit assumption that the "reproductive economy" can accommodate itself to whatever changes macro-policy introduces, especially to withdrawals of public services and subsidies and declines in public-sector employment and to rises in prices and taxes. Since it is women who undertake most of the work in the "reproductive economy," and in the organisation of community mutual aid, this is equivalent to assuming that there is an unlimited supply of unpaid female labour, able to compensate for any adverse changes resulting from macro-economic policy, so as to continue to meet the basic needs of their families and communities and sustain them as social organisations. (Elson 1994a:41–43)

Uniform Strategy Versus Socially Differentiated Villages

This chapter has highlighted the range of social relationships and uneven access to household and village resources in two locations in the Nile Delta. I have tried to indicate the inappropriateness of structural adjustment policies (SAP) in Egypt's countryside. I have done so by reinforcing the earlier responses from two other villages, namely, that peasant producers and landless labourers have anxieties and fears that are exacerbated by SAP: they are fears and anxieties that are shaped by the conditions of rural life, and by household and village relations of production and social reproduction, and that are ignored by the GoE and the IFIs.

A major problem with the strategy of economic liberalisation is that it has been a uniform strategy applied universally irrespective of the differences in Egyptian circumstances. Evidence from my case study villages indicates how the Egyptian countryside is socially differentiated. It

would therefore seem appropriate to have a differentiated view of village
and household needs and a nuanced reform strategy to promote agricultural growth and rural development suited to local relations of production and reproduction. Yet the emphasis of Egyptian state planners and
the international agencies is to try to standardise conditions of production in the countryside—to promote greater specialisation in crop production, and to integrate farming units—and in this there have been considerable strides made with the erosion of tenants' rights and the increase
in rents. The adjustment package also stresses the importance of standar-
dising technical conditions of production—put crudely, the application
of "green revolution" technology.

I have indicated the varied conditions of rural existence, of access to
land, and of incorporation into rural and urban markets, and I have discussed how the access to implements for farming are unevenly spread
throughout the countryside. I have also noted that across village communities, cropping patterns are variable. There has already been considerable disquiet regarding profiteering by middlemen who have taken advantage of market liberalisation and increased prices of inputs for
peasant producers. The increase in input prices has not been offset by
revenue for farm households that have insufficient land to generate sales
of high market value or that are without access to alternative sources of
cash to cover essential purchases.

The curbing of middleman power is one of the main policy comments
by respondents. And the need to curb the powers of relatively new and
unhindered power brokers in the village becomes a main issue for landless and poorer members of the sample—not surprisingly as the larger
landholders have started to usurp the roles of provider of inputs (and
employers of labour) that were previously performed by the hitherto
much maligned cooperative. The implementation of a uniform strategy
fails to grasp the intricate existing strategies for coping with agricultural
modernisation. And the uniform strategy fails to recognise that unless a
differential strategy for rural development is grasped, the impact will itself be uneven and divisive. My evidence suggests that the peasantry in
Kafr Tasfa and Kafr Saad have considerable insight into and awareness of
what is being promoted by the reform process. Respondents identified
similar problems within household circumstances and in terms of the deterioration of the village infrastructure. At a villagewide level villagers
showed initiative about trying to reduce the impact of things like poor
drainage, salination, and rising water levels. They had approached government for renovation of the system of covered drainage in Kafr Tasfa,
for example, but the project had foundered on the need for villagers to
fund the purchase of 6 *feddans* for the building of a drainage station. Gov-

ernment apathy and lack of finance were blamed for the villagers' initiative not coming to fruition.

Villagers were certainly looking for a lead from government to affect a reduction in the pace at which rents and prices were rising and to help in job creation. But villagers were also aware that fund-raising for mosque and social welfare provision was something that they would continue to do. Villagers were also looking for a lead from government in helping to raise the productivity of land and help with extension services. But this would have to be a universal service and not one directed only to wealthier families, as seems to have been the case in the past, when the politics of patronage and local connection seemed to shape the allocation of common resources like extension and cooperative services.

In contrast with a household dynamism of coping with change and transformation in the period of structural adjustment, government and IFI policy implemented in the 1990s was rooted in the view that having more people in the rural area is necessarily bad for the environment and productivity—hence the promotion of a policy of social engineering resulting from a belief in dispossession; in poor people's being limited in their time horizons because poverty induces short-termism with regard to resource management; in the idea that peasant livelihoods are simple and should be kept that way. That has led to the promotion of policies for uniform agricultural cropping and mechanisation (Chambers 1994).

This IFI and GoE characterisation blames the victims: standardisation of reform packages undermines local variety of household strategies, which has been the mainstay of Egypt's agricultural system. The current strategy for reform remains an attack on the rural poor. They are implicitly blamed for large families, shortsightedness, and failure to adopt modern technologies or reluctance to change cropping patterns.

It is also unwise, in a period when debate on the increasing fragility of the environment abounds, to simply promote modern farming techniques rather than recognise the importance of the varied and more sustainable farming systems, cropping patterns, and reliance upon the interrelationship between farming and wage labour employment used by resource-poor farmers. Among the resource-poor farmers and among those neglected by the GoE and IFIs in their plans for agricultural reform are women. I have already commented on the ways in which their activities are not fully recognised either by men in the countryside or by Cairo-based planners—again mainly men. And it is an issue where not only market liberalisation but also the new changes in the tenant-landlord relationship will undermine the ability of women to cope with declining conditions of existence. What should by now be clear in debates about the marginalisation of rural women is not the need for privatisation of land but the need for effective rights to land *utilisation* for the women who cultivate the land (Thompson 1991:121).

Notes

1. Compare discussion in Chapter 3 and the estimate that 90 percent of land-holdings are less than 5 *feddans*.

2. For a detailed discussion of rural livelihood strategies and methods for understanding them, see Chambers (1993), and for a fascinating case study in rural South Africa, see Carter and May (1999).

3. These findings are supported by the excellent detailed account of village and household transformation by Bach (1996, 1998). For an important discussion that questions the ways in which we understand the impact of "the market" on rural social formations see Mitchell (1998).

6

Egypt at a Turning Point

Egypt is now at a turning point. The economic reforms have not delivered the intended outcomes, and yet there is little indication that the GoE will manage to work with the IFIs to promote an alternative economic adjustment. The reforms began in Egypt's agricultural sector in the mid-1980s and were eventually matched in 1991 by ERSAP and a renewed programme with the IFIs in 1996. Macroeconomic targets set by the IFIs have helped stabilise the economy and reduce government expenditure, inflation, and budget deficits, although large-scale privatisation of state assets has failed to emerge and so, too, has significant economic growth. Attention has particularly focussed in agriculture on price and marketing reforms, the slashing of subsidies, and the promotion of cash crops for export. Land reform, favouring landowners and marginalising tenant interests, has also been central to agricultural transformation. Sustained and diverse growth has eluded Egypt's economy. Unemployment remains a central problem exacerbated by the economic reforms as levels of rural and urban poverty have also risen.

I have argued that the strategy for agricultural reform pursued by the IFIs and the GoE is flawed. It will not lead to sustained higher rates of agricultural output and greater food security, and neither will it address environmental issues like water logging, salination, and soil erosion. Instead, it will lead to greater rural inequality and social unrest as policymakers refuse to talk with the people that are most affected by the economic reforms. Heightened class conflict between landlords and tenants has been evident in the struggles over the land tenancy law. Although this unrest seems to be concentrated in only a minority of villages, perhaps 100 out of about 3,600, the level of repression that has been used to suppress opposition has been extraordinary, as has the collusion between landlords and security services and the absence of the rule of law.

Agricultural reform was certainly necessary, and so, too, was a proper reappraisal of the state's regulatory structures, which desperately needed overhauling. These issues, and others that I have raised, need to be examined in an era of economic and political reform. The problem is the way in which these issues have been addressed by the GoE and the IFIs and the assumptions they have made about the efficacy of the market and economic liberalisation to solve issues of agricultural productivity and sustainability.

It is also the case that the IFIs have failed to think through the possibility of alternative strategies of reform (see, for example, Cavanagh, Wysham and Arruda 1994; Griesgraber and Gunter 1996). They have instead embraced unquestioningly the Washington consensus of liberalisation and deregulation while simultaneously keeping the lid on political liberalisation, openness, transparency, and democratic governance. The GoE has accepted the menu of reform offered from Washington. Notwithstanding President Mubarak's rhetoric of opposition to the blanket implementation of the U.S.-led strategy, and the need for the Egyptianisation of economic liberalisation, discussion within important ministries regarding how to implement reforms (including the pace of reform) has not been visible. The GoE has not addressed and has failed to promote a viable alternative to structural adjustment.[1]

The failure to think through alternative strategies of economic reform and to engage with the specificities of the Egyptian countryside is particularly baffling when international criticism of the IFI strategies in the late 1990s at times reached siren pitch. Criticism has been extensive. It has raised issues of the continued neoliberal bias in World Bank and IMF models, and it has criticised perceived collusion between the IFIs and the private banking sector, in whose interest the international agencies are often perceived to work. Many of the IMF bailout operations from 1997 onwards can be understood as attempts of the IFIs to ensure repayment of short-term loans and sustain what is seen to be the integrity of the international financial system.

Beginning in mid-1997, the IMF became involved in five large rescue operations, but they all failed to deliver sustainable financial stability and economic growth in the countries concerned, while ensuring debt payment to creditors. The IMF bailed out Thailand in August 1997, Indonesia in November and Korea in December the same year, and Russia in 1998. At the start of 1999, a $41-billion rescue of the Brazilian economy, begun in November 1998, also failed to avert major financial instability in the world's eighth largest economy.

These "big" failures sit uneasily alongside the continuity of IFI policy implementation in terms of either crisis management or longer-term structural adjustment remedy. Despite a grudging recognition by the IMF in January 1999 of grave errors in its handling of the Asia crisis, and occasional hand-wringing by the World Bank—declared by its new president, investment banker John Wolfensohn, as an "open and ready-to-learn bank"—there is little evidence of seriousness of reform within the IFIs. This reluctance is at the level of policy and organisation.

The *World Development Report of 1997* (World Bank 1997), seemed to do the unthinkable: it recognised the importance of states to development, yet it remained clear on the superiority of state versus market and the greater efficacy of private investment than public enterprise in promoting economic growth. It also recognised that there were activities that private investors remained hesitant about, particularly in the area of public good provision, protecting and promoting environmental "assets" among other things. It noted that unemployment remained the greatest economic and social problem in the Middle East and that reforming the state and "downsizing" government and public corporations were resisted for this politically sensitive reason (World Bank 1997).

There seems to be confusion at the IFIs. Reluctance to think through the consequences of their *policy* failures by necessarily readdressing strategy is compounded by the second of their difficulties: a failure to apply to themselves the criticism that they level at the governments they work with, namely, the need for accountability, openness, transparency, and good governance. In Egypt, the IFIs may have colluded with the lack of transparency in government as it has suited their broad objectives of putting adjustment in place. Although there has been criticism of the slow pace of reform, and particularly of the reluctance for the GoE to privatise state assets, the authoritarian regime can ensure that the economic reforms remain in place despite the increased levels of inequality and poverty that they have generated.

In this concluding chapter, I argue that Egypt is at a turning point by highlighting the critique of adjustment that I have assembled. I reiterate the need to focus on what happens in the countryside during economic reform, to listen to farmers and their families, and to try to understand the *dynamics* of rural livelihoods. In short, I argue that the view of agricultural *modernisation* promoted in Egypt at the end of the 1990s will too readily promote land consolidation and rural unemployment. Moreover, this strategy runs alongside two other processes. The first of these is a historically naive view of development that is wedded to a view that Egypt's problems stem from a fragile environmental base. The policies that follow from such a crude formulation of the country's problems are investments in large development projects seen recently in the hype over Tushka rather than a recognition that Egypt's problems actually stem from unequal access to national resources and uneven regional and capitalist development. The second process that has been running alongside economic reforms has been a deliberalisation of the Egyptian political system and an increased authoritarianism. This has been shown in a whole range of government measures as I indicated earlier. It has been particularly felt in attacks on Islamists and tenants. I want to focus in this chapter on some of the implications that this authoritarianism has had for rural protest concerning Law 96. There is one other point that I need to make now. In policy terms this chapter is not an attempt to be prescriptive. Although I do conclude with an indication of a number of policy measures that could, under different circumstances, form part of a radical policy agenda, there is no obvious and simple policy alternative to the one promoted by the IFIs and the GoE. I have stressed the need to formulate policy around the interests of small farmers, an understanding of rural relations of production and reproduction, and the need in so doing to redress the historical imbalance created by uneven development. It must be recognised though that at the end of the 1990s, it seemed unlikely that this will take place. All policy agendas are dependent upon the balance of political and economic forces capable and willing to promote them. Although the development of a clearly vibrant and proactive set of rural social forces is much in evidence, it is unlikely to shape policy in a way that will reverse land tenure legislation and the narrowly focussed agenda of the MALR. The direction Egypt takes in the next millennium will depend on the balance of social and political forces inside the country as well as the role Cairo policymakers are able to carve out in the region and wider political economy.

Investing in Another Pyramid:
The Politics of Tushka

One of the series of problems and difficulties that farmers recounted in my fieldwork related to the broad area of environmental degradation. This is a theme that has been taken up nationally by the GoE and the IFIs. There does not, however, seem to be much fit between the local concerns and the national preoccupations. Egypt's perceived environmental crisis has been linked more and more with issues of economic reform. It has not been the purpose of SAPs to address environmental issues. Structural adjustment has addressed the mounting environmental costs of economic reform in much the same way as the World Bank finally came round on the issue of "social costs of adjustment."

The normal model that the World Bank applies to adjustment and the environment, as I noted in Chapter 5, is that because structural adjustment policies eliminate subsidies, change tariffs, and quota regimes, they will affect the types and quantities of resources used in the production process. This has had an effect in Egypt in terms of a fall in total aggregate fertiliser use. The World Bank model also suggests that as export cash crop production becomes more profitable for farmers, through higher producer prices, farmers will have an incentive to invest in the management activities that protect and enhance their "natural capital."

There are a number of problems with this model. Foremost among these is that linkages are assumed between policies and outcomes and that relationships are viewed as causal and linear and, of course, implicitly measurable: the emphasis is on allocative efficiency and on marginal change assuming a basically stable structure of the farming system. The model argues that the cause of environmental degradation is market failure *or* government failure. This characterisation has generated a very limited view of environmental degradation. For example, if we look at fertiliser use in Egypt, we know that since liberalisation there seems to have been a decline in overall demand. Yet what we do not know is how that fall in demand has been distributed across landholders. We also know little about whether the change in fertiliser use has actually affected optimal levels of application. And we generally know little about nonprice factors that shape the way farmers make decisions and that relate, too, to particular uneven access to resources.

Discussion of Egypt's environmental problems invariably begins with the recognition that less than 3 percent of its land area is cultivable and that the Nile provides 95 percent of the country's water resources. These environmental assets are set alongside Egypt's population of about 60 million and land density of more than 1,300 people per square kilometre. This has led the GoE to argue that "population and resource variables are set on a collision course . . . and dictate[s] a development strategy based on a more efficient use of limited natural resources" (Government of Egypt 1992:15). USAID has noted. "The root cause of Egypt's environmental problems is the extreme imbalance between Egypt's very limited arable land and water resources and its rapidly growing population"(USAID 1994:4).

The GoE's response to this characterisation of environmental crisis is to link scarcity of cultivated area with water availability. The GoE suggests that limited water has become polluted because of excessive and improper use: "Poor water management [leads] to the salinization of good agricultural land, reducing its productivity and requiring large investments for rehabilitation"(Government of Egypt 1992:15). Better resource management of scarce resources should now, it is argued by the IFIs and the GoE, be structured around incentives for conservation and better utilisation.

The concern that Egypt has an environmental crisis and the neo-Malthusianism of that characterisation culminated in legislation. The two important acts of legislation are Law 48 of 1982, which deals with the protection of the River Nile and Law 4 of 1994, which signalled for many the first legislation to promote a unified environmental policy. It was followed by additional measures in 1995 intended to confirm GoE determination to promote the environmental action plan and give teeth to the newly established Egyptian Environmental Affairs Agency (Government of Egypt 1992, 1995b).

Declared concern about the environment, however, has been dogged by the failure to enforce even limited mechanisms to restrict a range of environmental crises: soil erosion, water logging, salination, agricultural land encroachment by brick making, lead emissions, and so on. There has been some success in establishing a policy framework for controlling airborne pollution. Cairo is now recorded as having the highest rates of lead concentration—more than three times the level in Bangkok and Mexico City (although accuracy of the data is questionable)—and USAID has been at the fore in assisting the GoE in setting new targets for emissions, phasing out petrol subsidies in the hope of reducing demand, and establishing a regulatory authority to police these measures.

Yet there is little optimism, despite the rhetoric and the institution building to the contrary, that the GoE will in the near future be successful in winning its fight against environmental crisis in the urban centres, let alone in the crucial rural sectors. For it remains the case that even in the urban areas, business and governorate authorities seem to continue to collude in refusing to enforce environmental controls. As one commentator noted, "The environment is not their [GoE] first priority, what politicians need or require comes first, then comes the environment" (El Gazzar, quoted in *Al-Ahram Weekly,* 15–21 February 1996).

There is nevertheless evidence that a link is made by the IFIs and the GoE between environmental regulation (especially the strategy to price environmental assets like water and promote the privatisation of land) and the general economic reform strategy. While remaining critical of this position, a leading GoE environmental adviser noted, as early as 1994, that the linkages being made by the state are the result of considerable IFI pressure, regarding the efficacy of the economic reform process and the need for supply-side formulas to ameliorate Egypt's perceived environmental crisis. Government advisers, who also sit on the Intergovernmental Panel for Climate Change, remain unconvinced by the IFIs' conventionally orthodox strategy to restrict environmental entitlements to those who can pay. Their criticism seems to go unheard.

Egypt's recognition of environmental issues since 1990 has thus been driven by a number of pressures, including the IFI agenda for reform. An additional pressure has come from within the Egyptian polity itself. That has resulted from increased national recognition of struggles over local resources, levels of water logging, and salination of arable land—one estimate is that more than 2.4 million *feddans* of irrigated land suffers from salinisation aggravated by insufficient salt balance control.

A further pressure that has put environmental concerns on Egypt's national political agenda has been the international debate about global environmental change. Egypt's Framework of National Action Plan for Dealing with Global Warming (Government of Egypt 1995a) notes the obvious alarm at the impact that global warming may have on Egyptians living especially in the Delta. One projection for climate change by the year 2000 projects a 4-degree Celsius increase in temperature for Cairo. Another University of Cairo report argues that there will be a dramatic reduction in the flow of the Nile into Lower Egypt by up to 77 percent in a doubled carbon dioxide scenario (Government of Egypt 1995a:4; see also Delft Hydraulics 1991). A parallel study of the impact of rising tide levels of 0.5 metres in Lower Egypt suggests that millions of Egyptians might be displaced.

Despite volumes of research and activity that the GoE has promoted relating to environmental pressures, and especially to the possible impact of global environmental change, there are many shortcomings in the way its representatives formulate the problems confronting Egypt and the proffered strategies to ameliorate them. The first point to make is the lack of any hard evidence relating to what it is that constitutes an environmental crisis. Although there is in Egypt, as elsewhere, a strong belief that "Science knows best," there is little evidence of agreement about even basic issues regarding the total amount of arable land in Egypt (and as we have noted already, there is confusion regarding the numbers of owners and tenants and other categories of relationships with the land), the extent or meaning of degradation, and so on (compare World Bank figures for these issues, for instance, with Biswas 1995 and Kassas 1997).

Second, the GoE has been a reluctant convert to environmental protection, although the promise of donor money, especially after the 1992 Rio Earth Summit, has encouraged its change of mind. Yet despite legislation empowering governorate officials to fine offenders of air-borne pollution and the energy with which USAID, among other donors, has driven home the message about environmental crisis, IFI and GoE thinking is rooted in the preoccupation with supply-side formulas and particularly price incentives as *the* mechanism for transforming people's perceptions and actions to manage the environment. Moreover, most of the Environment Action Plan of 1992 seems to be simply a shopping list for donors, particularly concerned with urban issues of clean water and sewage disposal rather than pressures resulting from rising tide levels, the erosion of coastal defences, or villager concerns about health and hygeine, irrigation water, and water logging. For the World Bank, "Increased awareness of environmental problems and their consequences can motivate people to take action and increase their willingness-to-pay for environmental services" (World Bank 1994b:iv). In a further summary document, and with clear parallels with the way in which policy is driven in Egypt, the World Bank has argued that the forging of a partnership for environmental action will be driven by the private sector and involves the state reduction of subsidies; increases in the pricing of tariffs on energy, water, and sanitation; and the provision of land tenure to increase security for peasants (World Bank 1994b). This strategy is mirrored by the GoE, whose declared policy is to provide "incentives for proper management of the environment through appropriate pricing of inputs to encourage conservation and recovery/recycling" (Government of Egypt 1992:3).

There has also been a preoccupation in Egypt with viewing the environment in naturalistic terms. Officials, moreover, seem too willing to embrace the ethos of the 1992 Rio Earth Summit that "Spaceship Earth" is heading out of control and that Egypt is affected as its land area diminishes in relation to the numbers of people it has to sustain. Running alongside this view is the notion that the River Nile is the sole lifeblood of Egypt. This in many ways has been an environmentally determinist characterisation of Egypt's political economy for decades. It has also been the source of much recent popularist writing on Egypt (Kaplan 1996; compare Ikram 1980 and Waterbury 1979; contrast the exemplary critique by Mitchell 1995 and, more broadly, Englund 1998). The GoE has colluded in the view that it is the Nile and very little besides that maintains Egypt. This view helps to sustain the historical magic of Egypt as a hydraulic society and the continued need, therefore, for a powerful, omnipotent pharaonic president. This view was spelt out in early 1997 in the debate about the construction of a 500-mile Tushka canal in Upper Egypt. It was reiterated in January 1999 as much of the Egyptian press began supporting Hosni Mubarak for his fourth six-year term as President, confirmed by national referendum on 26 September 1999 when he was the only candidate. *Al Gomhoriya* staunchly defended President Mubarak's record including the imagination of projects like Tushka; Al Wafd, in contrast, likened the ambitious canal project to a bottomless pit into which Egypt was throwing money that it did not have (*Middle East Times*, Egypt Edition, 24 January 1999).

The Tushka proposal is to carry water to the New Valley governorate west of Luxor, where there are already about 150,000 settlers in four oases. That area represents just under 40 percent of Egypt—about 50 percent bigger than Britain—and the intention is to populate it further. The project led one commentator to note, "Moving to the desert is a must. There is no better way to inspire people than through a dramatic announcement. The president knows his people. Egyptians tend to join hands when they are inspired by an urgent national project" (Beshai, quoted in *The Financial Times*, 13 May 1997).

Although the new scheme is seen by its supporters to offer the outlet for Egypt's growing population and environmental relief for the valley either side of the Nile, the scheme also promises to bring with it many new hazards and further, rather than reduced, pressure on the Nile waters. The plan is to pump water from the Tushka reservoir using a pumping station to irrigate 500,000 *feddans* of land. Yet this scheme, personally embraced and promoted by President Mubarak, depends for its success on three crucial things. The first is availability of water. In 1996–1997 the Tushka reservoir was exceptionally filled by water from an overspill from Lake Nasser. That had only been possible because of unusually heavy rains closer to the head of the Nile in Ethiopia. The Tushka project is dependent upon the diversion of one-tenth of the 55.5 billion cubic metres of water that Egypt receives under the 1959 Nile waters agreement with Sudan and Ethiopia. And as peace settlements emerged in the hitherto war-ravaged greater Horn of Africa, the demand for increased shares of the Nile water seems probable. Indeed in February 1997, Cairo hosted a major conference, attended by all ten states with access to the Nile. The conference debated plans for securing access to Nile waters into the next millennium. As an adviser to the Canadian International Development Agency noted, "There are 250 million people living in the Nile basin and this will become 1bn by 2050. But the amount of water is exactly the same. More people will die very soon if they don't start to cooperate. The water those states receive is less than they need to live on, and this has been so since the 1950s" (Shady, quoted in *The Financial Times*, 27 February 1997).

The difficulty for the GoE, and its obvious concern, is that any new Nile waters agreement may adversely affect Egypt's development initiatives. The 1959 agreement was not based on equity, and with Ethiopia hitherto denied access to Nile waters, any development plans in Addis Ababa will affect access for other signatories to the agreement. This concern underpinned the Cairo conference need to raise about $100 million in aid to secure greater access to 6,750 kilometres of river water and to devise an equitable distribution of it. Yet, if Egypt goes ahead with the Mubarak scheme, it is possible that water drawn off to the New Valley will reduce the level of the Nile to less than the necessary 1.5 metres required for the draught of riverboats.

The second reason why the Tushka project is untenable is that there is no proper estimate of what its financial cost will be. Quoted figures have varied from $1 billion for the entire canal of 500 miles to Farafra to $1.9 billion for simply the first stage of 300 miles to Dakhla. This first stage will take an estimated ten years to build. If this project goes ahead—and it is likely, given the personal investment from Mubarak in terms of his own prestige, not dissimilar to Nasser's commitment to the Aswân High

Dam—it seems likely to suck in most available domestic income and donor assistance. The World Bank, for example, has already committed a total $200 million credit to the Agricultural Development Bank for reclamation in the New Valley, and Mubarak's close friend, Sheikh Zayed of Abu Dhabi, after whom the northern canal is named, is rumoured to have invested $12 million. In September 1998 the project received a boost from the Saudi prince Al-Walid Bin Talal. He is one of the biggest investors in Egypt, focussing on what he has declared to be the areas of high rates of return, "real estate, tourism and agriculture." He signed a contract to buy 120,000 *feddans* in the Tushka region, and he estimated that returns on his $1-billion investment would be 20 percent (*Al-Ahram Weekly*, 24–30 September 1998). But the GoE, it seems, promised to establish necessary infrastructure, including the extension of irrigation by 2001, and there is little evidence that this investment will either generate employment opportunities or produce for local consumption.

At a time of economic restructuring and the continued underdevelopment of resources and people in Upper Egypt, the investment in what many see as a "pyramid," not least because of its vulnerability to low Nile flows that will make it redundant, seems incredible. The value added of $1 billion (an amount equal to almost a third of Egypt's total net official development assistance in 1993), invested elsewhere in the productive economy in health and education for the forthcoming generations of Egyptians, would seem to the critics of the scheme a far more valuable investment. Total GoE investment in education in 1992 was about $1.5 billion (5 percent of GDP—which did rise to 5.6 percent in 1995) and in health in 1997 just 1.6 percent of GDP, an estimated $330 million (United Nations Development Programme 1996; World Bank 1994c, 1999).

The third reason why the scheme is flawed is that if resettlement is to take place on any meaningful scale, it must be on the basis of the willingness of the new settlers to live in the new lands and for those lands to be properly equipped with the necessities for life. A regular protest from settlers in Egypt's new lands is that once moved there, they and their needs are forgotten. The success of the Tushka canal, therefore, will not depend solely on the availability of investment capital to deliver the pumping stations and for there to be sufficiently high water levels to pump water to the desert. Its success will rest with the design and construction of a physical environment discussed with and suitable for new residents to develop sustainable livelihoods; there has been scarce attention to that. There has also been scarce attention to trying to discover what it is that new settlers' needs are and how continuity from settlers' positions in the old lands can be properly managed. It is of course in the government's own interest to ensure adequate consultation if it is serious about raising levels of productivity. Those increases in productivity will only come from successful settlers who are confident in new but stable environments. It might instead, however, be the case that the GoE strategy is really to keep settlers on new lands as effectively landless labourers (and labour migrants) who can work on the lands of absentee landlords—if this is the case then there is little need for consultation or for much local service provision.

Rural Protest: The Politics of Law 96 of 1992

In January 1999 the opposition Tagamu Party presented the Ministry of Agriculture and Land Reclamation with a petition of a quarter of a million signatures protesting against the full implementation of Law 96. Al Tagamu had equivocated its position on the new tenancy law, preferring to argue for its more gradual implementation rather than its nonimplementation. In this, its view was closer to that of the moderate Islamists, who supported the legislation because it defended the interests of private property. Both political groupings have been out of kilter with the majority of Egypt's small landholders and therefore have failed to take political advantage from opposing the legislation that has probably been the most significant since Nasser. Indeed, one British newspaper recounted the comments from a tenant fearful of the consequences of the full implementation of the land act: "Even our youth weep for Abdel Nasser, even though they never new him. With this government of thieves, God knows what will happen on October 1 [1997]" (Hirst 1997). These comments were very common during the transition period 1992–1997 and have continued since 1 October 1997, when the act became fully operational. In many respects the GoE must be content that the levels of unrest that were feared did not take place. It may also be true to say that the government also underestimated the level of violence associated with the new law, most of it emanating from the forces of law and (dis)order. Unrest has been considerable, and the might of security forces was used by overzealous governors eager to prove the suitability of their "no-nonsense" tactics to crush it. Government wrote up opposition to the land act as acts of "lawlessness." In so doing, the GoE and much of the semiofficial press were guilty of marginalising opposition and often reducing it to "terrorism" rather than legitimate acts of political opposition to what was seen as an unjust law.

The issue of privatisation of land tenure has become central to the economic reform process. There is little evidence, moreover, that acts of opposition to the land act have diminished since October 1997—although the form that it has taken may have been modified from open anger to more peaceful use of the courts and covert struggles. Yet getting an accurate account of the levels of unrest and opposition also remains difficult as it is not something governorate or security officials want to publicise. Part of the reason behind farmer changes in tactics recognises the strength of the security forces and the ability and confidence of landowners to have them at their disposal. Changes in land tenancy arrangements have generated winners and losers. The winners are landowners renting out land and farmers with more than 5 *feddans,* who can afford to pay increased rents and more easily make decisions about changes in cropping patterns that might generate increased income. Fellahin who are near-landless, who before 1997 were able to rent land, are now the class of farmers that is more likely to be dispossessed at a time when opportunities for off-farm income are diminishing.

The GoE seems to have been mindful of the implications for rural protest, but successful implementation of the act became a measure of GoE authority to deliver tough reforming legislation. Nevertheless, opposition has been stronger than the GoE probably imagined. And that opposition became not only a criticism of a state uninterested in its farmers but, by early 1999, a recognition by tenants and other small landholders that landlords were using the new law as a pretext to contest a whole range of landownership issues. These included contesting ownership of land-reform land that had been redistributed during the Nasser years and to contest ownership and access to religious land and property *(Al Awqaf).* Indeed, although more research is needed on this issue, it was already clear by early 1999 that the new tenancy act had opened a Pandora's box of claims and counterclaims to landownership. This conflict went far beyond simply issues of rented land to include, in addition to land controlled by the Ministry of Religious Endowments and agrarian reform land, ownership issues of land in the reclaimed areas and alluvial land (Land Centre 1999).

One of the possible consequences of the rush for land made by landlords and families still bearing grudges because of Nasser's redistributive reforms is a consolidation of power by landlords. Among those contesting the changes initiated by Nasser's agrarian reform is a family in Faiyum linked to a senior government official. This family seems to be seeking to regain access to land redistributed during the agrarian reform, and it may have used the opportunity of confusion surrounding the tenancy law to maximise its claim, yet the claim seems to be for land that has already been paid for by current holders to the Authority of Land Reform.

Changing the class status of the large landholders—enhancing and, in some cases, establishing for the first time obvious and real sources of economic power in the countryside—may polarise village and household differences and claims to local resources. Changes of tenure and higher rents will lead to greater social differentiation and rural landlessness, resulting from dispossession of small landholders not absorbed by urban growth. The policy reforms also assume that crop mix and levels of production will ipso facto redress the relationship between population growth and food production. As I noted in Chapter 5, one of the most vexing questions for village respondents who were small landholders was the likely outcome of the liberalisation of tenure. Peasants not only expressed anxiety but also declared aggression towards landlords who dispossessed and imposed rents that reduce and challenge the life chances of farmers.

In early 1997 a reporter in *El Sha'ab* noted that "the GoE had thrown a time bomb in the form of the new law in front of tenants. It had then retreated with fingers in her ears and with eyes closed in the hope that they would not witness an explosion". Ignoring the views of informed commentators, it seemed, the GoE was also ignoring the interests of about 2 million tenant farmers who supported up to 14 million family members.

As the transition period of Law 96 drew to a close in 1996–1997, the level of violence, underreported in the government press, increased. GoE reluctance to address mounting levels of rural violence against the tenancy legislation was challenged in May 1997 by two large demonstrations against the act in Daqahliya and Giza, which were put down by police. The GoE was also challenged by a May 1997 conference at which many peasant activists wanted to march on Tahrir Square in central Cairo to protest against tenant dispossessions. That meeting was also closed by security forces (*Le Monde*, 28 May–3 June 1997).

The threat to tenant farmers has been taken up by a newly established Cairo-based Land Centre. Established by lawyers in December 1996 to defend the rights of rural dwellers, the Land Centre has publicised the struggles emerging in Lower and Upper Egypt over the changes in the tenancy law. It has also pursued the coverage of the struggles by defending in court farmers threatened by dispossession and by more generally establishing a profile for the support of peasant human rights. In 1996, the Land Centre took unprecedented legal action against the MALR on behalf of fifty tenant farmers in Daqahliya. It argued for the provision of reclaimed land as compensation for dispossessed tenants according to Law 143 of 1981. The Land Centre also tried to establish a network of lawyers and support staff throughout Egypt to monitor the impact of the change in landlord-tenant relations (interviews with Land Centre staff, April, Cairo, 1997 and November 1998; Land Centre briefing documents).

Opposition to the land act has highlighted a broad range of rural protest. There have been demonstrations, acts of violence against landlords, acts of sabotage, and land occupation. Significantly, much of this

TABLE 6.1   Recorded Violence for the Period 1 January 1997–7 May 1997 Resulting From Opposition to the Implementation of Public Law 96 of 1992

Village	Governorate	Date	Killed	Injured	Arrested	Escaped arrest
Al-Shenawiq	Beni Suef	31/12/96	–	–	15	50
Lasiever	Kafr al Sheikh	24/1/97	–	12	5	–
Ezbat Al-Zeny	Al Daqahliya	12/3/97	–	11	90	–
Abu-Nassar	el Faiyum	10/4/97	4	52	29	47
El-Nemsa	Qena	Unavailable	–	9	Not determined	Not determined
Abu-Hagag	Al Beheira	30/4/97	–	–	6	–
Meet Nagy	Al Daqahliya	7/5/97	–	2	3	2
Other cases	Several	Several	1[a]	–	18	–
Total			5	86	167	99

[a]Violence was initiated in a village in Sharkia where a farmer was killed.

SOURCE: Reproduced with permission from the Land Centre, Cairo, 1997. Researchers: Karam Saber, Mahmoud Gaber Adel William, and Hisham Fouad.

protest has been spontaneous farmer-collective and individual opposition to the claims of landowners. And demonstrations have been organised across village and governorate boundaries without any interference from formal political parties. Towards the end of the transition period, farmers mobilised against landowners throughout much of Egypt. In January 1997 farmers in about twenty-five villages in the Nasser *markaz* of Beni Suef demonstrated against the law. The demonstration was a response to a court judgment that found against a farmer in Shatawya village and in favour of a landowner. The judgment led to what seems to have been the spontaneous mobilisation of 3,000 tenants who refused to recognise that they would have to leave the land voluntarily in October 1997 when the law became fully operational (*Afaq 'Arabia*, 16 January 1997:10).

Early in 1997 there was a report of the first murder resulting from proposed implementation of the law in Kafr al Sheikh (see Table 6.1). A landowner in Hamoul tried to reclaim his land shortly before harvest and was killed by his tenant. And in Kafr al Sheikh farmers resisting implementation of the act protested with robbery and sabotage, especially the destruction of crops. Many farmers reported to the Land Centre that they felt it incongruous that they would be dispossessed yet rehired as farm labourers, some after a generation or more of working the same piece of land. And other farmers in Daqahliya noted the prospect of a return to feudalism, remembering the days of the king and the "blue *Galabia*."

Violent opposition from tenants seemed most evident in governorates where there were large landholdings, as in Kafr al Sheikh and Daqahliya, which posed particular problems. The districts of Dekerniss and Madenet el-Nasser were extremely tense in early 1997, as a handful of large landowners tested the efficacy of the land law. Yet, despite the declared fears of many tenants of a return to feudalism, Mahmoud Heikal, the head of the local council in Madenet Nasser noted that the new law was fair, and that the tenants needed to thank God for the very many years that they had paid only nominal rent. In February 1997 *El Sha'ab* newspaper recorded that agricultural cooperatives had began distributing forms to landowners for them to indicate which land they owned, where it was located, and what was the name of the tenant. The forms were to be completed before July 1997, ready for the full implementation of the act the following October. The questionnaires were to prepare the tenants for their dispossession should they not comply with the new legislation—specifically the increase in rent and the foreclosure on rights of inheritance. Punishment for noncompliance was indicated to be appearance in the "rapid court," which would lead to the fining of the tenant, his or her imprisonment, and the transfer of the land to the owner by force. Legal challenges on behalf of more than 100 tenants were made to the MALR, which was legally bound to provide 5 *feddans* of reclaimed land for any dispossessed tenant (Land Centre 1997). There had, it seems, been hundreds of complaints from farmers in Kafr al Sheikh, Beni Suef, Daqahliya, and Giza, who felt threatened by the prospect of rapidly becoming homeless and hungry within months of Law 96 of 1992 being implemented.

In Daqahliya a bloody confrontation took place between tenants and a landowners who prematurely sold the land on which the tenants were working. In El-Zeni, the district of Dekerniss in Daqahliya, a landlord sold his 82 *feddans* that had been rented to 126 farmers, and he began to deliver the land to its new owner. To do this, the landlord required the help of the security forces, which surrounded the village with ten armoured vehicles. The protesting villagers were tear-gassed, and 90 were arrested: 7 were imprisoned for forty-five days 120 kilometres away from their village.

In July 1997 security force and government commentators began attributing rural opposition to the new act to "elements that want to destabilise the situation and take advantage of the farmers' discontent" (*Al-Ahram Weekly*, 10–16 July 1997). Characteristically, government officials attributed the cause of violence to Islamists. Disturbances near Beni Suef at the end of June 1997, when a local agricultural cooperative was burnt to the ground, were blamed on members of the Islamist Labour Party and the failure of local NDP representatives to explain the law properly to peasants. Major General Mahmoud Ramzi, assistant security chief of Beni Suef, noted that he had had advance warning of Islamist attempts to incite a disturbance, but that "knowing the peaceful nature of peasants, we did not wish to interfere and frighten them," but the Labour party "took advantage of their naive nature and their attachment to the land to spread misleading information about the law" (*Al-Ahram Weekly*, 10–16 July 1997). Violent protest and violent dispossession and arrest continued in 1998, however. That included Faiyum, Luxor, Sharkia, Menoufia, and Giza. In all these governorates security forces were used to promote the interests of landowners against legal tenants before disputes had been properly resolved by the courts.

Despite mounting rural opposition, the GoE failed to confront issues that have so vexed tenants and rural communities more generally against a perceived renewed order of landlordism. The GoE portrayal of rural discontent being whipped up by terrorist sympathisers, thereby making farmer resistance an issue of law and order rather than criticism of government policy, does not stand up to scrutiny. Table 6.2 clearly indicates the range of governorates where conflict over the land act continued throughout 1998, leading to at least 627 arrests, 289 injuries, and as many as 20 fatalities—and these are only the incidents that the Land Centre was able to report. The question needs to be posed, however, why the GoE put itself on a collision course with so many farmers and, in so doing, created conditions for wider issues of rural discontent to be manifested against the government? It may be that Prime Minister Kamal Al-Ganzouri was sensitive to that when he announced a mini-cabinet-reshuffle in July 1997. Among the new cabinet announcements, which reinforced the drive towards market liberalisation with the appointment of Youssef Boutros Ghali to the economics ministry, was the renaming of Mahmoud Sherif's portfolio from Minister of Local Administration to Minister of Rural Development. Ganzouri noted, "The new ministry aims to develop the rural areas which constitute a major and important sector in the structure of the Egyptian society" (quoted in *Al-Ahram Weekly*, 10–16 July 1997). There was no mention of the strategy to meet those aims or of increased resources to do it.

Another question needs to be addressed. Do we understand the type of political actions that many farmers have engaged in as a strategy or strategies to oppose the land law? One important set of observations focusses on urban political struggles defining the efficacy of the poor's strategies of "quiet encroachment." Asef Bayat (1997, 1998) has argued that quiet encroachment is "qualitatively different from defensive measures or coping mechanisms. . . . It represents a silent, protracted, pervasive advancement of ordinary people—through open-ended and fleeting struggles without clear leadership, ideology or structured organisation—on the propertied and powerful in order to survive" (Bayat 1997:5).

TABLE 6.2 Recorded Events of Violence Between Farmers and Police During 1998

Month	Governorate	Arrested	Injured	Deaths
January	Giza	14		
	Asyut	23		
	Sharkia	39		
	Minya	7	1	1
February	Daqahliya	7	1	
	Sharkia	56	32	1
	Suhag	5	18	
	Giza	21	20	
	Dumyat	42		
March	Sharkia	9	2	
April	Suez	7		
	Faiyum	29	3	1
May	Menoufia	43	8	
	Minya	7	6	
	Qalyubiya	4	9	
July	Minya	1	2	1
August	Sharkia	10	10	1
	Gharbia	14	6	2
	Asyut	9	11	
	Giza	11	7	2
September	Asyut	13	9	
	Giza	18	7	
	Qalyubiya	7	1	
	Qena	5	9	1
	Menoufia	5	3	
	Sharkia	8	3	
	Daqahliya	2	9	1
October	Qena	30	17	1
	Gharbia	54	23	
	Sharkia	20	2	3
	Beheira	7	4	
November	Menoufia	29	18	
	Gharbia	10	2	1
	Faiyum	7	2	1
	Sharkia	14	12	2
	Asyut	17	12	1
December	Sharkia	8	6	1
	Beheira	15	4	1
	Qena	4	3	1
Total		627	289	20

SOURCE: Adapted from a table produced by the Land Centre for Human Rights, Cairo, 1999. Reproduced with permission.

Bayat has argued (like others) that the Nasser legacy was one of a social contract, where the state provided basic necessities of life in exchange for popular support, "peace and consequently, demobilisation." This contract undermined oppositional politics and was dependent upon political passivity. The legacy is that political struggles have often taken the form of individualistic solutions to people's problems rather than class or group solidarities.

It would be wrong to argue that struggles in Egypt against many of the outcomes linked to structural adjustment have not been class-based. The factory occupations and protests against privatisation, especially in the textile industry, are just one example. Yet what Bayat offers is that "quiet encroachment" promotes struggles against the state and the powerful rather than, in his examples, against other city dwellers or neighbours. He talks about essentially political struggles around the poor, who may tap into state electricity supplies, promote demands for higher wages, and occupy or squat on land. And it may be that this strategy of "quiet encroachment" has also been part of the recent struggles over land.

Future discussion may focus on the extent to which many of the diverse struggles over land become part of an ongoing and uncoordinated political struggle demanding improved structures of governance and greater farmer representation. There has been the GoE Shorouk initiative for integrated rural development driven by the United Nations Development Programme (UNDP) and donor concern about better rural representation. The Shorouk programme has intended to close the development gap between urban and rural areas by improving local resource use and the performance of governmental and nongovernmental local institutions. It has been very ambitious in its declared aims and objectives. It was launched in 1994 with a view to including all Egyptian villages by 2002. Its life span is until 2017, and it has four main development areas: infrastructure, human resource development, economic development, and institutional development. Yet, although the language of the programme has been that of "popular participation" and "providing democratic channels for the participation of the rural population in the decision making process" (Institute of National Planning 1996:85), there is little evidence that it is delivering even the limited governance and institutional opportunities for farmers to voice their concerns to the GoE. A major difficulty with delivering anything along the lines of greater rural participation is GoE resistance to converting rhetoric into effective policy. On paper, the *Shorouk* initiative seems to hit all the right participatory buttons. In the countryside, there has been little evidence of mobilisation and popular participation, and the *Shorouk* relies overwhelmingly on government finance that has not been forthcoming.

The GoE and the IFIs have remained silent on the links between the economic reforms and the political reforms that many in USAID in Washington trumpeted following the "governance initiative" in 1990. Issues were flagged by USAID in Cairo in early 1992 to signal the importance of political reform:

> Much remains to be done to guarantee broad participation of Egyptian citizens in the political and economic processes of Egyptian society. This is even more critical as Egypt embarks on a programme of major economic reform. These reforms will not succeed if they do not appear to be equitable in their application. An open political system leads to more transparent decision-making and guarantees that the widest number of people can express their views, introducing an element of equity that might otherwise be missing. (USAID 1992a:9)

Despite this rhetoric, it was clear at the end of the 1990s that USAID understood the perceived need to implement economic reform *before* tinkering with Egypt's political structure.

Agricultural Modernisation: An Alternative

Notwithstanding my comment at the beginning of this chapter that I am not seeking to be policy-prescriptive in this conclusion regarding the consequences of economic reform in Egypt, there are a number of issues that do need to become part of any policy agenda. Central to the debate about agricultural reform in Egypt is what type of agricultural modernisation the country should pursue. On this issue Egyptian policymakers are guilty of a failure of imagination. It is clear from the characterisations of agricultural "decline" and "crisis" (two often-repeated terms in describing Egypt's agriculture) that what is at stake is nothing short of bringing the countryside into the modern era. This has been a preoccupation with commentators. One of the most widely read books on Egypt noted in its introductory chapter on the country's land and people that "isolationism and conservatism were the mainstays of fellah existence," and although the author noted, "Paradoxically though, the fellah has easily adapted to the most advanced methods of cultivation," these were brought to the peasant by his "city brothers." "Nonetheless, the fellah continued to construct his views and images of the universe, the mystery of life, and his relation to both of these through the earth and the mighty river" (Vatikiotis 1991:7). This view of Egypt's peasantry has done much to undermine rural people's inventiveness and the struggles that have sustained and promoted farmers' abilities to transform their environments. My discussion of the village data has challenged the view of the timeless Egyptian village and the implicit, if not explicit, laying of Egypt's rural crises at the door of peasant households. For although Vatikiotis is not alone in noting that "conservatism and insularity are manifested in the social practices of villagers, in their attachment to old agricultural methods, in their patience in adversity that derives from religious belief"(Vatikiotis 1991:9), it remains an ahistorical view lacking analytical rigour. It leads Vatikiotis to the view that "conservatism, isolation and a long established traditional social structure comprise what one might call Egypt's permanent 'Egyptianity'" (Vatikiotis 1991:9).

This view of Egyptian peasants and farmers is shared and built into policy planners' strategies for agricultural reform. It is in many ways a strategy for reform that *excludes* the peasant from the policies for modernisation for two reasons: the continued absence of any political mechanism to facilitate the flow of information and grievance from the countryside to policymakers locally at governorate or subgovernorate level or at the centre of the state, and the dominant view of agricultural modernisation.

The continued absence of political mechanisms to include peasants in the formulation of policy or of an arena in which peasant problems can be expressed remains a block to agricultural reform. Despite contemporary debates about the need for effective civil society and its relationship to political and economic liberalisation, Egyptian peasants have no effective institutional outlet to express their views. Egyptian politicians dismiss this criticism by continuing to express the myth that because, formally, a large percentage of political representatives in the Majlis, People's Assembly, is characterised as originating from the countryside, there is not a problem of rural representation. This disingenuous view was defended by the governor of El Minya, for example, at a seminar on the Egyptian countryside when he was called upon to slow the full implementation of the landlord-tenant law in 1997 (El Minya Workshop on Culture, Society and Economy in Rural Egypt, 3–7 April 1997). Instead, policies are directed to the dramatised concerns of environmental degradation and declining productivity, which are seen to have been *caused* by the peasant producer. Yet I have argued that the issues identified by the peasant producers themselves as obstacles to productivity and modernisation related mostly to access to land and farming inputs at costs that can be borne during a period of crisis. They also related to issues of rural infrastructure, employment, and notably educational opportunities for the children.

The IFI and GoE preoccupation with the market as Egypt's saviour is misguided and self-serving of the larger farmer and state official interests that want to sustain the status quo. It is a status quo that has already promoted a considerable concentration of landholdings that began prior to economic adjustment. Between 1961 and 1982, for example, the amount of leased and rented land fell from 40 percent to 25 percent. That meant that some 900,000 *feddans* passed from the hands of tenants into the hands of big landlords—the MALR accounting for 16.4 percent of that land. Although the declared rationale of policy is to release the energy and vibrancy of newly burgeoning entrepreneurial forces, the outcome will merely be to further empower those landowners and political forces that already exert authority in the countryside and in the state machine. And there is little example that the release of market forces will do anything in itself to undermine the level of state rent seeking that has characterised Egyptian politics for so long.

An important element of any alternative strategy for economic reform and agricultural transformation will be to recognise that the market per se is an inadequate instrument for economic growth. Markets are arenas of economic and political power. They empower as well as marginalise, and although changing the prices paid to farmers at the farm gate remains the preferred tool of reformers, it will not serve to promote sustainable growth. The reification of the market—or as Polanyi (1944) called it, the "tyranny of the market"—marginalises all other policy initiatives for reform. Egyptian policymakers, for example, have singularly failed to learn any historical lessons from the newly industrialised countries in Asia, which built their growth on land reform (of the more equitable variant) and protected local markets from the vagaries of changes in international crop prices. It is seen to be easier politically, and practically more efficient, to promote urban growth, which extends urban interests rather than promotes mechanisms for rural empowerment, effective decisionmaking, and efficient allocation of resources in the countryside. The empowerment of rural actors needs investment in rural infrastructure, roads, telecommunications, health, and education. Yet investment in these areas is often difficult to promote when the guiding view of modernity is urban rather than rural, industrial rather than agricultural. With a crude view of modernisation that seeks to continually channel resources into towns and cities rather than villages and rural households, there is little hope of effective and sustainable rural growth.

With the promotion of urban bias, the GoE and the IFIs fail once again to recognise the relative ease with which poverty alleviation and economic growth can be met by promoting policies favouring the countryside rather than the increased levels of investment targeted to the towns and cities. Planners have ignored the view that "a dollar of rural income, compared with a dollar of urban income, has three or four times the effect on poverty alleviation" (Timmer 1995:461). And there has been little recognition, either, of the significance of the many labour migrants from Egypt's countryside to the cities who seek work there and draw on urban services because of the continuing underdevelopment of the countryside.

This failure has been an even bigger omission by policymakers at a time of mounting Islamist opposition. Although there is no simple one-to-one relationship between recruitment to an agenda of radical Islam and increased rural poverty, it would be more likely for recruitment to increase if poverty intensified and Islamists had effective political structures of recruitment and were sympathetic to and understanding of rural interests and needs. The Islamist "strategy" of violence without widespread organic links with the rural poor is more effective in preventing the spread of radical Islam than Mubarak's security forces.

There seems to be a strategic amnesia among policymakers and advisers in Egypt with regard to agricultural development. The market is seen to have single-handedly delivered agricultural growth and increased productivity in the agricultural revolutions of Britain in the eighteenth and nineteenth centuries and of the United States after World War II. Yet, in both these cases, the market was peripheral to growth. In both cases, and elsewhere more recently in Southeast Asia, agricultural growth was the outcome of protected markets and active state intervention to preserve and defend and then to extend agricultural interests. The idea that the Egyptian state can now simply reduce its considerable activities and that the result will be sustained agricultural growth is untenable—at least if levels of rural welfare are not to continue to fall as dramatically as they have since 1991. For although the rationale is for the release of market forces to increase the effective use of land and thereby increase yields and the demand for rural labour as agricultural output increases, there has been little indication from either GoE evidence or my case studies that rural employment has improved with liberalisation. Indeed, the pressures on rural welfare levels has been intense, because of increased user charges for education and health and the costs of rural inputs outstripping the gains from increases in farm gate prices for smaller landholders, whose vulnerability to price changes is greater than that of larger landholders. The effects on the ability of that rural poor to extricate themselves from declining levels of welfare will undermine the reform strategy. This is not least because in the case of rural education, for instance, the impact of increasing levels of poverty have led families to withdraw children from school, as indicated by respondents in Kafr Saad and Kafr Tasfa. This will condemn society to low-productivity agricultural workers or, if they leave the countryside, to low-productivity urban workers or unemployed marginals.

It is on the issue of land, however, that the government has singularly failed to grasp the nettle of reform. The 1992 land law will only reinforce the interests of large landowners and promote speculation and landlessness. And although the government is committed to resettling expelled farmers in reclaimed desert land, the cost to the farmers of cultivating

that land, and of the social and cultural disruption caused by that reloca-
tion, is likely to prohibit its success.

What the GoE could have done instead is to promote a ceiling on landholdings above 5 *feddans*. There might be exceptions to that policy in the
new land and where large-scale cultivation delivers output of selected
important crops for strategic purposes and foreign exchange. But unless
ceilings are placed on land, pressures in the Delta and elsewhere will undermine the viability of an agricultural modernisation that is inclusive of
the farmers who work the land rather than exclusive of their interests
and livelihoods. It is essential for agricultural modernisation to be effective and sustainable, and for it to be informed by household farming
practices, the skills and methods of crop choice and labour process
shaped by farmers in their familial and village relationships. Agricultural
modernisation imposed or shaped by government decree or market
forces per se will be harsher and protracted, and it will bring to the fore
class antagonisms that even the authoritarian state might have difficulty
overcoming without continued resort to emergency legislation and abuse
of human rights.

If the history of Egypt has told us anything, it is that the agricultural
sector has managed to "deliver the goods" despite, rather than because
of, state intervention. And although state reforms in agriculture are desirable in facilitating infrastructural growth, moderating prices and incentive structures, and facilitating greater ease of the relationship between urban and rural workers, it is the farmers themselves who have
sustained the viability of production. It is the peasant farmers who must
be listened to and who must not be hindered in providing the initiative
and agricultural output that will sustain urban development and national economic growth. That agricultural growth will only be possible
and sustainable if a ceiling of 5 *feddans* is placed on landholdings. This is
a viable landholding for average-sized families, and it would undermine
the growth of an extractive class of rural landowners or absentee landlords, which will undoubtedly emerge and be reinvigorated by government strategy.

A redistributive land reform, however, is not on the political agenda.
Doreen Warriner's comments regarding pre-Nasserist Egypt seem to
have relevance for the late 1990s: "With the present [1948] distribution of
wealth and power, there is likely to be no measure of land reform, even
of a limited kind. Land reform must therefore wait upon political change,
and may one day become the main motive for revolution" (Warriner
1948:50). Although her comment regarding the clamour for land reform's
perhaps promoting revolution is doubtful, I noted earlier that many commentators would see the call for redistributive land reform as preposter-
ous. The alternative, however, is the promise of accelerated rural social

differentiation and the failure of urban economic growth to absorb the rural unemployed. It is indeed utopian to imagine that national economic growth will create employment for the 500,000-plus new entrants into the labour market each year. And although it might be seen to be equally utopian to suggest a land reform that would attack the vested interests of the holders of state power, and of their rural intermediaries, it is time that a debate highlighted what the probable outcome of the current strategy will be and why Egypt's political and economic future will continue to lie in the hands of its farmers. Without that debate, and without the placing on the agenda of peasant political as well as economic rights, the collusion between the IFIs and the GoE will merely postpone rather than prevent the possibilities of social conflict and political opposition to the state.

The start of a new strategy for rural development might begin by deemphasising supply-side issues—or the stock of Egypt's "environmental" (natural) assets—and begin with the demand side of the equation, namely, the quality of rural people's livelihoods (Redclift 1992a; Redclift and Sage 1994; Redclift and Benton 1994). Redclift, for example, has shown the importance of seeing environmental concern as part of agricultural policy and of involving "local people in policy objectives which they have had no real opportunity to influence" (Redclift 1992a:256). This is not a particularly new idea but he reminds us of the importance of understanding rural *politics*, of understanding the way in which it is constructed, and of understanding the way in which the rural poor formulate their interests. Opportunities for doing this in Egypt are minimal.

A new agricultural strategy requires a proper assessment of what factors contribute to social inequality. These factors include people's differential access to resources, their productive capabilities, and an indication of how these may change over time. These factors then provide a map of issues that can help inform policymakers of the way in which they can prevent poverty-creating destitution: primarily, the IFIs and the GoE will be required to understand the mechanisms of rural decisionmaking (Dasgupta 1993; Desai 1992). Dasgupta has also noted that there are many mechanisms of dispossession, including shifts in population size and density, predatory governments, and "thieving aristocracies" (Dasgupta 1993:292). He has further noted:

> Resource allocation mechanisms which do not take advantage of dispersed information, which are insensitive to hidden (and often not-so-hidden) economic and ecological interactions, . . . which do not take the long view, and which do not give a sufficiently large weight to the claims of the poorest within rural populations (particularly the women and children in these populations) are going to prove environmentally disastrous. (Dasgupta 1993:294)

The GoE and the IFIs are unable and unwilling to grasp the reality of rural struggles in Egypt because to do so would challenge the status quo. It would also require them to properly think through what creates the conditions for people's vulnerability to economic change and how the market alone cannot be used to protect the poor. The GoE and the IFIs do not have a theoretical perspective that can recognise the importance of understanding the ways in which farmers live. Fundamentally, what is happening in Egypt's countryside is a change in people's entitlements to rural assets and therefore their ability to withstand the acutest form of vulnerability: destitution.

Egyptian Agriculture at a Turning Point

Egyptian agriculture is now at a turning point that will in all likelihood lead to increasing rural social differentiation. That will fundamentally undermine the possibilities for the rural poor to continue to eke out an existence in the way that they have been able to since the 1950s. Safety nets are now being withdrawn. Market liberalisation is further monetarising the rural economy in ways that will make dependence upon access to the cash economy the single most important vehicle for safeguarding standards of living. Yet the market economy, especially at a time of economic contraction, penalises those with limited financial resources or limited access to cash.

Market-driven solutions to Egypt's problems neglect the existing ways in which rural people address their uneven access to resources. There is little attention paid to the way in which people cope with crisis and the impact of market failure. The international agencies have an incomplete characterisation of poverty and environmental degradation. Among other things, they have simply and crudely linked poverty with environmental degradation. They have focused on notions of peasant ignorance and poor technological know-how, and they reject any suggestion of the importance of common resource management, which is seen merely as an anachronism. Policymakers have failed to consider deeper issues of land reform and sociopolitical reform, which might include even very limited empowerment for farmers to shape and promote their own agendas for reform. This is to lose the great opportunity that the current period of transformation clearly offers while simultaneously posing political questions with which the GoE is unwilling to engage.

Notes

1. For an interesting debate on a possible attempt by Mubarak to promote "perestroika" within the NDP, see Brumberg (1992).

References

Abdel Aal, M. 1998. "Farmers and Cooperatives in the Era of Structural Adjustment." In Nicholas S. Hopkins and Kirsten Westergaard, eds., *Directions of Change in Rural Egypt*. Cairo: The American University in Cairo Press.

Abdel Fadil, Mahmoud. 1975. *Development, Income Distribution and Social Change in Rural Egypt 1952–1970: A Study in the Political Economy of Agrarian Transition*. Cambridge: Cambridge University Press.

Abdel Hakim, T. 1987. "Agriculture and State Policies in Egypt." In N. Bourenane and T. Mkandaware, eds., *The State and Agriculture in Africa*. London: Codesria.

Abdel Khalek, Gouda. 1988. *Stabilisation and Adjustment Policies and Programmes: Egypt*. Finland: World Institute for Development Economics Research.

_____. 1983. "The Open Door Economic Policy in Egypt: A Search for Meaning, Interpretation and Implications." In H. M. Thompson, ed., *Studies in Egyptian Political Economy: Cairo Papers in Social Science*, Vol. 2, 2nd ed.

Abu-Mandour, M. 1995. "Economic Reforms in Egyptian Agriculture; Reservations on Policies and Their Impact." Mimeo.

Abu-Zeid, M. 1993. "Egypt's Water Resource Management and Policies." In M. Faris and M. Khan, eds., *Sustainable Agriculture in Egypt*. Boulder and London: Lynne Rienner.

Adams, R. H., Jr. 1991. *The Effects of International Remittances on Poverty, Inequality, and Development in Rural Egypt*. Washington, D.C.: International Food Policy Research Institute.

_____. 1986a. "Bureaucrats, Peasants and the Dominant Coalition: An Egyptian Case Study." *Journal of Development Studies*, Vol. 22 (January), No. 2, pp. 336–354.

_____. 1986b. *Development and Social Change in Rural Egypt*. Syracuse, N.Y.: Syracuse University Press.

_____. 1985. "Development and Structural Change in Rural Egypt, 1952–1982." *World Development*, Vol. 13 (June, No. 6), pp. 705–723.

Africa Recovery. 1995 (December).

Ahmed, L. 1992. *Women and Gender in Islam: Historical Roots of a Modern Debate*. New Haven and London: Yale University Press.

Al-Ahram Weekly. 7 February 1992.

Al-Ahram Weekly. <http://web.ahram.org.eg/weekly/>.

Al-Guindy, M. Sidik, and E. Ariza-Nino. 1997. *Marketing and Pricing Policies for Nitrogen Fertilizers in Egypt*. Cairo: Ministry of Agriculture and Land Reclamation and USAID Agricultural Policy Reform Program and Reform Design Implementation.

Ali, K. A. 1998. "Conflict or Cooperation: Changing Gender Roles in Rural Egyptian Households." In N. S. Hopkins and K. Westergaard, eds., *Directions of Change in Rural Egypt*. Cairo: American University in Cairo Press.

Aliboni, R., Ali Hillal Dessouki, Saad Eddin Ibrahim, G. Luciano, and P. Padoan, eds. 1984. *Egypt's Economic Potential*. London: Croom Helm.

Amin, G. A. 1995. *Egypt's Economic Predicament. A Study in the Interaction of External Pressure, Political Folly and Social Tension in Egypt, 1960–1990*. Leiden: E. J. Brill.

_____. 1994. "Evolutions and Shifts in Egypt's Economic Policies: In Search of a Pattern." In A. Öncü, Ç. Keyder, K. Çaglar, and S. E. Ibrahim, eds. 1994. *Developmentalism and Beyond: Society and Politics in Egypt and Turkey*. Cairo: The American University in Cairo Press.

_____. 1987. "Adjustment and Development: The Case of Egypt." In S. El-Naggar, ed., *Adjustment Policies and Development Strategies in the Arab World*. United Arab Emirates, seminar proceedings 16–18 February, International Monetary Fund.

_____. n.d. *Madalat el-istisand al-Masri* (The Dilemma of the Egyptian Economy), trans. from the Arabic by S. Kaballo.

Amnesty International. 1998. *Amnesty International Report*. London: Amnesty International Publications.

Antle, J. M. 1993. "Agriculture in the National Economy." In G. M. Craig, ed., *The Agriculture of Egypt*. Oxford: Oxford University Press.

Assaad, R. 1997. "The Employment Crisis in Egypt: Current Trends and Future Prospects." In Karen Pfeifer, ed., *Research in Middle East Economics*, Vol. 2, pp. 39–36. Greenwich, Conn.: JAI Press.

Awny, M. M. 1996. "Small Enterprises as a Strategy for Development." Paper presented to the Conference on Egypt Today: State, Society and Regional Role. University of Manchester.

Ayubi, N. N. 1995a. "Etatisme Versus Privatization: The Changing Role of the State in 9 Arab Countries." Working Paper Series 9511. Cairo: Economic Research Forum.

_____. 1995b. *Over-stating the Arab State: Politics and Society in the Middle East*. London and New York: IB Taurus.

_____. 1993. "Government and the infrastructure in Egyptian Agriculture." In G. M. Craig, ed., *The Agriculture of Egypt*. Oxford: Oxford University Press.

_____. 1991a. *Political Islam, Religion and Politics in the Arab World*. London and New York: Routledge.

_____. 1991b. *The State and Public Policies in Egypt Since Sadat*. Political Studies of the Middle East, No.29. Reading, Mass.: Ithaca Press.

_____. 1988. "Domestic Politics." In L. C. Harris, ed., *Egypt: Internal Challenges and Regional Stability*. Chatham House Papers, No. 39. London: Royal Institute of International Affairs.

_____. 1980. *Bureaucracy and Politics in Contemporary Egypt*. London: Oxford University Press.

Bach, K. H. 1998. "The Vision of a Better Life: New Patterns of Consumption and Changed Social Relations." In N. S. Hopkins and K. Westergaard, eds., *Directions of Change in Rural Egypt*. Cairo: American University in Cairo Press.

_____. 1996. "New Spaces and Strategies for Social Reproduction in an Egyptian Village." Conference paper, conference on Egypt, Manchester University, 16–19 May. Organised by the University of Manchester, the Social Fund for Development, Cairo, and the Centre for Development Research, Copenhagen.

Badran, H. 1993. "Women's Rights as a Condition for Sustainability of Agriculture." In M. A. Faris and M. H. Khan, eds., *Sustainable Agriculture in Egypt.* Boulder: Lynne Rienner.

Badran, M. 1996. *Feminists, Islam, and Nation: Gender and the making of modern Egypt.* Cairo: American University in Cairo Press.

Bakker, I., ed. 1994. *The Strategic Silence, Gender and Economic Policy.* London: Zed Press.

Banerji, A. K. 1991. "Egypt Under Mubarak. The Quest for Stability at Home and Normalization Abroad." *Round Table,* Vol. 317, pp. 7–20.

Barkey, H. J., ed. 1992. *The Politics of Economic Reform in the Middle East.* New York: St. Martin's Press.

Baroudi, Sami. 1993. "Egyptian Agricultural Exports since 1973." *Middle East Journal,* Vol. 47 (Winter, No. 1), pp. 63–76.

Barratt Brown, M. 1995. *Africa's Choices After Thirty Years of the World Bank.* Harmondsworth, UK: Penguin Books.

Barratt Brown, M., and P. Tiffen. 1992. *Short Changed: Africa and World Trade.* London: Pluto Press.

Bates, R. 1983. *Essays on the Political Economy of Rural Africa.* Cambridge: Cambridge University Press.

_____. 1981. *Markets and States in Tropical Africa.* Berkeley and Los Angeles: University of California Press.

Bayat, A. 1998. *Street Politics: Poor People's Movements in Iran.* Cairo: American University Press.

_____. 1977. "Cairo's Poor: Dilemmas of Survival and Solidarity." *Middle East Report,* No.202 (Spring).

Baylies, C. 1995. "'Political Conditionality' and Democratisation." *Review of African Political Economy,* Vol. 22 (No. 65), 321–357.

Beetham, David. 1994. "Conditions for Democratic Consolidation." *Review of African Political Economy,* Vol. 21 (No. 60), pp. 157–172.

Bentley, C. Fred. 1993. "Sustainability of Agriculture in Egypt: A Non-Egyptian Perspective." In M. Faris and M. Khan, eds., *Sustainable Agriculture in Egypt.* Boulder and London: Lynne Rienner.

Benton, T., and M. Redclift. 1994. "Introduction." In M. Redclift and T. Benton, eds., *Social Theory and the Global Environment.* London and New York: Routledge.

Bernstein, H. 1990. "Agricultural 'Modernisation' and the era of Structural Adjustment: Observations on Sub-Saharan Africa." *Journal of Peasant Studies,* Vol. 18 (October, No. 1), pp. 3–35.

Berry, S. 1993. *No Condition Is Permanent.* Madison: University of Wisconsin Press.

Beshai, A. A. 1996. "Agriculture Versus Industry in Egypt." In D. Tschirgi, ed., *Development in the Age of Liberalization: Egypt and Mexico.* Cairo: American University Press in Cairo.

Bishay, F. K. 1993. "Integration of Environmental and Sustainable Development: Dimensions in Agricultural Planning and Policy Analysis." In M. Faris and M. Khan, eds., *Sustainable Agriculture in Egypt*. Boulder and London: Lynne Rienner.

Biswas, A. K. 1995. "Environmental Sustainability of Egyptian Agriculture: Problems and Perspectives." *Ambio*, Vol. 24 (February, No. 1), pp. 16–20.

_____. 1993. "Environmental Sustainability of Egyptian Agriculture." In M. Faris and M. Khan, eds., *Sustainable Agriculture in Egypt*. Boulder and London: Lynne Rienner.

Boserup, E. 1970. *Women's Role in Economic Development*. New York: St. Martin's Press.

Bromley, S. 1995. "Making Sense of Structural Adjustment." *Review of African Political Economy*, Vol. 22 (No. 65), pp. 339–348.

Bromley, S., and R. Bush. 1994. "Adjustment in Egypt? The Political Economy of Reform." *Review of African Political Economy*, Vol. 60, pp. 201–213.

Brown, N. 1991. "The Ignorance and Inscrutability of the Egyptian Peasantry." In F. Kazemi and J. Waterbury, eds., *Peasants and Politics in the Modern Middle East*. Miami: Florida International University Press.

_____. 1990. *Peasant Politics in Modern Egypt: The Struggle against the State*. New Haven and London: Yale University Press.

Brumberg, D. 1992. "Survival Strategies vs. Democratic Bargains: The Politics of Economic Reform in Contemporary Egypt." In H. J. Barkey, ed., *The Politics of Economic Reform in the Middle East*. New York: St. Martin's Press.

Bryceson, D. B. 1994. "Too Many Assumptions: Researching Grain Markets in Tanzania." In M. A. Mohemad Salih, ed., *Inducing Food Insecurity, Perspectives on Food Policies in Eastern and Southern Africa*. Seminar Proceedings, No. 30. Uppsala, Sweden: Scandinavian Institute of African Studies.

_____. 1993. *Liberalizing Tanzania's Food Trade*. Geneva and London: UNRISD and James Currey.

Burawoy, M. 1985. *The Politics of Production*. London: Verso.

Bush, R. 1995. "Coping with Adjustment and Economic Crisis in Egypt's Countryside." *Review of African Political Economy*, Vol. 22 (No. 66), pp. 499–516.

_____. 1994. "Crisis in Egypt: Structural Adjustment, food Security and the Politics of USAID." *Capital and Class*, Vol. 53 (Summer), pp. 15–37.

_____. 1992. "Agriculture in Jeopardy." *Middle East*, No. 211 (May), pp. 22–23.

Bush, R., S. Bromley, and M. Abou Mandour. 1996. *Al Iktisaad al Siyaasi lil-islah fi Misr: El Bank El Dowly wa-el-Zira'a wa-el-Fellahin (The Political Economy of Reform in Egypt: The World Bank, Agriculture and the Peasantry)*. Cairo: Al Mahroussa.

Bush, R., and M. Szeftel. 1994. "States, Markets and Africa's Crisis." *Review of African Political Economy*, Vol. 60, pp. 147–156.

Butter, David. 1992. "Egypt." *Middle East Economic Digest*, Special Report, 26 June.

Cardiff, Patrick, W. 1997. "Poverty and Inequality in Egypt." In Karen Pfeifer, ed., *Research in Middle East Economics*. Greenwich, Conn. and London: JAI Press.

Carter, M. R., and J. May. 1999. "Poverty, Livelihood and Class in Rural South Africa." *World Development*, Vol. 27 (No.1), pp. 1–20.

Casterline, J. B., E. C. Cooksey, and A-F. E. Ismail. 1989. "Household Income and Child Survival in Egypt." *Demography*, Vol. 1 (February 26), pp. 15–35.

Cavanagh, J., D. Wysham, and M. Arruda, eds. 1994. *Beyond Bretton Woods: Alternatives to the Global Economic Order.* London: Pluto Press.

Central Agency for Public Mobilisation and Statistics. 1991. *Statistical Yearbook 1991.* Cairo: Arab Republic of Egypt.

Chambers, R. 1994. "The Poor and the Environment: Whose Reality Really Counts?" Institute of Development Studies, Working Paper 3, United Kingdom.

_____. 1993. *Challenging the Professions: Frontiers for Rural Development.* London: Intermediate Technology Publications.

Chambers, R., and G. Conway. 1992. "Sustainable Rural Livelihoods: Practical Concepts for the 21st Century." Discussion Paper 296. Sussex, UK: Institute of Development Studies.

Chayanov, A. V. 1966. *On the Theory of Peasant Economy.* Homewood, Ill.: Richard D. Irwin.

Chomsky, N. 1992. "A View from Below." *Diplomatic History,* Vol. 16 (Winter, No. 1), pp. 85–94.

_____. 1991. *Deterring Democracy.* London: Verso.

_____. 1969. *American Power and the New Mandarins.* London: Penguin.

Choueiri, Youssef. 1991. "Syria and Egypt and the spoils of war." In John Gittings, ed., *Beyond the Gulf War: The Middle East and the New World Order.* London: Catholic Institute for International Relations in association with the Gulf Conference Committee.

Civil Society. 1995. Vol. 4 (December, No. 48).

Cleaver, K. A., and G. A. Schreiber. 1994. *Reversing the Spiral.* Washington, D.C.: World Bank

Cliffe, L. 1987. "The Debate on African Peasantries." *Development and Change,* Vol. 18, pp. 625–635.

Cochrane, S. H., and E. E. Massiah. 1997. "Egypt: Recent Changes in Population Growth, Their Causes and Consequences." Human Capital and Operations Policy Working Papers. World Bank <http://www.worldbank.org/html/hcovp/workp/wp_00049.htm>.

Commander, Simon. 1989. *Structural Adjustment and Agriculture: Theory and Practice in Africa and Latin America.* London: Overseas Development Institute in collaboration with James Currey and Heinemann.

_____. 1987. *The State and Agricultural Development in Egypt Since 1975.* London: Ithaca Press.

_____. 1984. "The Political Economy of Food Production and Distribution in Egypt: A Survey of Developments since 1973." Overseas Development Institute Working Paper No. 14. London: Overseas Development Institute.

Cooper, Mark. 1982. *The Transformation of Egypt.* London: Croom Helm.

Corbett, J. 1988. "Famine and Household Coping Strategies." *World Development,* Vol. 16 (No. 9), pp. 1099–1112.

Cornia, G. A. 1987. "Adjustment at the Household Level: Potentials and Limitations of Survival Strategies." In G. A., Cornia, R. Jolly, and F. Stewart, eds., *Adjustment with a Human Face,* Vol. 1. Oxford: Clarendon Press.

Cornia, G. A., R. Jolly, and F. Stewart, eds. 1987. *Adjustment with a Human Face,* Vol. 1. Oxford: Clarendon Press.

Craig, G. M., ed. 1993. *The Agriculture of Egypt.* Oxford: Oxford University Press.

Cuno, K. M. 1992. *The Pasha's Peasants: Land, Society and Economy in Lower Egypt, 1740–1858.* Cairo: American University in Cairo Press.

Dasgupta, P. 1993. *An Inquiry into Wellbeing and Destitution.* Oxford: Clarendon Press.

Deaver, M. V. 1996. "Military Industrialization of Egypt: Development, Debt, Dependence." In Karen Pfeifer, ed., *Research in Middle East Economics,* Vol. 1, pp. 127–148. Greenwich, Conn.: JAI Press.

Delft Hydraulics. 1991. *Implications of Relative Sea-Level Rise on the Development of the Lower Nile Delta, Egypt.* Pilot study for a quantitative approach, final report, prepared for the Commission of the European Communities, Brussels, and Coastal Research Institute, Alexandria.

Desai, M. 1992. "Population and Poverty in Africa." *African Development Review,* Vol. 4 (December, No. 2), pp. 63–78.

Dessouki, A. E. H. 1994. "Ideology and Legitimacy in Egypt: The Search for a "Hybrid Formula." In Öncü, A., Ç. Keyder, K. Çaglas, and S. E. Ibrahim, eds., *Developmentalism and Beyond: Society and Politics in Egypt and Turkey.* Cairo: American University in Cairo Press.

De Waal, A. 1989. *Famine That Kills.* Oxford: Clarendon Press.

Dreze, J., and A. Sen. 1989. *Hunger and Public Action.* Oxford: Clarendon Press.

Dwyer, K. 1991. *Arab Voices: The Human Rights Debate in the Middle East.* London and New York: Routledge.

Dyer, G. 1997. *State and Agricultural Productivity in Egypt.* London: Frank Cass.

_____. 1991. "Farm Size-Farm Productivity Re-examined: Evidence from Rural Egypt." *Journal of Peasant Studies,* Vol. 19 (October, No. 1), pp. 59–92.

Economist Intelligence Unit. 1998. *Egypt Country Profile.* London: Economist Intelligence Unit.

_____. 1996. *Egypt Country Profile.* London: Economist Intelligence Unit

_____. 1992. *Egypt Country Profile.* London: Economist Intelligence Unit.

Eilts, Hermann, Frederick. 1988. "The United States and Egypt." In William Quandt ed., *The United States and Egypt: An Essay on Policy for the 1990s.* Washington, D.C.: Brookings Institution.

El-Bendary, Azza, T. 1994. "The Egyptian Economic Crisis, Household Adaptations and Political-Religious Responses: A study in Two Egyptian Villages." Unpublished Ph.D. Dissertation. Ohio State University.

El-Gawhary, K. 1997. "Nothing More to Lose." *Middle East Report,* July-September, pp. 41–42, 48.

El-Ghonemy, M. Riad. 1998. *Affluence and Poverty in the Middle East.* London: Routledge.

_____. 1993. "Food Security and Rural Development in North Africa." *Middle Eastern Studies,* Vol. 29 (July, No. 3), pp. 445–466.

_____. 1992. "The Egyptian State and the Agricultural Land Market: 1810–1986." *Journal of Agricultural Economics. Vol.* 43 (May, No. 2), pp. 175–190.

_____. 1990. *The Political Economy of Rural Poverty: The Case for Land Reform.* London and New York: Routledge.

_____. 1967. *Land Policy in the Near East.* Rome: FAO.

El Guindy, Magdy, Ibrahim Sidik, and Edgar Ariza-Nino. 1997. "Marketing and Pricing Policies for Nitrogen Fertilizers in Egypt." Cairo: Ministry of Agriculture and Land Reclamation and USAID, Policy Reform Program and Reform Design Implementation.

El Kammash, Magdi M. 1968. *Economic Development and Planning in Egypt.* New York: Frederick A. Praeger.

El-Mahroussa. 1997. *Corruption.* Mimeo collection of Corruption cases in Egypt, 1995–1996 (in Arabic). Cairo: Al Mahroussa Publishing House.

El-Naggar, S. 1994. "The Victimised Nile." *Al-Wafd,* Vol. 1 (December), .

El-Naggar, S., ed. 1990. "Investment Policies in the Arab Countries." Paper presented at a seminar held in Kuwait, 11–13 December 1989. Washington: IMF.

_____. 1987. *Adjustment Policies and Development Strategies in the Arab World.* United Arab Emirates, seminar proceedings 16–18 February, International Monetary Fund.

El-Sadat, Mohemad Anwar. 1974. "The October Working Paper, April 1974." Cairo: Ministry of Information.

El-Sayyid, M. K. 1996. "Bureaucracy and Political Change in Egypt." In Dan Tschirgi, ed., *Development in the Age of Liberalization: Egypt and Mexico.* Cairo: American University Press in Cairo.

_____. 1990. *Privatization: The Egyptian Debate.* Cairo Papers in Social Science, Winter, Vol. 13, Monograph 4. Cairo.

El-Serafi, S. 1993. "The Agricultural Sector in the Context of Egypt's Structural Adjustment Program." In M. Faris and M. Khan, eds., *Sustainable Agriculture in Egypt.* Boulder and London: Lynne Rienner.

El-Shennawy. M. A. 1982. "Conclusions and Recommendations from the Conference on the Development of Egyptian Agricultural Exports." Agricultural Development Systems Project, Ministry of Agriculture and University of California. Mimeo.

Elson, Diane. 1994a. "Micro, Meso, Macro: Gender and Economic Analysis in the Context of Policy Reform." In Isabella Bakker, ed., *The Strategic Silence, Gender and Economic Policy.* London: Zed Books in association with the North-South Institute.

_____. 1994b. "People, Development and International Financial Institutions: An Interpretation of the Bretton Woods System." *Review of African Political Economy,* Vol. 21 (No. 62), pp. 511–524.

Elson, Diane, ed. 1991. *Male Bias in the Development Process.* Manchester: Manchester University Press.

_____. 1988. "Market Socialism or Socialization of the Market?" *New Left Review* (November-December, No. 172), pp. 3–44.

Elson, Diane, and R. Pearson. 1981. "'Nimble Fingers Make Cheap Workers': An Analysis of Women's Employment in Third World Export Manufacturing." *Feminist Review* (Spring, No. 7), pp. 87–107.

El-Tawil, Hosam. 1996. "Egypt's Democratic Margin." In Dan Tschirgi, ed., *Development in the Age of Liberalization: Egypt and Mexico.* Cairo: American University Press in Cairo.

Engberg-Pedersen, P., P. Gibbon, P. Raikes, and L. Udsholt. 1996. *Limits of Adjustment in Africa.* London: James Currey.

Englund, H. 1998. "Culture, Environment and the Enemies of Complexity." *Review of African Political Economy*, Vol. 25 (No. 76), pp.179–188.

Faris, M. A., and M. H. Khan, eds. 1993. *Sustainable Agriculture in Egypt*. Boulder and London: Lynne Rienner.

Fergany, N. 1998. "Unemployment and Poverty in Egypt." In M. A. Kishk, ed., *Poverty of Environment and Environment of Poverty*. Cairo: Dar El-Ahmadi lil Nasher.

Fletcher, Lehman B., ed. 1996. *Egypt's Agriculture in a Reform Era*. Ames: Iowa State University Press.

Friedmann, Harriet. 1993. "The Political Economy of Food: A Global Crisis." *New Left Review*, Vol. 197 (January-February), pp. 29–57.

_____. 1992. "Distance and Durability: Shaky Foundations of the World Food Economy." *Third World Quarterly*, Vol. 13 (No. 2), pp. 371–383.

_____. 1982. "The Political Economy of Food: The Rise and Fall of the Postwar International Food Order." In Michael Burawoy and Theda Skocpol, eds., "Marxist Enquiries." *American Journal of Sociology*, Vol. 88 (Special Suppl.), pp. S248-S282.

Friedmann, H., and P. McMichael. 1989. "Agriculture and the State System, the Rise and Decline of National Agricultures, 1870 to the Present." *Sociologia Ruralis*, Vol. 14, pp. 93–118.

Frischak, Laila, and Izak Atiyas, eds. 1996. *Governance, Leadership, and Communication*. Washington, D.C.: World Bank.

Fukuyama, F. 1992. *The End of History and the Last Man*. London: Hamish Hamilton.

Gala, S., Jr., and M. Fawzy. 1993. "Sustainability of Agriculture in Egypt: An Egyptian Perspective." In M. A. Faris and M. H. Khan, eds., *Sustainable Agriculture in Egypt*. Boulder and London: Lynne Rienner.

Galal, O., and A. Amina. 1984. "The State of Food and Nutrition in Egypt." Working Paper No. 1, October. Cairo: Nutrition Workshop on Identification and Prioritization of Nutritional Problems in Egypt, Ministry of Health and Nutrition Institute and UN Children's Fund. Mimeo.

Gayoso, Antonio. 1991. "Introduction from AID Officials." *Proceedings of Commission on Behavioural and Social Sciences and Education National Research Council*. Washington, D.C.: National Academy Press.

George, S. 1979. *Feeding the Few: Corporate Control of Food*. Washington, D.C.: Institute for Policy Studies.

Gibbon, P. Havnevik, K and Hermele, K. 1993. *A Blighted Harvest: The World Bank and African Agriculture in the 1980s*. London: James Currey.

Gibbon, Peter, Yusuf Bangura, and Arve Ofstad, eds. 1992. *Authoritarianism, Democracy and Adjustment: The Politics of Economic Reform in Africa*. Seminar Proceedings No. 26. Uppsala: Scandinavian Institute of African Studies.

Ginat, R. 1997. *Egypt's Incomplete Revolution. Lutfi al-Khuli and Nasser's Socialism in the 1960s*. London: Frank Cass.

Giugale, M., and H. Mobarak, eds. 1996. *Private Sector Development in Egypt*. Cairo: American University in Cairo Press.

Glavanis, K. 1990. "Commoditization and the Small Peasant Household in Egypt." In P. Glavanis and K. Glavanis, eds., *The Rural Middle East: Peasant Lives and Modes of Production.* London: Birzeit University and Zed Books.

Glavanis, Kathy R. G., and P. Glavanis, eds. 1990. *The Rural Middle East: Peasant Lives and Modes of Production.* London: Birzeit University and Zed Books.

_____. 1986. "'Historical Materialism or Marxist Hagiography?' A Response to a Positivist Critique." *Current Sociology,* Vol. 34 (No. 2), pp. 173–198.

_____. 1983. "The Sociology of Agrarian Relations in the Middle East: The Persistence of Household Production." *Current Sociology,* Vol. 31 (No. 2), pp. 1–109.

Göçek, F. M., and S. Balaghi, eds. 1994. *Reconstructing Gender in the Middle East: Tradition, Identity and Power.* New York: Columbia University Press.

Government of Egypt. 1995a. *Framework of National Action Plan for Dealing with Climate Change.* Cairo: Egyptian Environmental Affairs Agency.

_____. 1995b. "Taking Stock, Eight Years of Egyptian Agricultural Policy Reforms." Paper presented at Agricultural Policy Conference, Cairo, 26–28 March.

_____. 1992. *Environmental Action Plan.* Cairo.

Gramsci, Antonio. 1971. *Selections from the Prison Notebooks,* ed. Q. Hoare and G. N. Smith. London: Lawrence and Wishart.

Griesgraber, J. M., and B. G. Gunter. 1996. *The World Bank: Lending on a Global Scale.* London: Pluto Press.

Handoussa, Heba. 1994. "The Role of the State: The Case of Egypt." Working Papers Series, No. 9404. Cairo: Economic Research Forum.

_____. 1991. "Crisis and Challenge: Prospects for the 1990's." In Heba Handoussa and Gillian Potter, eds., *Employment and Structural Adjustment: Egypt in the 1990s.* Cairo: American University Press.

_____. 1990. "Egypt's Investment Strategy, Policies, and Performance Since the Infitah." In Said El-Naggar, ed., *Investment Policies in the Arab Countries.* Washington, D.C.: IMF.

Handoussa, Heba, and H. K. El-Din. 1995. "A Vision for Egypt in the Year 2012." Paper presented to workshop of Strategic Visions for the Middle East and North Africa, Gammerth, Tunisia, 9–11 June.

Handoussa, Heba, and Gillian Potter, eds. 1991. *Employment and Structural Adjustment: Egypt in the 1990s.* Cairo: American University Press.

Hansen, B. 1991. *The Political Economy of Poverty, Equity, and Growth, Egypt and Turkey.* Oxford: Oxford University Press, published for the World Bank.

Harris, Lillian. 1988a. "Conclusions." In Lillian Harris, ed., *Egypt: Internal Challenges and Regional Stability.* Chatham House Papers, No. 39. London: Royal Institute of International Affairs.

Harris, Lillian, ed. 1988b. *Egypt: Internal Challenges and Regional Stability.* Chatham House Papers, No. 39. London: Royal Institute of International Affairs.

Harrison, M. 1982. "Chayanov's Theory of Peasant Economy." In John Harriss, ed., *Rural Development Theories of Peasant Economy and Agrarian Change.* London: Hutchinson University Library for Africa.

_____. Harrison, M. 1975. "Chayanov and the Economics of the Russian Peasantry." *Journal of Peasant Studies,* Vol. 2 (No. 4), pp. 389–417.

Healey, John, and Mark Robinson. 1992. *Democracy, Governance and Economic Policy*. London: Overseas Development Institute.

Henry, C. M. 1997. *The Mediterranean Debt Crescent: Money and Power in Algeria, Egypt, Morocco, Tunisia, and Turkey*. Cairo: American University in Cairo Press.

Hinnebusch, R. 1993. "Class, State and the Reversal of Egypt's Agrarian Reform." *Middle East Report*, September-October.

_____. 1990. "The Formation of the Contemporary Egyptian State from Nasser and Sadat to Mubarak." In Ibrahim M. Oweiss, ed., *The Political Economy of Egypt*. Washington, D.C.: Center for Contemporary Arab Studies, Georgetown University.

Hirst, D. 1997. "Egypt's Peasants Yearn for Nasser." *The Guardian*, 7 October, p. 13.

Hollist, W. L., and F. Tullis, eds. 1987. *Pursuing Food Security: Strategies and Obstacles in Africa, Asia, Latin America and the Middle East*. Boulder and London: Lynne Reinner.

Holt, R., and T. Roe. 1993. "The Political Economy of Reform: Egypt in the 1980s." In R Bates and A. Krueger, eds., *Political and Economic Interactions in Economic Policy Reform*. Oxford: Basil Blackwell.

Hopkins, N. S. 1999. "Irrigation in Contemporary Egypt" In Alan Bowman and Eugene Rogan, eds., *Agriculture in Egypt from Pharaonic to Modern Times*. Oxford: University Press.

_____. 1993. "Small Farmer Households and Agricultural Sustainability." In M. A. Faris and M. H. Khan, eds., *Sustainable Agriculture in Egypt*. Boulder and London: Lynne Rienner.

_____. 1988. *Agrarian Transformation in Egypt*. Boulder: Westview Press.

Hopkins, N. S., S. Mehenna, and B. Abdelmaksoud. 1982. "The State of Agricultural Mechanisation in Egypt: Results of a Survey, 1982." Report to the Ministry of Agriculture, Cairo.

Hopkins N. S., and Kirsten Westergaard, eds. 1998. *Directions of Change in Rural Egypt*. Cairo: American University in Cairo Press.

Humana, H. 1992. *World Human Rights Guide*, 3rd ed. New York and Oxford: Oxford University Press.

Hussein, 'Adil. 1981. *The Egyptian Economy from Independence to Dependency, 1974-1979*. Beirut: Dar al-Kalimah lil-Nashr.

Hussein, M. A. 1989. "The Effect of Increasing Food Cost on the Behaviour of Families Towards Feeding Their Members." Nutrition Institute Cairo and the Catholic Relief Services, Egypt, Program.

Hyden, G. 1986. "Discussion: The Anomaly of the African Peasantry." *Development and Change*, Vol. 17 (No. 4), pp. 677–705.

_____. 1983. *No Shortcuts to Progress: African Development Management in Perspective*. Berkeley and Los Angeles: University of California Press.

_____. 1980. *Beyond Ujamaa in Tanzania*. Berkeley and Los Angeles: University of California Press.

Ibrahim, S. E. 1996a. *Egypt Islam and Democracy: Twelve Critical Essays*. Cairo: American University in Cairo Press.

_____. 1996b. "Reform and Frustration in Egypt." *Journal of Democracy*, Vol. 7 (October, No. 4), pp. 125–135.

_____. 1994. "Egypt's Landed Bourgeoisie." In A. Öncü, Ç. Keyder, K. Çaglas, and S. E. Ibrahim, eds. 1994. *Developmentalism and Beyond: Society and Politics in Egypt and Turkey.* Cairo: American University in Cairo Press.

Ibrahim, S. E., and H. Löfgren. 1996. "Successful Adjustment and Declining Governance? The Case of Egypt." In Leila Frischak and Izak Atiyas, eds., *Governance, Leadership, and Communication.* Washington, D.C.: World Bank.

Ikram, K. 1980. *Egypt: Economic Management in a Period of Transition: The Report of a Mission Sent to the Arab Republic of Egypt by the World Bank.* Baltimore and London: John Hopkins University Press, for the World Bank.

The Independent, 29 March 1993.

Institute of National Planning. 1996. *Egypt: Human Development Report.* Cairo: Institute of National Planning, Government of Egypt.

International Labor Office. 1991. *The Challenge of Job Creation in Egypt: Report of the ILO Multidisciplinary Mission on Return Migrants from the Gulf.* Geneva: ILO.

International Monetary Fund. 1997. *Annual Report of the Executive Board for the Financial Year Ended April 30 1997.* Washington, D.C.: IMF.

Jabber, P. 1986 "Egypt's Crisis, America's Dilemma." *Foreign Affairs,* Vol. 64 (Summer), pp. 960–980.

Jacobs, M. 1994. "The Limits to Neoclassicism: Towards an Institutional Environmental Economics." In M. Redclift, and T. Benton, eds. 1994. *Social Theory and the Global Environment.* London and New York: Routledge.

Joffe, George. 1993. "Foreign Investment and Economic Liberalization in the Middle East." In T. Niblock and E. Murphy, eds., *Economic and Political Liberalization in the Middle East.* London: British Academic Press.

Kaplan, R. D. 1996. *The Ends of the Earth.* London: Papermac.

Karam, Azza, M. 1998. *Women, Islamisms and the State: Contemporary Feminisms in Egypt.* London: Macmillan Press.

Kasfir, N. 1987. "Are African Peasants Self-Sufficient?" *Development and Change,* Vol. 17 (No. 2), pp. 335–357.

Kassas, M. 1997. "Environment and Social Transformation" *The Environmentalist,* Vol. 17, pp. 63–67.

Kazemi, Farhad, and J. Waterbury, eds. 1991. *Peasants and Politics in the Modern Middle East.* Miami: Florida International University Press.

Keddie, Nikki. 1992. "The End of the Cold War and the Middle East." *Diplomatic History,* Vol. 16 (Winter, No. 1), pp. 95–103.

Keddie, Nikki, and B. Baron, eds. 1991. *Women in Middle Eastern History: Shifting Boundaries in Sex and Gender.* New Haven and London: Yale University Press.

Kerr, J. M. 1994. "Institutional Barriers to Policy Reform in Egypt: The Case of the Agricultural Machinery Industry." *World Development,* Vol. 22 (No. 6), pp. 877–888.

Khedr, H., R. Ehrich, and L. B. Fletcher. 1996. "Nature, Rationale and Accomplishments of the Agricultural Policy Reforms, 1987–1994." In L. B. Fletcher, ed.,1996. *Egypt's Agriculture in a Reform Era.* Ames: Iowa State University Press.

Kienle, Eberhard. 1998. "More Than a Response to Islamism: The Political Deliberalization of Egypt in the 1990s." *Middle East Journal,* Vol. 52 (Spring, No. 2), pp. 219–235.

Kishk, M. A. ed., *Poverty of Environment and Environment of Poverty.* Cairo: Dar El-Ahmadi lil Nasher.

_____. 1994. "Rural Poverty in Egypt: The Case of Landless and Small Farmers' Families." In H-G. Bohle, ed., *Worlds of Pain and Hunger, Geographical Perspectives on Disaster Vulnerability and Food Security.* Saarbrucken: Verlag Breitenbach.

_____. 1986. "Land Degradation in the Nile Valley." *Ambio,* Vol. 15 (No. 4), pp. 226–230.

Korayem, K. 1997. "Activity Report." Cairo: Markaz el Ard. Mimeo, translated from Arabic.

_____. 1994. "Poverty and Income Distribution in Egypt." Cairo: Third World Forum. Mimeo.

_____. 1991a. "The Egyptian Economy and the Poor in the Eighties." Cairo: Institute of Planning, Arab Republic of Egypt. Mimeo.

_____. 1991b. "Ta'rif Mahdowdi el Dakhl in Masr" (The Definition of the Limited-Income Groups in Egypt). *Masr el Mua'sira (Contemporary Egypt),* No. 425, pp. 5–29.

Land Centre. 1999. "Activity Report." Cairo: Markaz el Ard. Mimeo.

Leach, M., S. Joekes, and C. Green. 1995. "Editorial: Gender Relations and Environmental Change." *Institute of Development Studies Bulletin,* Vol. 16 (January, No. 1), pp. 1–9.

Lenin, V. I. 1964. *The Development of Capitalism in Russia.* Moscow: Progress.

Lesch, A. 1990. "Egyptian Labor Migration." In Ibrahim Oweiss, ed. *The Political Economy of Contemporary Egypt.* Washington, D.C.: Georgetown University, Center for Contemporary Arab Studies.

Lewis, R. 1996. *Gendering Orientalism, Race, Femininity and Representation.* London: Routledge

Lipton, Michael. 1991. "Market Relaxation and Agricultural Development." In Christopher Colclough and James Manor, eds., *States or Markets? Neo-Liberalism and the Development Policy Debate.* Oxford: Clarendon Press.

Löfgren, H. 1996. "The Cost of Managing With Less: Cutting Water Subsidies and Supplies in Egypt's Agriculture." In Karen Pfeifer, ed., *Research in Middle East Economics,* Vol. 1. Greenwich, Conn., and London: JAI Press

_____. 1993. "Liberalizing Egypt's Agriculture: A Quadratic Programming Analysis." *Journal of African Economies,* Vol. 2 (No. 2), pp. 238–260.

Mabro, R. 1974. *The Egyptian Economy 1952–1972.* Oxford: Clarendon Press

Mamdani, M. 1996. "Peasants and Democracy in Africa." *New Left Review* (March-April, No. 156), pp. 37–49.

Mansfield, P. 1969. *Nasser's Egypt.* Harmondsworth, UK: Penguin African Library.

Martelo, E. M. 1996. "Modernization, Adjustment, and Peasant Production: A Gender Analysis." *Latin American Perspectives.* Vol. 23 (Winter, Issue 88, No. 1), pp. 118–130.

Martin, M. J. 1993. "Systems of Agricultural Production in the Northern Littoral Region." In G. M. Craig, ed., *The Agriculture of Egypt.* Oxford: Oxford University Press.

Meillassoux, C. 1981. *Maidens, Meal and Money: Capitalism and the Domestic Economy.* Cambridge: Cambridge University Press.

Mernissi, F. 1985. *Beyond The Veil: Male-Female Dynamics in Muslim Society.* London: El Saqi Books.

Meyer, G. 1998. "Economic Changes in the Newly Reclaimed Lands: From State Farms to Small Holdings and Private Agricultural Enterprises." In N. S. Hopkins and K. Westergaard, eds., *Directions of Change in Rural Egypt.* Cairo: American University in Cairo Press.

Middle East Watch. 1992. *Behind Closed Doors: Torture and Detention in Egypt.* New York: Middle East Watch.

Ministry of Agriculture, Livestock and Fishery Wealth and Land Reclamation. 1993. Guidelines and recommendations from conference, 28–29 November.

Ministry of Agriculture and Land Reclamation and USAID. 1995a. "Conference Proceedings & Recommendations." Agricultural Policy Conference: Taking Stock, Eight Years of Egyptian Agricultural Policy Reforms, 26–28 March, Cairo. Mimeo.

_____. 1995b. "The Egyptian Agricultural Policy Reforms: An Overview." Agricultural Policy Conference: Taking Stock, Eight Years of Egyptian Agricultural Policy Reforms, 26–28 March, Cairo. Mimeo.

Ministry of Agriculture and Land Reclamation. 1989–1990. *Agricultural Census, Volume of Total Republic.* Cairo: Government of Egypt.

Mitchell, T. 1998. "The Market's Place." In N. S. Hopkins and K. Westergaard, eds., *Directions of Change in Rural Egypt.* Cairo: American University in Cairo Press.

_____. 1995. "The Object of Development: America's Egypt." In J. Crush, ed., *Power of Development.* London and New York: Routledge.

_____. 1991a. "America's Egypt, Discourse of the development industry." *Middle East Report,* Vol. 21 (No. 2, March-April), pp. 18–34.

_____. 1991b. "The Representation of Rural Violence in Writings on Political Development in Nasserist Egypt." In F. Kazemi and J. Waterbury, eds., *Peasants and Politics in the Modern Middle East.* Miami: Florida International University Press.

Mohtadi, Hamid. 1995. "Environment and Sustainable Development; Problems, Policies and Institutions." Paper presented to the workshop on Strategic Visions for the Middle East and North Africa, 9–11 June, Tunisia, organised by Economic Research Forum for the Arab Countries, Iran and Turkey, Cairo.

Morsy, Soheir A. 1986. "US Aid to Egypt: An Illustration and Account of US Foreign Assistance Policy." *Arab Studies Quarterly.* Vol. 8 (Fall), pp. 358–389.

Moser, C. O. N. 1993. *Gender Planning and Development: Theory, Practice and Training.* London and New York: Routledge.

Mosley, P., J. Harrigan, and J. Toye. 1991. *Aid and Power: The World Bank and Policy Based Lending,* 2 vols. London: Routledge.

Moursi, T. A. 1993. "The Role and Impact of Government Intervention in Egyptian Agriculture." In G. M. Craig, ed., *The Agriculture of Egypt.* Oxford: Oxford University Press.

Moustapha, Samir M. n.d. "American Food Aid and Its Impact on the Egyptian Economy." Cairo: Institute of National Planning, Memo 1328. Mimeo.

Murton, J. 1997. "Sustainable Livelihoods in Marginal African Environments? The Social and Economic Impacts of Agricultural Intensification in Makueni District, Kenya." Draft paper presented to Economic and Social Research Centre conference on Sustainable Livelihoods in Marginal African Environments, 10–11 April, Sheffield University, UK.

Nada, Atef Hanna. 1991. "The Impact of Temporary International Migration on Rural Egypt." *Cairo Papers in Social Science,* Vol. 14 (Fall), Monograph 3, Cairo.

Nassar, H. A. 1992. "Bat al Athar al Ijtimayya li prnamij al-Islah al Iqtisadi fi Misr" (Some Social Effects of the Economic Reform Programs in Egypt). Paper presented to the Department of Economic Conference on the Economic Reform and Its Distributive Effects, 21–23 November, University of Cairo, Faculty of Economics and Political Science.

Nassar, S. 1993. "The Economic Impact of Reform Programs in the Agricultural Sector in Egypt." Cairo: Ministry of Agriculture, Livestock and Fishery Wealth and Land Reclamation, Economic Affairs Sector. Mimeo.

National Security Council. 1984. Document No. 5432/1, 3 September 1954. Washington, D.C.: U.S. Department of State, Foreign Relations of the United States.

Niblock, T., and E. Murphy, eds. 1993. *Economic and Political Liberalization in the Middle East.* London: British Academic Press.

Niblock, Tim. 1993. "International and Domestic Factors in the Economic Liberalization Process in Arab Countries." In Tim Niblock and Emma Murphy, eds., *Economic and Political Liberalization in the Middle East.* London: British Academic Press.

Nygaard, D., and R. H. Adams, Jr. 1994. "Maintaining Food Security in Egypt During and After Agricultural and Food Policy Reform: A Synthesis." Washington, D.C.: International Food Policy Research Institute. Mimeo.

Okonjo-Iweala, N. 1992. "The Structural Adjustment Program and Its Impact on Egyptian Agriculture." Paper presented at International Conference Sustainability of Egyptian Agriculture in the 1990s and Beyond, 15–19 May.

Okonjo-Iweala, N., and Y. Fuleihan. 1993. "Structural Adjustment and Egyptian Agriculture: Some Preliminary indications of the Impact of Economic Reforms." In M. A. Faris and M. H. Khan, eds., *Sustainable Agriculture in Egypt.* Boulder and London: Lynne Rienner.

Oman, M. A. 1993. "Effects of Eliminating Agricultural Subsidies in Egypt." *Egyptian Review of Development Planning,* Vol. 1 (Nos. 1, 2), pp. 4–39.

Öncü, A., Ç. Keyder, K. Çaglas, and S. E. Ibrahim, eds. 1994. *Developmentalism and Beyond: Society and Politics in Egypt and Turkey.* Cairo: American University in Cairo Press.

Onyeji, S. C., and Günther Fischer. 1994. "An Economic Analysis of Potential Impacts of Climate Change in Egypt." *Global Environmental Change,* Vol. 4 (No. 4), pp. 281–299.

Osman, M. A. 1993. "Effects of Eliminating Agricultural Subsidies in Egypt." *Egyptian Review of Development Planning,* Vol. 1 (Nos. 1, 2), pp. 4–39 (in Arabic).

Oweiss, I. M., ed. 1990. *The Political Economy of Egypt.* Washington, D.C.: Center for Contemporary Arab Studies.

Owen, Roger. 1986. "Large Landowners, Agricultural Progress and the State in Egypt, 1800–1970: An Overview with Many Questions." In A. Richards, ed., *Food, States, and Peasants: Analyses of the Agrarian Question in the Middle East.* Boulder and London: Westview Press.

Oxfam. 1994. *Embracing the Future . . . Avoiding the Challenge of World Poverty.* Oxford: Oxfam Policy Department.

Pearson, R. 1992. "Gender Matters in Development." In T. Allen and A. Thomas, eds., *Poverty and Development in the 1990s.* Oxford: Oxford University Press.

Polanyi, Karl. 1957. *The Great Transformation,* rev. ed. Boston: Beacon Press. (Originally published in 1944.)

Pripstein-Posusney, Marsha. 1997. *Labor and the State in Egypt: Workers, Unions, and Economic Restructuring.* New York: Columbia University Press.

Quandt, William B., ed. 1988. *The United States and Egypt: An Essay on Policy for the 1990s.* Washington, D.C.: Brookings Institution.

_____. 1990 *The Middle East Ten Years After Camp David.* Washington, D.C.: The Brookings Institution.

Radwan, S., and E. Lee. 1986. *Agrarian Change in Egypt: An Anatomy of Rural Poverty.* London: Croom Helm.

Ragab, Hasan. 1995. "Egypt's New Draconian Press Law: A Tale of Two Sons." *Review of Political Economy* (No. 66), pp. 592–595.

Raikes, P. 1988. *Modernising Hunger.* London: Catholic Institute for International Relations, James Currey and Heinemann.

Redclift, M. 1992a. "A Framework for Improving Environmental Management: Beyond the Market Mechanism." *World Development,* Vol. 20 (No. 2), pp. 255–259.

_____. 1992b. "Sustainable Development and Global Environmental Change, Implications of a Changing Agenda." *Global Environmental Change,* Vol. 2 (March, No. 1), pp. 32–42.

Redclift, M., and T. Benton, eds. 1994. *Social Theory and the Global Environment.* London and New York: Routledge.

Redclift, M., and C. Sage, eds. 1994. *Strategies for Sustainable Development: Local Agendas for the Southern Hemisphere.* Chicester, UK: Wiley.

Refaat, Essam. 1991. "Egypt Charts New Economic Path." *Africa Recovery,* Vol. 5 (December, No. 4), pp. 30–35.

Richards, Alan. 1993a. "Economic Imperatives and Political Systems." *Middle East Journal.* Vol. 47 (Spring, No. 2).

_____. 1993b. "Food, Jobs, and Water: Participation and Governance for a Sustainable Agriculture in Egypt." In M. A. Faris and M. H. Khan, eds., *Sustainable Agriculture in Egypt.* Boulder and London: Lynne Rienner.

_____. 1993c. "Land Tenure." In G. M. Craig, ed., *The Agriculture of Egypt.* Oxford: Oxford University Press.

_____. 1991a. "Agricultural Employment, Wages and Government Policy During and After the Oil Boom." In H. Handoussa and G. Potter, eds., *Employment and Structural Adjustment: Egypt in the 1990s.* Cairo: American University Press.

_____. 1991b. "The Political Economy of Dilatory Reform: Egypt in the 1980s". *World Development,* Vol.19 (December, No. 12), pp. 1721–1730.

_____. 1987. "Food Problems and State Policies in the Middle East and North Africa." In W. L. Hollist and F. Tullis, eds., *Pursuing Food Security: Strategies and Obstacles in Africa, Asia, Latin America and the Middle East.* Boulder and London: Lynne Reinner.

Richards, Alan, ed. 1986a. *Food, States, and Peasants: Analyses of the Agrarian Question in the Middle East.* Boulder and London: Westview Press.

_____. 1986b. "Introduction." In A. Richards, ed., *States, and Peasants: Analyses of the Agrarian Question in the Middle East.* Boulder and London: Westview Press.

_____. 1982. *Egypt's Agricultural Development, 1800–1980: Technical and Social Change.* Boulder: Westview Press.

Richards, Alan, and John Waterbury. 1990. *A Political Economy of the Middle East: State, Class and Economic Development.* Boulder: Westview Press.

Rueschemeyer, D., E. V. Stephens, and J. D. Stephens. 1992. *Capitalist Development and Democracy.* Cambridge, UK: Polity Press.

Ruf, T. 1993. "The History of Agricultural Development." In G. M. Craig, ed., *The Agriculture of Egypt.* Oxford: Oxford University Press.

Saad, R. 1999. "State, Landlord, Parliament and Peasant: the Story of the 1992 Tenancy Law in Egypt." In Alan Bowman and Eugene Rogan, eds., *Agriculture in Egypt From Pharaonic to Modern Times.* Oxford: University Press.

Sadowski, Y. 1991. *Political Vegetables? Businessmen and Bureaucrat in the Development of Egyptian Agriculture.* Washington, D.C.: Brookings Institution.

Safadi, R., ed. 1998. *Opening Doors to the World: A New Trade Agenda for the Middle East.* Cairo: American University in Cairo Press.

Salih, M., ed. 1994. *Inducing Food Insecurity, Perspectives on Food Policies in Eastern and Southern Africa.* Seminar Proceedings No.30. Uppsala, Sweden: Scandinavian Institute of African Studies.

Sandbrook, R. 1986. "State and Economic Stagnation in Tropical Africa." *World Development,* Vol. 14 (No. 3), pp. 319–332

Sarris, A. H. 1985. "Food Security and Agricultural Production Strategies Under Risk in Egypt." *Journal of Development Economics,* Vol. 19 (No. 1/2), pp. 85–111.

Saunders, Lucie Wood, and Sohair Mehanna. 1993. "Women-Headed Households from the Perspective of an Egyptian Village." In Joan P. Mencher and Anne Okongwu, eds., *Where Did All The Men Go? Female Headed/Female-Supported Households in Cross-Cultural Perspective.* Boulder: Westview Press.

_____. 1986. "Village Entrepreneur: An Egyptian Case." *Ethnology,* Vol. 25 (January, No. 1), pp. 75–88.

Sayed-Ahmed, M. Abdel-Wahab. 1993. "Relations Between Egypt and the USA in the 1950s." In Charles Tripp, ed., *Contemporary Egypt: Through Egyptian Eyes. Essays in Honour of P. J. Vatikiotis.* London: Routledge.

Schulze, R. C. 1991. "Colonization and Resistance: The Egyptian Peasant Rebellion, 1919." In Farhad Kazemi and J. Waterbury, eds., *Peasants and Politics in the Modern Middle East.* Miami: Florida International University Press.

Seddon, David. 1990. "The Politics of Adjustment: Egypt and the IMF, 1987–1990." *Review of African Political Economy,* Vol. 47 (Spring), pp. 95–104.

_____. 1986. "Commentary on Agrarian Relations in the Middle East." *Current Sociology,* Vol. 34, pp. 151–169.

Sen, A. 1981. *Poverty and Famine: An Essay on Entitlement and Deprivation.* Oxford: Clarendon Press.

Shafik, N. 1994. "Multiple Trade Shocks and Partial Liberalization: Dutch Disease and the Egyptian Economy." Working Papers Series, No. 9503. Cairo: Economic Research Forum.

Shukrallah, Hani. 1989. "Political Crisis and Political Conflict in Post 1967 Egypt." In Charles Tripp and Roger Owen, eds., *Egypt Under Mubarak*. London and New York: Routledge.

"Sisters in the Wood: A Survey of the IMF and the World Bank." 1991. *The Economist* (Suppl. 12, October).

Soliman, Raefat. 1992. "Bridging the Food Gap." *Al-Ahram Weekly*, 18–24 June, pp. 28–30.

Sparr, P., ed. 1994. *Mortgaging Women's Lives*. London: Zed Press.

Springborg, Robert. 1993. "Egypt." In Tim Niblock and E. Murphy, eds., *Economic and Political Liberalization in the Middle East*. London: British Academic Press.

_____. 1991. "State-Society Relations in Egypt: The Debate over Owner-Tenant Relations." *Middle East Journal*, Vol. 45 (Spring, No. 2), pp. 232–249.

_____. 1990. "Rolling Back Egypt's Agrarian Reform." *Middle East Report*, Vol. 20 (September-October, No. 5), pp. 23–30.

_____. 1989. *Mubarak's Egypt: The Fragmentation of the Political Order*. Boulder: Westview Press.

Stephens, R. 1971. *Nasser*. Harmondsworth, UK: Penguin.

Streeton, Paul. 1993. "Markets and States: Against Minimalism." *World Development*, Vol. 21 (No. 8), pp. 1281–1298.

Subramanian, S., E. Sadoulet, and A. de Janvry. 1994. "Structural Adjustment and Agriculture: African and Asian Experiences." FAO Economic and Social Development Paper No. 124. Rome: Food and Agriculture Organisation of the United Nations.

Sullivan, Denis J. 1997. "American Aid to Egypt Without Development." <http://www.mepc.org/sullivan.htm#2> 14 February.

_____. 1990. "The Political Economy of Reform in Egypt." *International Journal of Middle East Studies*, Vol. 22, pp. 317–334.

Thompson, C. B. 1991. *Harvests Under Fire: Regional Co-operation for Food Security in Southern Africa*. London: Zed Books.

Thomson, Anne M. 1983. "Egypt: Food Security and Food Aid." *Food Policy* (August).

Tiffen, M., M. Mortimore, and F. Gichuki. 1994. *More People, Less Erosion: Environmental Recovery in Kenya*. Chichester, UK: Wiley.

Timmer, C. Peter. 1995. "Getting Agriculture Moving: Do Markets Provide the Right Signals?" *Food Policy*, Vol. 20 (October, No. 5), pp. 455–472.

Tomich, T. P. 1992. "Sustaining Agricultural Development in Harsh Environments: Insights from Private Land Reclamation in Egypt." *World Development*, Vol. 20 (No. 2), pp. 261–274.

Toth, J. 1999. *Rural Labor Movements in Egypt and Their Impact on the State, 1961–1992*. Cairo: American University in Cairo Press.

_____. 1991. "Pride, Purdah, or Paychecks: What Maintains the Gender Division of Labor in Rural Egypt?" *International Journal of Middle East Studies*, Vol. 23, pp. 213–236.

Tripp, Charles, and Roger Owen, eds. 1989. *Egypt Under Mubarak*. London and New York: Routledge.

Tschirgi, Dan, ed. 1996. *Development in the Age of Liberalization: Egypt and Mexico*. Cairo: American University Press in Cairo.

Tullis, F. L., and W. L. Hollist, eds. 1986. *Food, the State and International Political Economy.* Lincoln: University of Nebraska Press.

United Nations Development Programme. 1996. *Human Development Report.* Oxford: Oxford University Press.

United Nations Development Programme, Food and Agriculture Organization, and International Bank for Reconstruction and Development. 1986. Mission to Review the Technical Assistance Requirements in the Agriculture and Food Security Sector, background paper, 8 January–5 February, Cairo.

USAID. 1998a. "USAID/Egypt Agriculture." <http://www.info.usaid.gov/eg/econ.htm>.

_____. 1998b. "USAID/Egypt Economic Growth Overview." <http://www.info.usaid.gov/eg/econ-ovr.htm>.

_____. 1992a. *Congressional Presentation, Fiscal Year 1992.* Washington, D.C.: USAID.

_____. 1992b. *Congressional Report, 1992.* Washington, D.C.: USAID.

_____. 1992c. *Country Programme Strategy FY 1992–1996: Egypt.* Cairo: USAID.

_____. 1992d. *Country Program Strategy FY 1992–1996: Agriculture.* Cairo: USAID.

_____. 1992e. *Country Program Strategy FY 1992–1996: Economic Reform.* Cairo: USAID.

_____. 1992f. *Country Program Strategy FY 1992–1996: Private Sector.* Cairo: USAID.

_____. 1992g. *Country Program Strategy FY 1992–1996: Environment.* Cairo: USAID.

_____. 1992h. *Congressional Presentation for Fiscal Year 1992.* Washington, D.C.: USAID.

_____. 1991a. *Democracy and Governance.* Washington, D.C.: USAID.

_____. 1991b. Implementing AID Privatization Objectives. Cairo: USAID. Mimeo.

_____. 1990. *Agriculture Briefing Paper.* Cairo: USAID.

_____. 1990. *U.S. Economic Assistance to Egypt, Status Report, April 1990.* Washington, D.C.: USAID.

USAID and the Government of Egypt. 1995. "The Egyptian Agricultural Policy Reforms: An Overview." Paper presented at Agricultural Policy Conference, Taking Stock, Eight Years of Egyptian Agricultural Policy Reforms, 26–28 March. Mimeo.

U.S. Embassy, Cairo. 1994. *Foreign Economic Trends, January.* Cairo: U.S. Embassy

_____. 1991. *Foreign Economic Trends, April.* Cairo: U.S. Embassy.

Vatikiotis, P. J. 1991. *The History of Modern Egypt: From Muhammad Ali to Mubarak,* 4th ed. London: Weidenfeld and Nicolson.

Wade, R.1990. *Governing the Market.* Princeton: Princeton University Press.

_____. 1996. "Japan, the World Bank, and the Art of Paradigm Maintenance: The East Asian Miracle in Political Perspective." *New Left Review,* Vol. 217 (May-June), pp. 3–36.

Wallenstein, Peter. 1976. "Scarce Goods as Political Weapons: The Case of Food." *Journal of Peace Research,* Vol. 13, pp. 287–298.

Wallerstein, Mitchel B. 1980. *Food for War-Food For Peace: US Food Aid in a Global Context.* Cambridge, Mass., and London: MIT Press.

Ward, P. N. 1993. "Systems of Agricultural Production." In G. M. Craig, ed., *The Agriculture of Egypt*. Oxford: Oxford University Press.

Warriner, D. 1962. *Land Reform and Development in the Middle East*. London: Royal Institute of International Affairs.

_____. 1948. *Land and Poverty in the Middle East*. London: Royal Institute of International Affairs.

Waterbury, John. 1993. *Exposed to Innumerable Delusions: Public Enterprise and State Power in Egypt, India, Mexico, and Turkey*. Cambridge: Cambridge University Press.

_____. 1992. "The Heart of the Matter? Public Enterprise and the Adjustment Process." In Stephen Haggard and Robert R. Kaufman, eds., *The Politics of Adjustment*. Princeton: Princeton University Press.

_____. 1991. "Twilight of the State Bourgeoisie?" *International Journal of Middle East Studies*, Vol. 23, pp. 1–17.

_____. 1989. "The Political Management of Economic Adjustment and Reform." In Joan M. Nelson and contributors, *Fragile Coalitions: The Politics of Economic Adjustment*. Third World Policy Perspectives, No. 12. New Brunswick, N.J.: Overseas Development Council.

_____. 1985. "The 'Soft State' and the Open Door: Egypt's Experience with Economic Liberalization, 1974–1984." *Comparative Politics*, Vol. 18 (October, No. 1), pp. 65–83

_____. 1983. *The Egypt of Nasser and Sadat: The Political Economy of Two Regimes*. Princeton: Princeton University Press.

_____. 1979. *Hydropolitics of the Nile Valley*. Syracuse, N.Y.: Syracuse University Press.

Weinbaum, M. G. n.d. "The Interface of Western and Patrimonial Bureaucracies: US Economic Aid to Egypt 1975–83." Cairo: USAID. Mimeo.

Weyland, P. 1993. *Inside the Third World Village*. London: Routledge.

Williams, G. 1995. "Modernizing Malthus: The World Bank, Population Control and the African Environment." In Jonathan Crush, ed., *Power of Development*. London and New York: Routledge.

World Bank. 1999. *1998/99 World Development Report*. Oxford: Oxford University Press.

_____. 1997. *World Development Report 1997*. Oxford: Oxford University Press

_____. 1996a. Press Release. "News Release No. 96/25/mena." <http://www.worldbank.org/html/extdr/extme/9725men.htm>.

_____. 1996b. *World Development Report 1996*. Oxford: Oxford University Press.

_____. 1994a. Background documents, Consultative Group Meeting, 25–26 January, Paris. Cairo: Arab Republic of Egypt. Mimeo.

_____. 1994b. "Middle East and North Africa Environmental Strategy: Towards Sustainable Development." Middle East and North Africa Region, Report No. 13601MNA, November 14.Washington, D.C.: World Bank.

_____. 1994c. *World Development Report 1994*. Oxford: Oxford University Press.

_____. 1992a. "Arab Republic of Egypt: An Agricultural Strategy for the 1990s." Agricultural Operations Division, Country Department, II, Middle East and North African Region, Report No. 11083-EAT, 11 December. Washington, D.C.: World Bank. Mimeo.

_____. 1992b. *World Development Report.* Oxford: Oxford University Press.

_____. 1991a. *Egypt: Alleviating Poverty During Structural Adjustment, A World Bank Country Study.* Washington, D.C.: World Bank

_____. 1991b. *World Development Report.* Oxford: Oxford University Press.

_____. 1990. *World Development Report.* Oxford: Oxford University Press.

_____. 1989a. *Sub-Saharan Africa: From Crisis to Sustainable Growth.* Oxford: Oxford University Press.

_____. 1989b. *Trends in Developing Economies.* Washington, D.C.: Oxford University Press.

_____. 1988. *Adjustment Lending: An Evaluation of Ten Years of Experience.* Policy and Research Series. Washington, D.C.: World Bank.

_____. 1980. *World Development Report.* Oxford: Oxford University Press.

_____. 1960. *World Development Report.* Oxford: Oxford University Press.

Yapp. M. E. 1996. *The Near East Since the First World War: A History to 1995,* 2nd ed. London and New York: Longman.

York, E. T., Jr. 1993. "Achieving and Maintaining a Sustainable Agriculture." In M. Faris and M. Khan, eds., *Sustainable Agriculture in Egypt.* Boulder and London: Lynne Rienner.

Young, K., C. Wolkowitz, and R. McCullagh, eds. 1981. *Of Marriage and the Market.* London: CSE Books.

Zaki, Moheb. 1994. *Civil Society and Democratization in Egypt 1981–1994.* Cairo: Konrad Adenauer Stiftung and Ibn Khaldoun Center.

Index